THE MACMILLAN WILD FLOWER BOOK

THE MACMILLAN

Wild Flower Book

Descriptive Text by

CLARENCE J. HYLANDER

Illustrations by

EDITH FARRINGTON JOHNSTON

THE MACMILLAN COMPANY • NEW YORK

Printed in the United States of America

First Printing

Printed by the Great Lakes Press Corp., Rochester, New York

Introduction

Colorful fields of golden daisies, wooded hillsides covered with pink laurel, flaming banks of wild azaleas, patches of white violets and purple hepaticas beneath the trees, giant red lilies by a wayside stream—these are only a suggestion of the generous bounty of the wild flowers. The spectacular beauty of masses and the intricate delicacy of individual flowers rival the most elaborately arranged garden of cultivated flowers. How few of us fully appreciate these flowers, recognize their individual characteristics, call them by name, or experience the satisfaction of searching out rare specimens!

Here in this book is a panorama of the wild flowers with which nature so generously decorates the land throughout the year. Beautiful water colors have caught these flowers in all their color, pattern and texture, to make such lifelike portraits that the flowers can easily be identified in their natural habitat, and also studied with increasing pleasure at each turning of the book pages.

Edith Farrington Johnston was given a full palette of colors to portray these native plants. She traveled far to secure her models and when necessary had the freshly picked flowers shipped to her by air. With a botanist's eye for accuracy and the artist's appreciation of beauty, she has produced a group of paintings which are remarkable not only for their verity but also for their artistic design.

The accompanying text was planned to provide the specific information every flower lover needs—common names, botanical names (the nomenclature of Gray's *Manual of Botany,* 1950, has been followed), size, appearance, habitat and geographical location. Starting with the Common Cattail, and then the Jack-in-the-pulpit and Sweet Flag of the simple Arum family, the arrangement follows through the course of gradual plant development to the closing pages of the Star-Thistle, Tall Coreopsis and Gumweed of the Composite family, covering over five hundred individual flowers that grow wild in the region from the East Coast to the Rocky Mountains, and often beyond, and from Florida to southern Canada.

It is not surprising that one's first experience in attempting to identify a wild flower is apt to be frustrating when we realize that in such a large area as eastern United States alone, there are uncounted millions of individual flowering plants belonging to at least four thousand different kinds, or species. However, the identification of flowers is a science, which means that we can make use of the scientific method in discovering the species to which an individual flower belongs. This brief introduction presents this scientific method as it is applied to the recognition of wild flowers. In essence it is simply knowing *what to look for* by careful observation, and interpreting accurately *what you see.*

A basic fact, recognized at once, is that no two individual plants are exactly alike; but at the same time we can notice that some plants which are very similar may differ only in minor aspects. A group of these individuals which have many traits in common and which differ only in such minor ways as may be attributed to environmental conditions (such as type of soil, available moisture, sunlight, etc.), is known as a species. The species is generally found in a definite geographic area. Identification of a species is relatively easy when, as with Bloodroot, it has no near relatives. When closely related species do exist, such as among the Milkworts, it is more difficult.

The final step in using the scientific method to identify a particular flower is to decide the species to which it belongs. Since some 500 species are described in this book, to save time one must use a better method than looking through all the illustrations and matching the pictures against the flower in question. A time-saving method is the system of classifying species into larger groups of related individuals.

Related species are grouped into a category known as a *genus* (plural, *genera*). All of the various species of violet are grouped together in the genus called Viola; the same is true of all the different kinds of Trillium, which are grouped in the genus called Trillium.

Just as species are grouped for convenience into genera, a number of related genera can be grouped into a *family.* Sixty-two such families are included in this book. Each is described in its proper place in the text—the Violet family, for instance, at the head of the section describing all violets; the Bean family introducing all the peas and beans. In addition, on page 465 is a brief guide to help the reader in determining the principal classifications. Families often possess some outstanding characteristics, or combination of characteristics, which help to identify its members; such are the spadix and spathe inflorescence typical of the Arum family, the parallel-veined leaves and distinctive flowers of the Iris family, the winged flower and two-valved pod of the Bean family.

The correct method in identifying flowers would then be first to determine the family to which the unknown belongs; second to determine the genus within the family; and finally to determine the species. It is a process of gradually narrowing down the number of possible groups to which the plant may belong.

For accurate identification it is necessary to use scientific names instead of common names. Common names vary in different localities; the flower that is called May Apple in one region may be called Mandrake in another place. The same common name is sometimes applied to two different flowers. Swamp Pink is the common name for two different genera of wild flowers. Common names are often preferable for use in talking about flowers which one already has identified; but common names cannot be relied on as "identification tags" for recognition purposes.

Ordinarily, in common language, an adjective combined with a noun indicates the species and genus; for example we say "Fringed Gentian", the "fringed" referring to a particular species of the "gentian" genus. The same principle is applied in scientific usage, except that the genus name comes first and the species second. Fringed Gentian becomes *Gentiana crinita,* the "crinita" being the specific designation equivalent to "fringed". Since such scientific names are international, there can be no other *Gentiana crinita* anywhere in the world. Closed Gentian, another species of the same genus, is *Gentiana andrewsii.*

At this point we need to know what features are of value in placing an unknown flower in a particular family, genus and species.

The identification of a flowering plant is generally based upon a combination of five characteristics: (1) the habit of growth, (2) the leaf form and arrangement, (3) the flower structure and type of inflorescence, (4) the nature of the fruit, and (5) the preferred habitat.

Thus it is essential to observe more than the flowers. If the plant is to be identified before or after the flowers develop, the additional features are even more important.

1. *Habit of Growth*

Flowering plants vary in their growth habits. A number are *annuals*; that is, they grow from seed, reach maturity, and produce flowers and seeds in the course of one growing season. Then they die. Annuals are usually soft-stemmed and relatively small in size. Some flowering plants are *biennials*, carrying out the complete life cycle in two years and then dying. A great number of wild flowers are *perennials*, living from year to year, producing flowers and seeds annually. Some perennials are soft-stemmed and herbaceous, living through the winter by means of underground organs which may be thickened roots, as in the Wild Potato Vine; bulbs, as in Wild Onion and Wood Lily; corms, as in Jack-in-the-pulpit; or rhizomes, as in Clintonia and Trillium. Other perennials are woody; these are the vines and shrubs such as Trumpet-creeper, Bittersweet, New Jersey Tea, and Rhododendron.

The annual type of growth habit is exemplified by Partridge pea, Purple Gerardia, Painted Cup and Common Nightshade. Evening-primrose is representative of the biennial group. The perennials include most of the wild flowers; typical perennials are Cardinal-flower, the Mints, the Gentians, and Wintergreen.

Other aspects of growth concern erect, prostrate, trailing, or climbing habits and the occurrence of branching.

2. *Leaf Form and Arrangement*

A typical leaf consists of a thin flattened portion or *blade* and a supporting stalk known as a *petiole*. If the leaf has no stalk it is said to be *sessile*, as can be seen in the upper leaves of the Evening-primrose. A *simple* leaf has a blade which is undivided, or, if divided into segments, the subdivisions do not reach the midrib of the leaf. Simple leaves are found among Violets and Asters, to mention a few. Other leaves have blades which are divided into smaller leaflets; these are known as *compound* leaves. Compound leaves are common in the Rose and Bean families. If the leaflets radiate out from the petiole like the fingers of a hand, the leaf is said to be *palmately compound*, as in Lupine, Clover and Five-finger. If the leaflets are arranged opposite each other, feather-like, the leaf is *pinnately compound*; this is seen in Vetchling, Trumpet-creeper, Partridge pea and Goat's Rue.

Some leaves arise from a short stem, or directly from the crown of the root, surrounding the base of the flowering stalk. Such leaves are known as *basal* leaves and are exemplified by Saxifrage and Hawkweed; they often form a compact rosette as in Mullein. When leaves grow in the erect stems they generally follow one of three patterns of arrangement. If only one leaf arises at a point on the stem, the leaves are said to be *alternate,* as in False Solomon's-seal. If the leaves appear in pairs they are known as *opposite,* as in Boneset and Honeysuckle. When three or more leaves grow at the same level on the stem, they are *whorled,* as in Indian Cucumber-root.

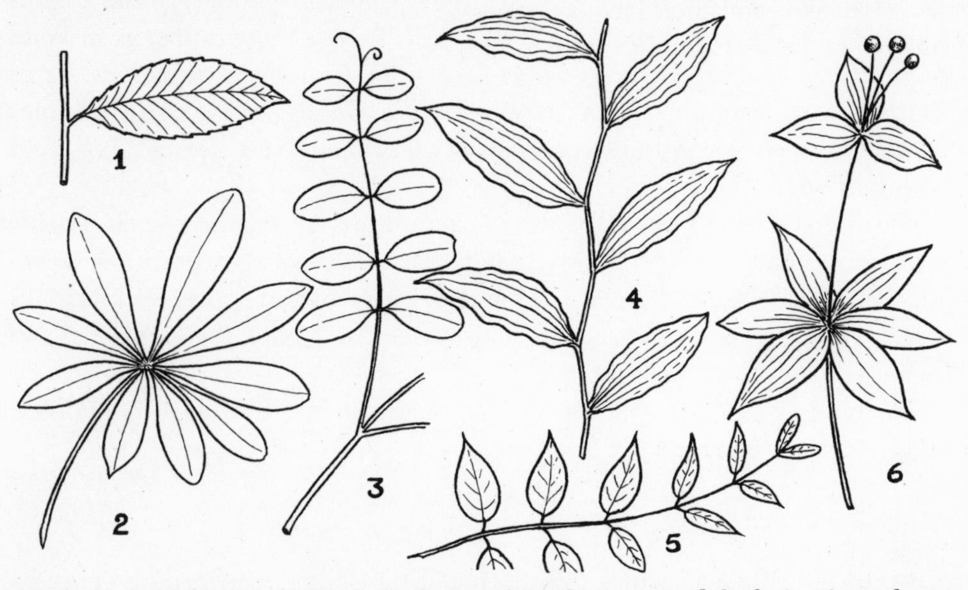

***Figure 1. Leaf Form:* 1, simple leaf; 2, palmately-compound leaf; 3. pinnately-compound leaf, each composed of numerous leaflets. *Leaf Arrangement:* 4, alternate; 5, opposite; 6, whorled.**

The leaf shape is another important identification feature. If the blade is considerably longer than broad, grass-like and with parallel margins, it is said to be *linear,* as in Phlox, Cattail, and Iris. If the margins are not parallel and the blade tapers to a pointed tip, the leaf is *lanceolate,* as in the Milkweeds. If the blade is but a little longer than broad, with parallel sides, it is said to be *oblong,* as in some Blueberries. A broad egg-shaped leaf is *ovate,* as in the Trilliums. An *oval* leaf is found in Showy Orchis. *Elliptic* leaves are typical of Turtlehead. Many leaves have a *cordate* or heart-shaped outline.

The leaf margin is also a clue to the plant's identity. If the margin is not indented in any way, the leaf is *entire*. Rounded indentations in the margin results in a *lobed* leaf, represented by Bloodroot and Compass-plant. The margins of many leaves are variously *toothed*; some teeth are delicate and fine, others are large and coarse. Currant is a good example of a toothed leaf.

In summarizing the use of leaf form and arrangement in identifying a plant, we should remember to notice (1) whether the leaves are simple or compound, (2) whether they grow alternately, opposite or in whorls, (3) the leaf shape, and (4) the leaf margin. A combination of these leaf features will often give considerable assistance in placing the unknown flowering plant in the correct family, genus or species.

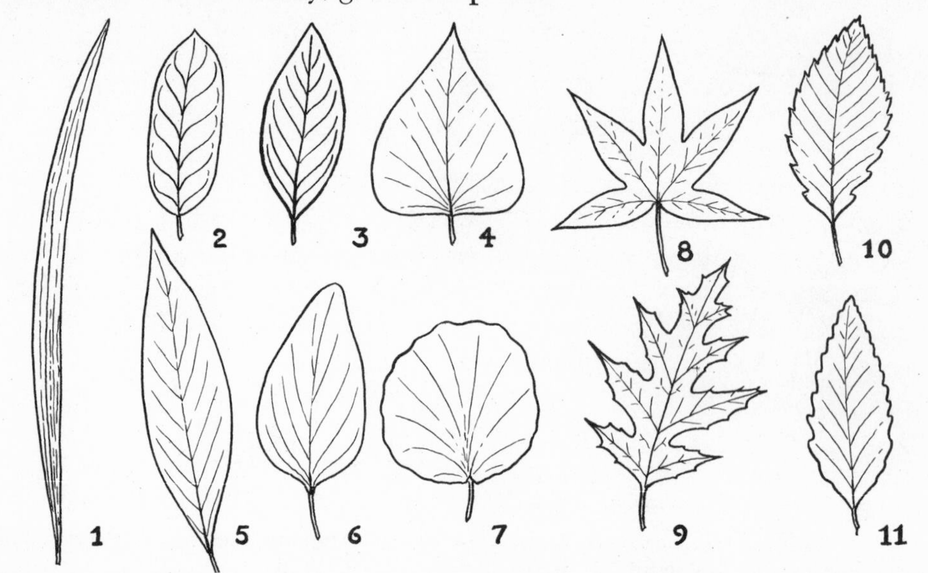

***Figure 2. Leaf Shape:* 1, linear; 2, oblong; 3, elliptic; 4, deltoid or triangular; 5, lanceolate; 6, ovate; 7, orbicular or round. *Leaf Margin:* 8, palmately-lobed; 9, pinnately-lobed; 10, sharp-toothed or serrate; 11, rounded-toothed or crenate.**

3. *Flower Structure and Type of Inflorescence*

Technically a flower is the reproductive structure which produces fruit and seeds. This is slightly different from the popular usage which often means the entire plant, as when we speak of the "wild flowers of the United States." Many flowers are brilliantly colored, but such a feature is not necessarily the criterion of a flower. Some flowers are an inconspicuous green or brown; others are small and easily overlooked. Still others, in themselves insignificant, are associated with colored accessory parts, as in Jack-in-the-pulpit, Bunchberry and Pearly Everlasting.

A typical flower consists of four parts. In the center is the *pistil* in which the seeds are formed and from which all or part of the fruit is developed. Its tip may be a striking feature of the flower, as in Pitcher-plant and Blue Flag. Surrounding the pistil is a group of *stamens* which produce the powdery yellow pollen. Stamens are sometimes a conspicuous portion of the flower, as in Meadow Rue. In the majority of flowers, however, it is the floral envelope or *perianth* which is the showy portion. This may consist of undifferentiated colored segments as in Lily flowers, or it may be differentiated into an inner *corolla* and an outer *calyx*.

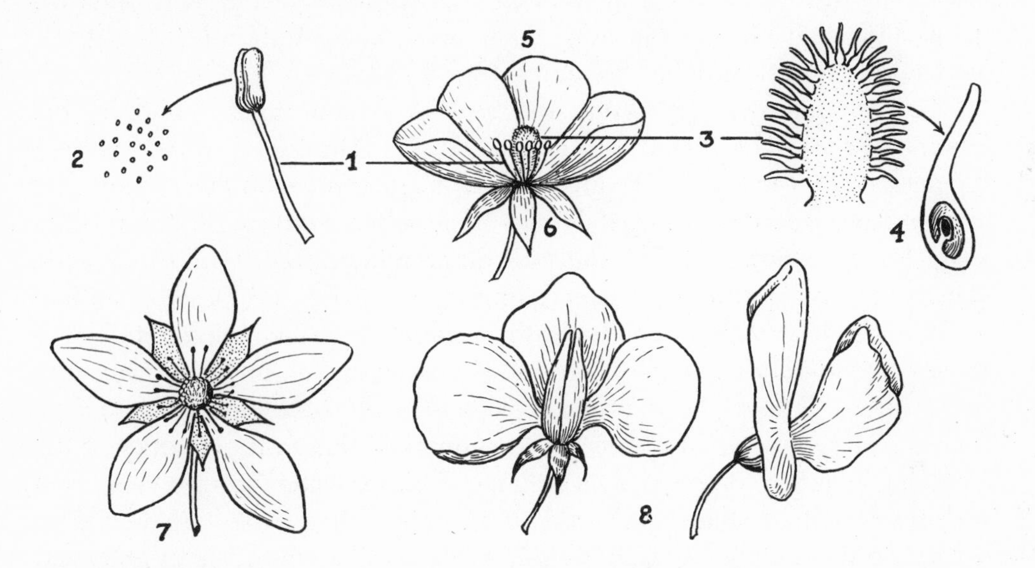

Figure 3. Flower Parts: **1, stamens; 2, pollen grains from stamens; 3, pistils (as in a buttercup); 4, ovule or egg in ovary at base of pistil; 5, petals, forming corolla (some corollas are formed of lobes instead of separate petals); 6, sepals, forming calyx.** ***Flower Symmetry:*** **7, regular flower; 8, one kind of irregular flower (a pea), front and side view.**

The calyx is usually green and may consist of separate segments known as *sepals*. However, the calyx is the conspicuous portion of the Dutchman's-pipe flower, and the sepals are the colored flower parts in Marsh Marigold and Hepatica. The corolla is usually the colored portion of the flower; its segments are known as *petals*. Thus a complete flower consists of pistil, stamens, petals and sepals in that order. Occasionally leaf-like structures or bracts are present beneath the flower, adding to its conspicuousness. Such are the red-tipped bracts of Painted Cup, the white spathe of Water Arum and the white petallike bracts of Bunchberry.

Not all flowers possess all of these floral parts, or the same numbers of each. Hence it is possible to identify many flowering plants by careful observation of the flower structure. In some families there is no perianth, as in the Spurges and Cattails. In others the perianth is present but not differentiated into calyx and corolla, as in the Lily family. In most cases there is both a calyx and corolla, but again there may be a great variation in the number of petals and sepals, and the degree of their fusion with each other. The Buttercup and Rose families include many species with separate petals and sepals; in the Morning-glory and Composite families the petals are fused to form a tubular or funnel-shaped corolla.

Another important feature is the type of symmetry exhibited by the flower when seen from the front. In some flowers (Buttercup, Rose families) the petals, also the sepals, are alike in shape and size; such flowers are said to be *regular*. In others the petals may be grouped to form an upper and a lower lip to the flower, or be otherwise differentiated from each other; such flowers are *irregular,* and are exemplified by the Mint and Orchid families.

When a flower grows singly at the summit of the flowering stalk it is known as a *solitary* flower; this type of flowering is seen in Moneywort and the Trilliums. Many plants produce flowers in clusters known as *inflorescences.* The type of inflorescence is often another clue to the identity of the flowering plant. A *raceme* is an inflorescence in which the flowers, each with its own short stem, are borne on an unbranched stalk; this is typical of the Forget-me-not. A *spike* is somewhat similar, with an unbranched stalk, but the individual flowers are sessile; often the spike forms a compact pencil-like or club-shaped inflorescence; examples of a spike are Pickerelweed and Ladies'-tresses. In a *spadix* the flowers are borne on a fleshy axis, as in Jack-in-the-pulpit. An *umbel* is a flat-topped inflorescence in which the flower stems originate at the same point at the tip of the flowering stalk, but the outer (lower) flowers have longer stems than the inner ones. This is best seen in Queen Anne's Lace and Milkweed. A *cyme* is a type of inflorescence in which each flower terminates a stem which arises in turn from the axil of another stem. A *panicle* is a spreading cluster formed by racemes with a branching axis.

A very complex type of inflorescence is the *head*; it is a feature of the largest family of flowers described in this book—the Composites. In a head the flowers are arranged compactly on a flat, hemispherical or cone-shaped receptacle beneath which is a cluster of leaf-like bracts; this is spiny in the Thistles. The flowers of a Composite head may be of two kinds, one tubular with a single strap-shaped segment, the other being tubular with a minutely lobed margin. In a Daisy, the strap-shaped flowers form a rim of white petal-like structures around the head, and the tubular yellow flowers with lobed margins form the central disc. Such an inflorescence is often mistaken for a single flower. Details of the Composite flower will be discussed when the family is described and illustrated.

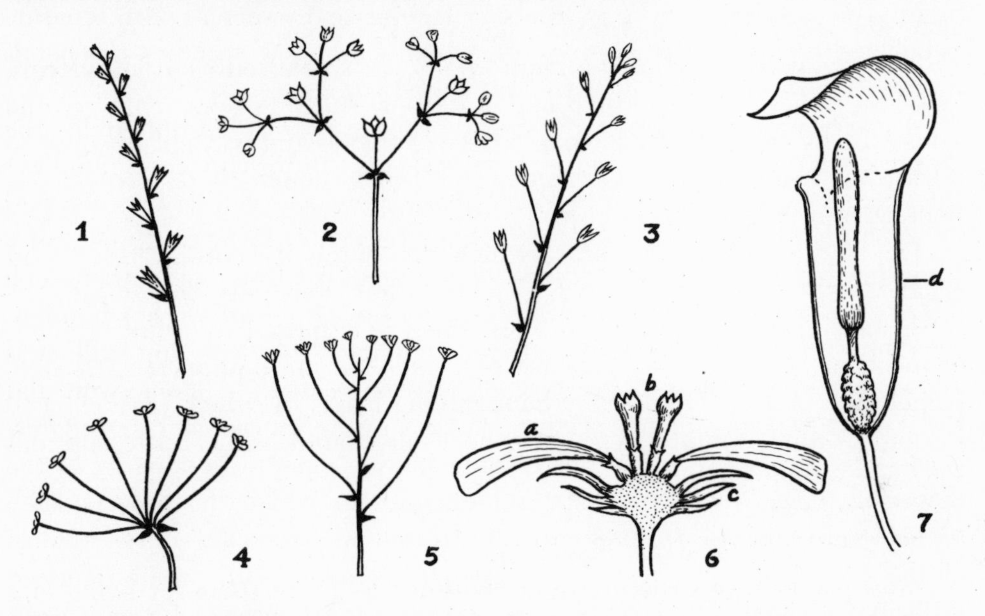

Figure 4. Types of Inflorescence: **1, spike; 2, cyme; 3, raceme; 4, umbel; 5, corymb; 6, head (in section) with ray-flower (a), disk-flower (b), and involucre of separate bracts (c); 7, spadix with spathe (d).**

Thus in using the structure and arrangement of the flowers as an aid in identifying the plant, you should notice (1) whether there is a perianth or not, (2) whether the perianth has accessory colored parts or not, (3) the condition of the perianth segments, as separate or fused sepals and petals, (4) whether the flowers are regular or irregular, and (5) the type of inflorescence.

4. *The Nature of the Fruit*

The fruit is normally formed from the ovary, which is the swollen portion at the base of the pistil. Some ovaries are partitioned into two or more compartments, or cells, which may be discerned if the structure is cut crosswise with a razor blade. The eggs, or ovules, within the ovary become the seeds of the mature fruit.

In many families the fruits are important identification features. Some are fleshy, some are dry. Among the fleshy fruits are the *berry,* as in Trillium; the *drupe,* with a single hard "stone" containing the seed in the center, as in plums and cherries; and the *aggregate fruit,* as in blackberries. Such fruits are usually dispersed by animals, which drop the hard-coated seeds along the way as they feed on the fleshy pulp.

The two-valved *pod* of the Bean family is also classed as a fleshy fruit, as is the *follicle* of Columbine and Larkspur, splitting open only on one side. A fleshy *capsule* may have a variety of shapes and ways of opening to release the seeds. In Wild Geranium and Touch-me-not there are two distinct types of trigger mechanism.

Dry fruits include the *nuts,* which are borne by certain trees, and *achenes,* which are small, hard, dry structures, generally containing one seed each. Their size and weight suit them to dispersal by wind, gravity, or mechanical means. The achenes of Dandelion are equipped with silky parachutes; in Tick Trefoil they have minute hooks by which they cling to fur and clothing. Simpler types of achenes are found in the Buttercup and Buckwheat families.

5. *The Nature of the Habitat*

Most plants have structures and abilities which suit them for living in a particular kind of environment, or *habitat.* Each habitat has its characteristic amount of water, light, and exposure to the elements. Water is of prime importance, and the amount of water in the environment is used to classify plants into hydrophytes, mesophytes, and xerophytes. Hydrophytes are plants living in, on, or near the water. Mesophytes live in mediumly moist habitats, such as shaded ravines and dense woods. Xerophytes can survive the arid and sunny habitats where soil water is at a minimum.

Hydrophytes are common in the Arum family (Skunk Cabbage, Water Arum), the Pickerelweed family (Pickerelweed and Water Hyacinth), the

Iris family (Blue Flag), the Water Lily family and the Bladderwort family. Some of these flowering plants float on the water, some are rooted in the bottom of ponds, and others grow in swampy soil.

Mesophytes include the majority of our wild flowers. They are the summer wild flowers of woods and thickets, many of them in the Lily, Orchid, Buttercup, and Gentian families. Species in this group vary in their water requirements, but in general they do not grow in swamps, or as aquatics in streams and ponds; neither do they tolerate the extremely dry and sunny habitats of waste lands and roadsides.

Xerophytes are often weeds, since they are relatively insensitive to their living conditions. Some grow in sand and gravel, as Sand Verbena and Mullein. Many grow in burned over areas; in this group are most of the naturalized European species. A great many of the Composites have xerophytic tendencies, as is evidenced by their numbers in dry fields, pastures and roadside banks. Some xerophytes live in salt marshes; a good example of this type is Marsh Rosemary.

The more of these features and characteristics you can observe, the easier it will be to place each new wild flower in its proper genus or species. The more you know of the flowers, the more you can enjoy them. To call any wild flower book complete, is to presume on the tremendous scope of nature itself, but the five hundred plants covered in this volume represent a large share of the wealth of our more conspicuous native plants.

Clarence J. Hylander

The Artist wishes to acknowledge with great appreciation the help and encouragement of many friends and acquaintances in the preparation of the paintings for this book.

To Dr. H. A. Gleason, now Curator Emeritus at the New York Botanical Garden, who prepared the original list of flowers to be covered, and checked each drawing for accuracy as it was finished, and to Mrs. Gleason who provided many specimens from her wild garden. To E. J. Alexander of the New York Botanical Garden, who helped greatly with advice and identification; also to Dr. Frances E. Wynne, and Harry Ahles, there, for the many flowers that they furnished. And to Dr. Henry K. Svenson, then Curator at the Brooklyn Botanic Garden, who supplied a number of rare plants.

Special thanks are due Mr. and Mrs. S. Le Roy King for placing their famous garden and their dauntless car at the service of this book, all one summer, and to Mary Strong who furnished a much needed workroom.

To many, many friends who gave the artist the freedom of their woodlands to collect the wild flowers—Carol H. Woodward, Eloise Luquer, Mrs. Ralph Langley, Mrs. Perle Boyd Bascom, and others. To Florence Robinson and Bernard Duncan, friends in the South who sent fresh specimens. And to innumerable others whose encouragement, advice and criticism made the preparation of these illustrations a memorable experience.

Edith Farrington Johnston

THE MACMILLAN WILD FLOWER BOOK

PLATE 1

(*left*) **Common Cat-tail,** ***Typha latifolia*** (*right*) **Sweet Flag,** ***Acorus calamus***

PLATE 2

Jack-in-the-pulpit, *Arisaema triphyllum*

The Cattail Family

Typhaceae

Rare is the swamp, either fresh-water or brackish, which is not edged with the close ranks of tall grasslike leaves of the cattails. There is only one genus, with four species, to represent the Cattail family in the United States. The tiny brownish flowers, appearing in June, are closely crowded on a fleshy stalk in a type of flower cluster known as a spadix. Each flower by itself is very simple, lacking both petals and sepals; the sexes are separated, some flowers being pistillate, others staminate.

COMMON CATTAIL PLATE 1

Typha latifolia *Typhaceae*

This member of the family is one of the most widespread of our flowering plants, being found throughout the United States from coast to coast. The erect stems reach a height of eight feet and sometimes even more, and bear narrow swordlike leaves. The inflorescence resembles a cylindrical club, an inch in diameter and six to twelve inches in length, with a velvety brown texture resulting from the closely packed flowers. The basal portion consists of the crowded pistillate flowers, the terminal portion bears the staminate flowers. In autumn each "cat tail" is transformed into a fluffy mass of wind-dispersed seeds.

The Arum Family

Araceae

The margins of ponds and swamps, as well as muddy and wet habitats generally, are also the home of members of the Arum family. As in the cattails, the flowers are small and inconspicuous, borne on the fleshy stalk of a spadix. In many members of the family this is surrounded by a colorful and conspicuous leaflike structure known as a spathe. Large tuberous rootstocks are present, some of which have a bitter, burning taste because of the presence of calcium oxalate crystals in the sap. The Arum family is a large one, including about 1,000 species; most of these are tropical in their range. Our native species, found in the eastern and central states, some of them also in the Northwest, include the six following flowers.

SWEET FLAG

PLATE 1

Acorus calamus

Araceae

This species of the Arum family gets its name from the sweet taste of the insides of the stalks. It is also known as Calamus and Flagroot, the former because of the drug calamus which is secured from the rootstocks. In appearance Sweet Flag resembles an iris (whose native species are known as "blue flag"); like iris, the leaves are narrow and sword-shaped, and grow stiffly erect to a height of three feet. The small flowers are crowded in a cylindrical mass on a spadix several inches in length, growing out at an angle from the stem. Each club-shaped inflorescence has a leaflike spathe extending behind and above it. Fleshy rootstocks which grow in tangled clumps often several feet in extent have long been used as a country remedy for indigestion. When sliced and boiled with a sugar syrup to candy them, Sweet Flag rootstocks made a primitive kind of sweetmeat. Flowers appear in spring and summer; these become dry berrylike fruits in autumn. Sweet Flag occurs from New England to Florida, and ranges westward to the plains and northwestward to Oregon.

PLATE 3

Water Arum, *Calla palustris*

PLATE 4

Skunk Cabbage, ***Symplocarpus foetidus***

JACK-IN-THE-PULPIT PLATE 2

Arisaema triphyllum *Araceae*

This familiar spring flower is so named because of the appearance of the inflorescence in the center of the pulpitlike spathe. It is also known as Indian Turnip because of its edible, turnip-shaped, underground "bulbs" which are botanically known as corms. Jack-in-the-pulpit plants reach a height of from one to several feet, and bear one or two rather long-stalked leaves, each divided into three leaflets. Very small greenish-yellow flowers are crowded on the lower part of the spadix, invisible because of the enveloping base of the spathe. The lower blossoms are pistillate, the upper staminate. The terminal portion of the colorfully striped spathe arches over the rest of the flowering structure. In late summer the spathe withers away and reveals a cluster of bright red berries at the base of the former spadix. The starchy corms, when eaten raw, have an unpleasant acrid taste. However, they formed a staple diet of the Indians, who boiled them to serve with venison; the boiled corms were also dried and ground into a meal for use in baking cakes or making gruel.

WATER ARUM PLATE 3

Calla palustris *Araceae*

In some localities known as Wild Calla, this striking native flower inhabits the cold bogs and pond margins of our more northern states. Glossy-green leaves, somewhat heart-shaped, which arise from long, buried rootstocks, are clustered fairly close to the ground or above the water surface. In their midst appear the inflorescences, each resembling a flower with a single large white petal. However, the seeming petal is actually a spathe surrounding the usual cylindrical spadix, characteristic of other members of the Arum family. The spadix is a compact mass of small yellow flowers which appear in late spring and early summer; they become transformed into clusters of red berries in autumn. The range of the Wild Calla is from New England to New Jersey, west to Minnesota. It is also found from Newfoundland to Alaska.

SKUNK CABBAGE

PLATE 4

Symplocarpus foetidus

Araceae

This widespread member of the Arum family has a twofold claim to distinction—its time of flowering and its scent. It is one of the most intrepid of the early flowers, often forcing the pointed tips of its cone-shaped spathes upward through the partly frozen soil long before any other signs of spring enliven the woodland scene. Later the leaves, if crushed, and also the spathes, emit as unpleasant an odor as is likely to be encountered in the plant kingdom. The Skunk Cabbage populates depressions and hollows in fields and open woods wherever there is an abundance of soil water. The simple leaves, which are large, coarse, and strongly veined, appear after the hooded flowers have developed. Hidden within each spathe is the characteristic cylindrical spadix with its inconspicuous flowers. After the flowers have matured, the small brown fruits form a hard rounded mass which is developed from the enlarged base of the spadix. Skunk Cabbage can be found from New England south to Georgia and west to the Mississippi valley, wherever there is swampy ground.

DRAGONROOT

PLATE 5

Arisaema dracontium

Araceae

This close relative of the jack-in-the-pulpit, also a spring flower of low moist ground, is far less common. Known in some parts of the country as Green Dragon, this member of the family bears a single large compound leaf divided into three sets of leaflets, each made up of five or more divisions. The flowering structure is unusual in that the narrow spathe which surrounds the spadix does not completely cover it; a slender whiplike tip of the spadix projects far beyond the spathe itself. The inconspicuous flowers are clustered around the base of the spadix and thus are hidden from view. In autumn the reddish orange berry clusters become evident, as the spathe withers away. Dragonroot is common from Florida to Texas, and occurs locally as far north as New England and west to the Great Lakes states.

PLATE 5

Dragonroot, *Arisaema dracontium*

PLATE 6

(*left*) Golden Club, *Orontium aquaticum* (*right*) Yellow-eyed Grass, *Xyris flexuosa*

GOLDEN CLUB

PLATE 6

Orontium aquaticum

Araceae

This is another spring-flowering species with a fondness for swamps, ponds, and streams. The bluish-green leaves, moored by long stems to the buried rootstocks, often float on the surface of the water. The flowers appear between April and June. Unlike most of its relatives, the Golden Club has a small, inconspicuous, and short-lived spathe. By flowering time there remains only the elongated spadix, covered with the small golden-yellow flowers. Each flower produces a small blue bladderlike fruit containing a single seed. Most common from Florida to Louisiana, the Golden Club can be found sparingly northward to New England and west to Minnesota.

The Yellow-Eyed Grass Family

Xyridaceae

A small group of rushlike plants, the Yellow-eyed Grass family has but a single genus in the United States. Of this there are a dozen species here; most of the rest are tropical in distribution. Narrow leaves are clustered around the base of a leafless flowering stalk topped by a head of small flowers. Familiar from Texas eastward is the common Yellow-eyed Grass.

YELLOW-EYED GRASS

PLATE 6

Xyris flexuosa

Xyridaceae

Wet fields and bogs are the home of this small grasslike plant. The narrow linear leaves, four to twelve inches in length, usually form a twisted cluster and arise from a bulblike base. The flowering stalks, as long as the leaves and frequently rising above them, bear terminal heads of small flowers. Each flower has three petals and three sepals, and reaches a width of a quarter of an inch. The flowers appear in early summer, from June through August; later they become capsules enclosing minute seeds. This Yellow-eyed Grass can be found from Maine to Forida, and west to the plains states. The other species are very similar.

The Water Plantain Family

Alismataceae

Shallow water of ponds and swamps is the natural home of the Water Plantain family. Its members are aquatic perennials with large leaves and erect stalks bearing clusters of flowers, each flower with its parts in three's. The most familiar genus, with sixteen species in eastern United States, is the Arrowhead.

ARROWHEAD — PLATE 7

Sagittaria latifolia — *Alismataceae*

Sometimes known as Broad-leaved Arrowhead, this plant of pond and stream margins and roadside ditches can be recognized when not in blossom by its large pointed leaves with acute basal lobes. It is this peculiar leaf shape which has given the species its common name. The flowers appear during the summer; each inflorescence is borne on a stout stem, one to three feet tall, with the flowers in groups of three. The individual flowers consist of three large white petals which soon drop off and three sepals which are green and persistent. The flowers in the upper portion of the inflorescence are usually staminate, the lower ones pistillate. Arrowhead has stout underground stems, or rhizomes, which have a high starch content and are edible. This feature was early discovered by the American Indians throughout the country, who boiled or roasted the tuberous roots as we use potatoes. In fact, the men in the Lewis and Clark Expedition subsisted on them as a substitute for bread.

PLATE 7

Arrowhead, *Sagittaria latifolia*

PLATE 8

(*left*) **Dayflower,** ***Commelina communis*** (*right*) **Spiderwort,** ***Tradescantia virginiana***

The Spiderwort Family

Commelinaceae

Chiefly tropical in occurrence, this family includes two genera which are commonly encountered in the eastern half of the United States. The plants have jointed, often branching stems, bearing alternate parallel-veined leaves. The flowers are grouped in small clusters, and are characterized by having their parts in three's. The ornamental Wandering Jew (Zebrina) is a trailing member of the Spiderwort family, with silvery green or striped leaves and pairs of rose-red flowers.

DAYFLOWER PLATE 8

Commelina communis *Commelinaceae*

A native of Asia, the Dayflower (so named because of the short life of its blooms) has escaped to become a wild flower of roadsides and ditches throughout eastern United States. It is a sprawling plant with the habit of forming roots at the nodes of the jointed stems; the simple lanceolate leaves of a smooth dark green sheathe the stem and are three to five inches long. Dayflowers die to the ground each winter, but survive in the underground tubers, which are provided with many fibrous roots. The flowers, produced near the tips of the branches throughout the summer months, are characterized by an irregular corolla and calyx. Two of the three unequal blue petals are larger than the third. A leaflike green bract can be found at the base of each flower. In autumn the flowers become transformed into small capsules, each containing several brown seeds.

SPIDERWORT PLATE 8

Tradescantia virginiana *Commelinaceae*

Spiderwort, with lilylike foliage and large flowers, is a taller plant than the dayflower. The narrow long-pointed leaves may reach a length of twelve inches, and the flower a diameter of two inches. Other names for this flower are Spider Lily and Bluejacket. It prefers to grow in the rich soil of woods, although when cultivated it may escape to roadsides. The flowers are symmetrical, with a regular corolla bearing three petals each of the same shape and size. The flowers last only a very short while, opening in the morning and often withering by noon. Spiderwort is an early summer flower, the blossoms appearing in June. Its range is from southern New England and New York to the Carolinas and west to Minnesota and Arkansas.

The Pickerelweed Family

Pontederiaceae

Members of this family are not numerous, being about twenty-eight in number; they are represented in the eastern portion of the United States by only half a dozen kinds. All are aquatic plants, either floating on the surface of the water or rooted in the mud; the stems arise from thick rootstocks which float beneath the surface or are buried in the mud and anchored there by numerous fibrous roots. Attractive flowers are grouped in clusters, which in some species are in compact spikes like hyacinths. Members of the family are often grown as ornamentals in water-lily pools and in large aquaria. Their irregular, six-parted flowers of attractive coloring have an orchidlike appearance. Some of the species, however, are such rampant growers that they may become serious aquatic weeds.

PLATE 9

Pickerelweed, *Pontederia cordata*

PLATE 10

Water Hyacinth, *Eichornia crassipes*

PICKERELWEED

PLATE 9

Pontederia cordata

Pontederiaceae

This aquatic perennial is a familiar sight in the shallow coves of ponds and along the borders of small streams. The large glossy-green and heart-shaped leaves are as attractive as the erect spikes of blue flowers. Each individual flower is tubular, with a two-lipped corolla. The upper lip consists of three lobes, of which the middle lobe is the largest; the lower lip is made up of three narrow and spreading lobes. The flowers are clustered in an inflorescence with a fleshy axis, arising from a leaflike spathe. The flowering period is a long one, beginning in spring and extending into early autumn. Pickerelweed can be found from New England to Florida and west to Minnesota and Oklahoma. Their leaves are sometimes blotched with irregular markings like splashes of ink.

WATER HYACINTH

PLATE 10

Eichornia crassipes

Pontederiaceae

One of the most striking sights greeting a northerner visiting Florida for the first time is the floating islands and smaller masses of Water Hyacinths which make a meadow of the smaller ponds, choke the surface of small streams for miles, and drift continuously along the broad St. John's River on its way to the sea. This attractive nuisance in our Southern States had its home in South America, whence it was introduced as a garden pool ornamental.

Water Hyacinth has adapted itself to a floating existence, its clusters of leaves being buoyed up by the inflated leaf-stalks which resemble bladders. From the base of each cluster hangs a pendulous mass of gray-brown roots, which obtain all the nourishment for the plant from the water. When the water level drops, depositing the plants on the mud, the roots function as normal roots and bury themselves in the ground. The rosettes of leaves produce erect clusters of large, slightly irregular flowers, with six lobes, varying in color from pale lilac or purple to white. The flowers appear in spring and persist through summer. The present range of this aquatic immigrant is from Georgia around the Gulf of Mexico to Texas.

The Lily Family

Liliaceae

The Lily family is one of the best known of the native American wild flower groups, its attractive flowers forming an important part of the flora of the entire country. We find a wide variety of plants in the family. In addition to the twenty-six wild flowers described and illustrated on the following pages, the Lily family includes such favorite ornamentals as the hyacinth and tulip; such food plants as asparagus, chives, leek and onion; the unusual succulent aloe; and the picturesque dagger-leaved yucca. It is a large family of some 4,000 species, most of them perennials rising from underground bulbs, corms or tubers. The leaves are narrow, often grasslike, and can be recognized by their parallel veins. The flowers consist of the usual calyx and corolla, but in most species the three sepals are colored like the three petals, so that a lily flower has generally six similarly colored segments.

Asparagus is an Old World genus, with an unusual characteristic. The leaves are reduced to small scales, so that the green threadlike branches function as leaves in manufacturing food for the plant. Thus the delicate dissected "foliage" of asparagus, as well as that of the misnamed "asparagus fern" of florists, is actually a spray of green branches. Asparagus flowers are green and small. The edible portion of the plant consists of the succulent shoots, the papery scales of which are degenerate leaves.

The native homes of the various tulips cover a wide region from the Mediterranean to Siberia, as well as in China and Japan. From some 50 species, horticulturists have produced the great number of varieties prized by gardeners. Tulips grow from large underground bulbs, which are actually compressed stems clothed with fleshy, overlapping, scalelike leaves. In spring this bulb produces the green leaves and erect stalks which bear the flowers, each with six colored sepals and petals. Another ornamental in the family, the hyacinth, has also been under cultivation for centuries. Its native home was Greece and Syria. The basal cluster of leaves and the erect, highly scented flower cluster arise, as in the tulips, from a bulb.

PLATE 11

(*left*) **Smooth Solomon's-seal,** ***Polygonatum canaliculatum*** (*right*) **Wild Onion,** ***Allium stellatum***

PLATE 12

(*left*) Dwarf White Trillium, *Trillium nivale* (*right*) Prairie Wakerobin, *Trillium recurvatum*

WILD ONION

PLATE 11

Allium stellatum

Liliaceae

Like its cultivated relatives, Wild Onion is a strongly-scented plant growing from a bulb. The slender and tapering leaves are often soft and hollow. The stiffly erect flowering stalk produces at its summit an inflorescence known as an umbel, in which the stems of the individual flowers all arise from a common center like the ribs of an umbrella. Each small flower has a regular perianth of three sepals and three petals, all similar in appearance. Wild Onion grows on rocky slopes and ridges in the central states, from Ohio and Illinois to Texas. The flowers appear in summer. A related species (*Allium cernuum*) known as the Nodding Wild Onion grows on roadside banks and hillsides from New York to the Carolinas, and west to the Dakotas. Bulbs of wild onions have a very strong flavor, but can be eaten if parboiled. Small amounts of either leaves or bulbs can be used to flavor soups. The Meadow Garlic (*Allium canadense*), common in low meadows throughout the eastern states, as its name implies, has strongly scented leaves. Chives is an onion species native to northern Europe; the leaves are used in salads and soups; the plants are low-growing, and form dense clumps with violet-colored flowers. In the species of Allium known as leek the leaves and slender bulbs together are used in cooking; it is a native of the Mediterranean region, and is cultivated more frequently in Europe than in this country.

HAIRY SOLOMON'S-SEAL

PLATE 11

Polygonatum biflorum

Liliaceae

This graceful member of the Lily family flowers in spring, together with such other woodland species as bellwort and trillium. The unusual name comes from the shape of the scar left by each year's stalk on the rhizome. Its favorite habitat is the rich valley floor and moist slopes of open woods and thickets. The slender stems are often zigzag in appearance, but always arch over at the tip; along the stems are borne nearly opposite leaves, oval and pointed at the tip. The inconspicuous greenish flowers hang in pairs (occasionally singly or in fours) from the leaf axils. The long tubular base of the flower gives an appearance of being in bud even when mature; the margin of each flower has six short lobes. By midsummer the flowers have formed dark-blue berries, each about a quarter of an inch in diameter. Hairy Solomon's-seal can be found from New England and New York south to Florida and Texas, and west to Iowa and Nebraska.

SMOOTH SOLOMON'S-SEAL — PLATE 18

Polygonatum canaliculatum — *Liliaceae*

This member is one of the tallest plants in the Lily family, its sturdy stems sometimes rising to a height of six feet. It is partial to moist thickets and woods, especially the neighborhood of river banks. The simple leaves are oval in outline, and grow alternately on the erect stems. Clusters of two to eight drooping flowers appear in spring, in the axils of the leaves. Each flower has a long tubular base with six marginal lobes. It is a rank-growing plant compared with the other Solomon's-seals. The fruit is a bluish-black berry. Smooth Solomon's-seal grows from southern New England to the Carolinas, and extends westward to Missouri and Oklahoma.

TWISTED STALK

Streptopus roseus — *Liliaceae*

This greatly resembles a Solomon's-seal in its zigzag stalk and oval, pointed leaves; the plants may reach a height of several feet. Single flowers (occasionally pairs) hang from the axils of the leaves; they are rose or purple in color, less than half an inch in length, and with longer, sharper segments of the margin than in Solomon's-seal. In autumn Twisted Stalk is very conspicuous because of its bright red berries. This species thrives in thick woods of our cooler regions, from southern Labrador southward in the mountains to Georgia and westward to Michigan.

PLATE 13

(*upper left*) **Wild Lily-of-the-Valley, *Maianthemum canadense***
(*upper right*) **Star-of-Bethlehem, *Ornithogalum umbellatum***
(*below*) **Yellow Clintonia, *Clintonia borealis***

PLATE 14

(*left*) Wild Hyacinth, *Camassia scilloides* (*right*) Indian Cucumber-root, *Medeola virginiana*

PRAIRIE WAKE-ROBIN

PLATE 12

Trillium recurvatum — *Liliaceae*

The Trilliums, or Wake-robins, are as familiar harbingers of spring as the hepaticas and bloodroots. All of the Trilliums have three conspicuous spreading or reflexed sepals, and usually three colored petals. The name, which comes from the Latin for "three," refers to this characteristic number in the floral parts and in the whorls of leaves. About a dozen different kinds of Trillium grow in eastern United States. The Prairie Wake-robin has a stout erect stem arising from a horizontal rhizome. At its summit develop three simple and broadly rounded leaves. From the center of the whorl arises a single flower with reflexed sepals and erect petals. This species has a range from Ohio to Iowa, southward to the Gulf States.

DWARF WHITE TRILLIUM

PLATE 12

Trillium nivale — *Liliaceae*

Also known as Snow Trillium, this species is smaller than its relatives, being only four or five inches in height. The narrow oval leaves are relatively small, an inch or two in length. Each flower stands erect, firmly supported by the cuplike calyx of three sepals. The Dwarf White Trillium is one of the earliest of the genus to flower, the first blooms often appearing in March and the blossoming continuing through May. This member of the Trillium group is most frequently found in rich soil, on shaded ledges in the woods. Its home is from Pennsylvania to Kentucky, west to Minnesota.

WHITE TRILLIUM

PLATE 25

Trillium grandiflorum — *Liliaceae*

If our explorations lead us to ravines and wooded slopes where the soil is rich with humus, we are likely to find the colonies of White, or Large-flowered Trillium—considered by many to be the most striking species in the genus. The erect plants reach a height of a foot or more, bearing at the top three broadly rounded leaves with pointed tips. The flowering stalk, rising in the center of the foliage, is short and stout, and supports the single flower. Pure white when they first appear, the petals gradually change in color so that after a few weeks they become pink or dull rose. The petals are much longer than the green sepals. In this species the berry, almost an inch in diameter, is a blue-black color. White Trillium can be found principally from New England to the Carolinas and westward to Wisconsin and Minnesota. It flowers from April to June.

RED TRILLIUM — PLATE 26

Trillium erectum — *Liliaceae*

This is the common Wake-robin or Birthwort, familiar flower of early spring in woods and thickets from Maine to upland Georgia, and west to Michigan. The unpleasant scent of the flower has also given it the name of Stinking Benjamin; the stout brown rhizome undoubtedly accounts for the other common name of Squawroot. Usually about a foot in height, the Red Trillium has exceptionally large leaves, up to seven inches in length and often as wide as long. A slightly arching flower stalk bears the single flower, which has three brownish pointed sepals and three petals varying in color from crimson to dark purplish brown. The fruit is an oval red berry.

PAINTED TRILLIUM — PLATE 27

Trillium undulatum — *Liliaceae*

This is a northern species which prefers cold damp woods and the acid soil of bogs. Tall slender stems, often sixteen to eighteen inches high, bear the usual set of three leaves, in this case bluish-green and terminating in long tapering tips. The flowers, either erect or arching slightly, have narrow green sepals and broad, wavy petals, the latter white marked with magenta. Painted Trillium flowers appear in April and bloom on into June; the bright red berry, developing in late summer, is oval in shape and three-sided. This species grows in the region between eastern Canada, the mountains of the Carolinas, Manitoba, and the Great Lakes states.

PLATE 15

Soapweed, *Yucca glauca*

PLATE 16

Turk's-cap Lily, *Lilium superbum*

NODDING WAKE-ROBIN

Trillium cernuum *Liliaceae*

The flower of this trillium, as its name suggests, is unusual in being drooping rather than erect. The plants reach the same size as the painted trillium, but have paler green leaves. The single flower, an inch in diameter, has narrow pointed sepals and white or pinkish petals which are recurved and edged with a wavy margin. The fruit is a reddish-purple berry. The Nodding Wake-robin grows in rich damp woods, preferring peaty soil; it can be found from Newfoundland to Georgia and west to Wisconsin. The flowers, which have a very sweet scent, appear in June in the northern states, a month earlier farther to the south.

TOADSHADE

Trillium sessile *Liliaceae*

Like the prairie wakerobin this species has its flowers sessile—that is, without an individual stalk. The oval leaves, terminating in blunt tips, are often a mottled green. The three sepals tend to be spreading while the narrow petals are more erect. One variety has green petals. Toadshade grows in rich woods from western New York southward and westward to Georgia, Mississippi, Arkansas, Missouri and Illinois.

The various species of Trillium are a welcome addition to a wild-flower garden, but need care in transplanting. Most difficult to bring into the garden is the painted trillium, while the white trillium is perhaps the easiest. A prime requirement is rich peaty soil, on the acid side for painted trillium. The best time for bringing them into the garden from the woods is in autumn when the tuberlike rhizomes can be dug up without injury to any above-ground parts; these rhizomes should be planted at least four inches deep. When grown from seed, four or five years are required for the plants to produce flowers. All trilliums do best in a shaded spot, with ample moisture in the soil.

WILD LILY OF THE VALLEY — PLATE 13

Maianthemum canadense — *Liliaceae*

This low-growing member of the Lily family is also known as Two-leaved Solomon's-seal and Canada Mayflower. A slender, often zigzag stem rarely more than six inches in height bears one to three oval, pointed leaves whose basal lobes surround the stem. Very small flowers form an open cylindrical cluster at the top of the stem; each individual flower, less than a quarter of an inch in diameter, consists of four segments instead of the family's customary units of three. The flowers appear in May, and continue to bloom through June. The fruit is a speckled berry, at first greenish or brown, later becoming pale red. Wild Lily of the Valley thrives in cool, moist woods, and can be found from Labrador southward to the uplands of Georgia and Tennessee, and west to Iowa.

YELLOW CLINTONIA — PLATE 13

Clintonia borealis — *Liliaceae*

Also known as Dogberry and Corn-lily, this short-stemmed plant arises from a creeping rhizome which produces a basal cluster of two to five large glossy-green leaves. From May until midsummer the plants send up leafless flowering stalks a foot or more in height, which bear at the tip a small cluster of three to six flowers. Occasionally plants can be found which develop a second flower cluster below the terminal one. Each flower is about an inch in length, with six equal and spreading greenish-yellow segments. The fruits are conspicuous objects in the woods in late summer and autumn, being shiny dark blue berries. Yellow Clintonia grows in moist woods from Labrador to the mountains of Georgia and Tennessee and westward to Minnesota. A related species with small, speckled white flowers and black berries, known as White Clintonia (*Clintonia umbellulata*) grows in the rich woods of New York and Ohio, southward to Georgia and Tennessee.

PLATE 17

Indian Poke, *Veratrum viride*

PLATE 18

Hairy Solomon's-seal, *Polygonatum biflorum*

STAR-OF-BETHLEHEM

PLATE 13

Ornithogalum umbellatum *Liliaceae*

Star-of-Bethlehem is a succulent bulb-forming plant introduced from Europe into our northern states, and frequently found as an escaped plant in roadside grassy areas from Newfoundland to Nebraska and as far south as Mississippi. The underground bulb produces a cluster of slender basal leaves, and an erect flowering stalk tipped with a cluster of star-shaped flowers. Each flower has six segments, faintly marked with green on the back. Flowers appear in May and June, and produce rounded-angular capsule fruits later in the summer. Star-of-Bethlehem is one of the poisonous members of the Lily family, all parts reputed to be harmful if eaten.

WILD HYACINTH

PLATE 14

Camassia scilloides *Liliaceae*

This member of the Lily family is also known as Eastern Camass, or Squill. It is an onionlike plant arising from a bulb and bearing narrow grasslike leaves. Some consider it one of the most beautiful of our wild flowers; its blooming period is May and June. A leafless flowering stalk, reaching a height of eighteen inches, produces at its summit a loose cluster of star-shaped flowers each with six segments. The native Wild Hyacinth grows mostly in open woods, fields and meadows from Pennsylvania south to Alabama and westward to Iowa and Texas.

INDIAN CUCUMBER-ROOT

PLATE 14

Medeola virginiana *Liliaceae*

A tall erect plant, one to two feet in height, Indian Cucumber-root is distinctive because of the two whorls of leaves which clothe the stem. The lower whorl consists of five to nine oval leaves with tapering base and pointed tip. Young plants, when only this whorl of leaves is present, resemble small umbrellas. The upper whorl, near the top of the stem, is made up of three smaller leaves; from this whorl arises a drooping cluster of several to nine flowers. Each flower is given a spidery appearance by the six projecting brown stamens and the spreading three-parted style. The flowers appear in May and June; after fertilization the flower stalks become erect and bear dark purple berries in an upright position, in the center of the upper leaf whorl. Indian Cucumber-root prefers moist woods, over a wide range from Quebec to Florida and west to the Mississippi river. The name refers to the thick, white tuberlike rootstock which may reach a length of three inches, its brittle nature and cucumberlike flavor.

SOAPWEED — PLATE 15

Yucca glauca — *Liliaceae*

The genus Yucca includes some of the most peculiar, even grotesque, flowering plants of our southwestern states. Soapweed is the only species which is found also in Iowa and Missouri and as far north as the Dakotas. The stem lies partially on the ground, with its tip upturned sufficiently to support a crown of swordlike leaves which are rigid and sharp-tipped. The flowering stalk, up to three feet in height, bears an open cluster of showy flowers; each flower consists of six similar segments, which are broad with a minute point at the tip.

Along the eastern coastal plain occurs Adam's-needle or Silkgrass (*Yucca filamentosa*). This has a similar basal cluster of sharp-pointed leaves, radiating in all directions from the short stem; it produces a taller flowering stalk, sometimes ten feet in height, and bearing a larger cluster of creamy-white flowers. Soapweed and Adam's-needle both grow in dry sandy locations, beach dunes, and old fields. In Florida and the adjacent states two additional species of Yucca add a picturesque touch to the pine-lands, dry fields, and beaches. These attain the size of small trees, and have either unbranched or branched erect stems reaching a stature of ten or fifteen feet, completely armed with the needle-sharp, rigid, succulent leaves. They are very distinctive when in blossom, the flowering stalk arising from the top of the stem with a dense cluster of large flowers, often five or six feet in height. The flowers are produced during the early summer months, later giving rise to capsules filled with black seeds. One of these southern species is known as Spanish Bayonet (*Yucca gloriosa*), another Spanish Dagger (*Yucca aloifolia*).

PLATE 19

False Solomon's-seal, ***Smilacina racemosa***

PLATE 20

(*left*) **Yellow Dogtooth Violet,** ***Erythronium americanum*** (*right*) **White Dogtooth Violet,** ***Erythronium albidum***

FALSE SOLOMON'S-SEAL

PLATE 19

Smilacina racemosa — *Liliaceae*

Another local name for this robust plant is Wild Spikenard; it is a large member of the Lily family, reaching a stature of three feet under ideal growing conditions. The stem is erect and characteristically zigzag, bearing alternate oval leaves and a large terminal cluster of small flowers. Each flower has six spreading oblong segments. The flowers can be found from May through July. False Solomon's-seal prefers wooded slopes and moist bluffs. In autumn the flower cluster becomes a mass of red berries, which are conspicuous in the thinning woods. A related species, Three-leaved Solomon's-seal (*Smilacina trifolia*) is more slender, recognizable by the three sheathing leaves and the small cluster of white flowers. It grows in wet woods from New England to Pennsylvania, west to Michigan.

BUNCHFLOWER

Melanthium virginicum — *Liliaceae*

This tall perennial, characterized by a stout erect stem three to five feet high, bears grasslike leaves which are often a foot in length. Small greenish yellow flowers, which turn brown as they grow older, each possess six spreading segments with narrowed bases. The flowers are grouped in an open terminal cluster, and appear during the summer. The Bunchflower can be found in wet woods and meadows from southern New York to Florida and Texas. The nearest relative in the Lily family is Indian poke (Pl. 17).

FALSE ASPHODEL

Tofieldia glutinosa — *Liliaceae*

This is another member of the Lily family with narrow grasslike leaves; it is a smaller plant, rarely reaching a height of more than twelve inches. The narrow leaves grow in a basal tuft or cluster, from which rises a slender flowering stalk bearing at its tip a small cylindrical cluster of white flowers.

Each individual flower is about a quarter of an inch in diameter, with six oblong segments. False Asphodel flowers can be found in June and July, in the marshes and bogs where it has its home. It is a fairly rare plant, ranging from Newfoundland to New York, southward in the mountains and west to Minnesota.

TURK'S-CAP LILY

PLATE 16

Lilium superbum

Liliaceae

The true lilies are members of the genus Lilium, which includes some seventy species with showy flowers common to the North Temperate zone. Few wild flowers are so delicately and strikingly colored, and several of the species adapt themselves well to transplanting in a wild-flower garden. The Turk's-cap Lily is one of the taller members of the genus, plants normally reaching a height of five or six feet and often eight. The lower leaves are whorled, the upper ones sometimes in pairs. Nodding flowers, usually in pairs, appear on erect stalks from July through early September. As many as fifty may occur on a single plant. The Turk's-cap Lily can be found in wet meadows and swampy woods from New England to Alabama.

CANADA LILY

PLATE 23

Lilium canadense

Liliaceae

Also known as Meadow or Wild Yellow Lily, this lily is slightly smaller in size than the Turk's-cap, being usually two to four feet in height. The rootstock produces several scaly white bulbs, which aid in reproduction of the species. The lancelike pointed leaves grow in whorls of four or more, although alternately placed leaves sometimes occur. At the top of the stem one to many nodding flowers are developed, at the ends of long flowering stalks. The six perianth segments are ordinarily recurved. The Canada Lily grows in wet meadows and open woods in the cooler portions of the East, from the Gaspé peninsula to Ohio south to the mountains of Kentucky. It flowers between mid-June and early August.

PLATE 21

Daylily, *Hemerocallis fulva*

PLATE 22

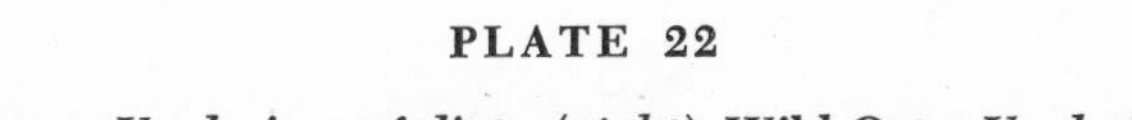

(*left*) **Bellwort,** ***Uvularia perfoliata*** (*right*) **Wild Oats,** ***Uvularia sessilifolia***

WOOD LILY

PLATE 24

Lilium philadelphicum *Liliaceae*

Known in some localities as Wild Red Lily, this member of the genus bears its flowers erect rather than nodding, as in the two preceding species. The plants are smaller, also, rarely growing taller than three feet. Like the other lilies, it grows from an underground bulb. Whorls of three or more slender pointed leaves grow at intervals on the erect stem. At the top of the stem a single flower (occasionally several) will develop, three to four inches in size. Wood Lilies thrive in drier habitats than the others, being found often in open woods and clearings. Their range is from southern Canada to North Carolina, west to Kentucky.

In the southern states, from North Carolina around the coastal plain to Louisiana, grows a close relative of the wood lily, known as the Leopard Lily or Pine Lily (*Lilium catesbaei*). This species is found in moist pine-lands and swampy woods, where it flowers in late summer. The erect flowers, red and growing singly on the stems, have segments which are rounded and taper to slender basal portions. Another southeastern species is the Carolina Lily (*Lilium michauxii*), with nodding flowers very similar to those of the Turk's-cap; the leaves are blunter and more broadly rounded. The Carolina Lily frequents pine and oak woods, from Virginia to Florida and Louisiana.

Many varieties of lilies are grown by florists and by gardeners. Most familiar is the Easter Lily (*Lilium longiflorum*) whose fragrant white blossoms are used as decorations at weddings and other functions. The native home of the Easter Lily is China and Formosa; it has been introduced into Bermuda where many of our plants now are grown. It is estimated that annually millions of bulbs are imported from these countries for forcing by American florists. The Tiger Lily (*Lilium tigrinum*) also comes from the Far East, its native home being China and Japan. Of all the introduced lilies this is one of the hardiest and easiest to grow. Plants often escape and establish themselves as roadside wild flowers. A spectacular, and also familiar, cultivated species is the Showy Lily (*Lilium speciosum*) which bears white flowers which are tinged with pink in the center and spotted with red.

INDIAN POKE

PLATE 17

Veratrum viride — *Liliaceae*

Also known as American or False Hellebore, this is one of the tallest and rankest appearing of the eastern members of the Lily family, some plants growing to a height of eight feet. The stout unbranched stems bear alternate leaves which are strongly veined and accordion-pleated; leaves reach a length of twelve inches. The fairly small flowers are densely clustered on the top of the stem. Flowers appear in early summer, and later produce three-lobed capsules. Indian Poke is one of our few poisonous wild flowers. The perennial rootstock possesses a toxic alkaloid which is fatal to sheep and other grazing animals. The plant should be carefully avoided by humans too. Poisoning symptoms from ingestion include abdominal cramps, difficulty in walking, general paralysis, and convulsions. Indian Poke grows in swampy meadows and woods, from Quebec to Georgia, westward to Minnesota.

YELLOW DOGTOOTH VIOLET

PLATE 20

Erythronium americanum — *Liliaceae*

A familiar wild flower of early spring in the eastern states, this common member of the Lily family is also known by a variety of other, actually more appropriate names: Trout Lily, Fawn Lily, Yellow Adder's-tongue. It is a low-growing plant with little or no stem, rising from an underground corm. The narrow pointed leaves, mottled with brown, seem to spring directly from the earth. Between the leaves rises a short flowering stem, six to twelve inches tall, bearing a single nodding flower with six recurved or spreading segments which may reach a length of several inches. Dogtooth Violets grow in rich woods and meadows, often forming extensive beds to the exclusion of other plants. The first flowers appear in March, and flowering continues on through June. This species ranges from New Brunswick to Florida and west to Ontario and Oklahoma.

PLATE 23

Canada Lily, *Lilium canadense*

PLATE 24

Wood Lily, ***Lilium philadelphicum***

WHITE DOGTOOTH VIOLET — PLATE 20

Erythronium albidum — *Liliaceae*

Very similar to the yellow dogtooth violet in general habit, this species has leaves more rarely mottled and flowers which are pinkish to bluish white. It flowers somewhat later, from April to June, but is a less common species. Its range is from southern Ontario to Georgia, west to Missouri and Oklahoma.

DAYLILY — PLATE 21

Hemerocallis fulva — *Liliaceae*

A native of Europe and Asia commonly grown in gardens in the United States, the Daylily often escapes to become a roadside wild flower. It can also be found in meadows and along the edges of thickets. The plants have narrow irislike leaves several feet in length, growing in a basal cluster. The flowering stalks are leafless and grow to a height of four or five feet. At their tips develop six to twelve flowers on short stalks; the funnel-shaped blooms are four to five inches in length, with the three outer segments flat and straight-margined, the three inner segments wavy-margined. The flowering period begins in May and lasts through July. Individual flowers are short-lived, hence the name Daylily.

BELLWORT — PLATE 22

Uvularia perfoliata — *Liliaceae*

Also known as Strawbell, this inconspicuous flower of rich woods and thickets grows from a short underground rhizome; the oval-pointed leaves are smooth, with the base of the leaf growing around the stem. Full-grown plants reach a height of twelve to twenty inches, with a forking stem sparsely clothed with leaves. The terminal flowers, one or few in number, are drooping, with a bell-shaped perianth of six similar segments. Flowering from late April to early June, the Bellwort can be found from southern Ontario to Florida, Alabama and Louisiana.

WHITE CAMASS

Zigadenus glaucus *Liliaceae*

The linear grasslike leaves of this genus of the Lily family grow on the lower parts of the slender stem, usually a foot or two in height. The creamy white flowers, tinged with green on the backs of the segments, grow in an open cluster at the top of the stem, appearing during late summer and early autumn. It thrives on lime soils and ledges from Quebec to Virginia and North Carolina, westward to the Great Lakes region. Related species in the western states, known as Death Camass, have foliage, flowers and seeds which are very poisonous to grazing animals.

WILD OATS

PLATE 22

Uvularia sessilifolia *Liliaceae*

This species is also known as the Sessile-leaved Bellwort; it has slender stems which rarely exceed twelve inches in height. The oblong or slightly tapering leaves are a pale green on the undersurface. Drooping flowers, an inch or slightly less in length, are characterized by the same similar six segments as in the bellwort. Wild Oats is an inconspicuous flower of moist woodlands, flowering from April to June, and found from New Brunswick to Georgia, westward to North Dakota and Alabama.

LARGE-FLOWERED BELLWORT

Uvularia grandiflora *Liliaceae*

The largest of the bellworts, this species has leaves whose bases grow around the stem, as in the Strawbell. Plants reach a height of twenty inches, but are usually around a foot tall. The drooping and slender bell-shaped flowers are a lemon-yellow color and an inch or slightly more in length; they can be found from April to June in rich woods from Quebec to North Dakota and from Georgia to Oklahoma.

PLATE 25

White Trillium, *Trillium grandiflorum*

PLATE 26

Red Trillium, ***Trillium erectum***

The Amaryllis Family

Amaryllidaceae

The Amaryllis family is a group of lilylike plants distinguished from the lilies by having the ovary of the flower attached to the calyx and the stamens attached to the inside of the corolla tube. In the Lily family the ovary is free from the calyx, a condition which is known as a "superior ovary." The plants in the Amaryllis family are perennials growing from rootstocks, bulbs, or corms; the leaves are narrow and grasslike; and the flowers have a perianth of six segments, in some species with a tubular base. Native wild flowers in the family include yellow star grass, Atamasco lily, spider lily, and crinum lily, also the century plants. Such garden ornamentals as the narcissus, jonquil, and daffodil are also in the group.

The genus Narcissus is native to the Mediterranean region, central Europe, and the Orient. Various species in the genus have been under cultivation as ornamentals for many centuries. The bulbs are planted in late summer or early autumn, and the spearlike leaves penetrate the earth with the first warm days of spring. The flower consists of six spreading segments and a tubular base, and a peculiar trumpet- or cup-shaped crown known as a corona. Paper-white narcissi bear showy white flowers with a small corona and spreading segments. The similar Chinese sacred lily is yellow. Jonquils have small clustered creamy white or yellow flowers with small cup-shaped coronas. The familiar daffodils have white, cream, or yellow flowers with a long conspicuous corona and proportionally smaller perianth segments.

YELLOW STAR-GRASS PLATE 28

Hypoxis hirsuta *Amaryllidaceae*

A low-growing and stemless plant with grasslike leaves. Yellow Star-grass grows from a short cormlike rhizome. The leaves are often hairy, and tend to obscure the shorter flowering stalks which are only four or five inches in height. The terminal flower cluster consists of a few inconspicuous flowers, each star-shaped with six regular segments. Yellow Star-grass prefers the dry soil and sunny habitats of meadows and open thickets. The flowers first appear in late spring and persist through late summer; the plants occur from New England to Florida, west to North Dakota and Texas.

ATAMASCO LILY — PLATE 28

Zephyranthes atamasco — *Amaryllidaceae*

Also known as Zephyr Lily, this low-growing stemless member of the Amaryllis family rises from an underground bulb, producing a few slender grasslike leaves which are bright green and shiny. A short flowering stalk, rarely more than twelve inches tall, bears a terminal and usually erect lily-like flower whose six segments are partially fused at the base to form a tubular perianth. Colonies of these bright little flowers spring up in moist grassy places and meadows along the edge of woods, resembling the cultivated crocus in habit of growth. Atamasco Lilies bloom from April through June, and can be found from Virginia southward to Mississippi and Alabama.

SPIDER LILY — PLATE 29

Hymenocallis occidentalis — *Amaryllidaceae*

The six long, slender perianth segments give the flower of this species a spidery appearance, explaining the common name. The base of the perianth is funnel-shaped, and in the center of the flower is a peculiar crown which forms a cup-shaped structure uniting the base of the stamens. Spider Lilies have long irislike leaves a foot or more in length; the slender flowering stalk produces a cluster of three to six flowers which are very showy. This species is very water-loving, and therefore is found along marshy banks of streams and similar habitats; its range is from Georgia to Alabama, west to Missouri and Illinois. The flowering period is early May through September.

PLATE 27

Painted Trillium, *Trillium undulatum*

PLATE 28

(*left*) Yellow Star-grass, ***Hypoxis hirsuta*** (*right*) Atamasco Lily, ***Zephyranthes atamasco***

CRINUM LILY

PLATE 30

Crinum americanum *Amaryllidaceae*

Another name for this attractive wild flower is Florida Swamp Lily, referring to its partiality for wet habitats. It is one of the tallest members of the Amaryllis family, its flowering stalk reaching a height of four feet. The simple leaves, which are basal, are narrow and grasslike. Several fragrant large flowers are borne in a terminal cluster. Each flower has a funnel-shaped base and long spreading petals and petallike sepals. The American species is one of sixty which make up the genus, most of them tropical in distribution. The Crinum Lily flowers throughout late spring and continues all summer; its home is from Florida to Texas.

AMERICAN ALOE

Agave virginica *Amaryllidaceae*

This is a representative of an interesting genus of the Amaryllis family characterized by thick succulent leaves which grow in a basal cluster. In the American Aloe these leaves may be purple-spotted as well as the more usual green. A flowering stalk, three to six feet tall, bears fragrant greenish-yellow flowers in a loose terminal cluster. The funnel-shaped perianth of each flower terminates in six lobes or segments. American Aloe, found in sandy and open woods from Virginia to Florida and Texas, blooms throughout the summer months. Relatives of this species, known as "century plants," are familiar sights in the southern and southwestern states. The huge succulent leaves, sharply pointed and often edged with teeth, form unusual ornamental groupings, and develop treelike flowering stalks twenty or thirty feet high. Many species flower once and then die. Since it usually takes plants twenty to thirty years to develop their huge stalks of blossoms, they are popularly considered to flower "once in a century."

The Iris Family

Iridaceae

The Iris family, with 1,500 species, is another large group. While it is represented by four genera in the United States, a greater number is found in Africa, which is the center of distribution for the family. The group consists of perennials reproducing by rhizomes, bulbs or corms from which grow solitary stems with narrow swordlike leaves which are parallel-veined. The flowers, whether occurring singly or several in a cluster, are often very showy. The characteristic feature of the family is found in the flowers, which have inferior ovaries as in the Amaryllis family but only three stamens instead of six. Sepals and petals are colored more or less alike.

Two ornamental genera in this family, in addition to the genus Iris itself, have become favorites with American gardeners. Plants of the genus Crocus have been introduced from the Mediterranean region and southwestern Asia. Their erect funnel-shaped flowers seem to rise directly out of the ground amid grasslike leaves. The genus Gladiolus is a large one, with its native home in Africa and Asia; the showy flowers grow in crowded spikes, each flower with unequal segments to the perianth, some of which form hoods over the throat of the flower. Interest in this member of the Iris family has resulted in the development of more than ten thousand horticultural varieties, and the formation of the American Gladiolus Society.

Of the four native North American genera in the Iris family, most common are the irises themselves and the blue-eyed grasses.

SOUTHERN BLUE FLAG PLATE 31

Iris hexagona *Iridaceae*

This iris has larger flowers than the common blue flag found farther north; it grows to the same size as the red iris. The basal portions of both petals and sepals are often tinged with green. The Southern Blue Flag grows in swamps and roadside ditches from South Carolina to Florida, and west to Missouri.

PLATE 29

Spider Lily, *Hymenocallis occidentalis*

PLATE 30

Crinum Lily, *Crinum americanum*

RED IRIS

PLATE 31

Iris fulva — *Iridaceae*

This is a tall plant with large, simple, sword-shaped leaves and a zigzag stem, reaching a height of three or four feet. Short-stemmed flowers are borne erect in a terminal cluster. Each flower consists of three spreading or recurved colored sepals, three smaller petals, and an unusual development in the form of colored petallike stigmas. The basal portions of the petals and sepals are united into a tube. The color of this species is variable, from orange and copper to salmon-pink and scarlet. Like most members of the genus Iris it prefers the moist soil of marshes, ditches, and wet fields. The flowers appear in May and June. Red Iris is a southern species, being most common from Alabama to Georgia.

COMMON BLUE FLAG

PLATE 32

Iris versicolor — *Iridaceae*

This is the Blue Flag of margins of streams and ponds, found throughout the eastern states from New England to Virginia and west to Minnesota, where from May to August the erect and trim flower clusters add color to moist roadside areas and fields. Round smooth stems rise to a height of two or three feet, bearing typical iris flowers with six perianth segments and a tubular base. The plants crowd together to form a miniature thicket of tapering swordlike leaves. Because of the presence in the rootstock of a bitter resinous substance which causes intestinal upsets, this species is also known in some localities as Poison Flag.

NARROW BLUE FLAG

Iris prismatica — *Iridaceae*

This is a more slender species than the common blue flag, characterized by more narrow grasslike leaves. The blue flowers, veined with yellow, have narrow perianth segments which are more spreading than those of the common blue flag. The Narrow Blue Flag also grows in marshes and swamps, but is found in a more restricted area, between Maine and Delaware. Because of its preference for brackish or saline habitats, it is more common along the coast than inland.

BLUE-EYED GRASS PLATE 33

Sisyrinchium angustifolium *Iridaceae*

A tufted grasslike plant, common to meadows and grassy hillsides, this species is an inconspicuous member of the Iris family—a miniature of its more impressive relatives. The leafy portions of the plant are hidden among the grasses, being rarely more than six or ten inches in height. The stiffly erect stems bear small starlike flowers, a quarter to a half an inch in breadth, in a small cluster from a green leaflike bract. The six spreading perianth segments are all petallike. Blue-eyed Grass first flowers in May, and flower-bearing plants can be found throughout the summer, from southeastern Canada to Florida and Texas, as well as in the plains states.

The Canna Family

Cannaceae

The Canna family is a small one, with but one genus of some sixty species centering in the West Indian and Central American region. The members of this family are large coarse perennials growing from a tuberous rhizome. Leafy bracts occur on the flowering stalk. The elliptic to oblong foliage leaves are pinnately veined, with a prominent midrib. Floral development is unusual in that the stamens are colored and petallike, adding to the effect of the perianth with its three greenish or purple sepals and three erect petals.

PLATE 31

(*left*) **Red Iris, *Iris fulva*** (*right*) **Southern Blue Flag, *Iris hexagona***

PLATE 32

Common Blue Flag, *Iris versicolor*

GOLDEN CANNA

PLATE 33

Canna flaccida

Cannaceae

Wild Canna, or Golden Canna, is a marsh-dwelling plant related to the familiar ornamental cannas of gardens. The showy flowers are borne in a small terminal cluster, and they begin to open in early spring. Golden Canna is a southern species, being found only from South Carolina to Florida.

The Orchid Family

Orchidaceae

Orchids are the aristocrats of the plant kingdom; in their floral structure they represent one of the climax developments in plant evolution. The Orchid family, which is most abundant in the tropics, is a large one, with ten to fifteen thousand, perhaps twenty thousand species. The members of the family found wild in eastern United States are predominantly terrestrial —that is, they grow with their roots (generally tuberous) in the ground. Among these are the lady's-slippers, fringed orchids, ladies'-tresses, pogonia, calypso, and swamp pink. The tropical species, among which are a few rare representatives in Florida, are chiefly epiphytic—that is, they live as growths on other plants, mainly trees. Epiphytes do not injure the plant to which they attach themselves, but merely use it for support. Epiphytic orchids have peculiar swollen leaf-stalks and aerial hanging roots covered with a water-absorbing tissue. In tropical forests such orchids form aerial gardens on the limbs of the trees.

The orchid flower itself is a complex structure, with three petallike sepals and three petals which, when looked at from the front, form an irregularly shaped flower with the upper and lower portions different. One of the petals has become a conspicuous lip with a special function of secreting nectar and attracting insects. The expensive orchid of the florist is usually some species or variety of Cattleya, which is native to tropical America and especially abundant in Brazil. The showy flowers have large membranous or fleshy petals with a lobed lip whose edges are frequently rolled to form a tube around the fused column of stamens and pistil. In color these orchid flowers vary from purple to rose, lilac and white. The closest native relative to the tropical epiphytes is the Greenfly Orchid (*Epidendrum*) found on live oaks and magnolias in Florida and Louisiana; its green-and-purple flowers grow in clusters amid tufted stems bearing elliptical leaves.

MOCCASIN-FLOWER — PLATE 34

Cypripedium acaule — *Orchidaceae*

The Lady's-slippers or Moccasin-flowers are easily recognizable by the inflated sac which forms the lip of the flower. This stemless pink Lady's-slipper has two large simple oval leaves with parallel veins rising from the base of the flowering stalk, which grows six to twelve inches high. The single drooping flower appears in May and June. This species prefers the dry acid soil of sandy or rocky woods and thrives in the company of either pines and hemlocks or deciduous trees. It can be found from Newfoundland to Saskatchewan and south to Georgia and Alabama.

YELLOW LADY'S-SLIPPER — PLATE 37

Cypripedium pubescens — *Orchidaceae*

Also known as Downy Lady's-slipper, this species bears leaves along its stem, each leaf oval and pointed, and up to six inches in length. The flowering stalks reach a height of two feet or more, bearing at their tips nodding flowers with long twisted sepals and an inflated saclike lip. Inside the top of the sac is a tuft of white hairs. In various forms the Yellow Lady's-slipper is found from April to June in rich moist woods from Quebec to Yukon and southward to the southern and southwestern states.

PLATE 33

(*left*) **Golden Canna,** ***Canna flaccida*** (*right*) **Blue-eyed Grass,**
Sisyrinchium angustifolium

PLATE 34

Mocassin-flower, *Cypripedium acaule*

SHOWY LADY'S-SLIPPER — PLATE 36

Cypripedium reginae — *Orchidaceae*

This is one of the largest and most spectacular of our native terrestrial orchids. The stout stem grows to a height of three feet, and may be leafy to the top. Elliptic leaves, tapering to pointed tips, reach a length of eight inches. One to three flowers grow at the summit of the plant, conspicuous in their bicolored attire. Because of its spectacular beauty this species has been picked unwisely by those who are not satisfied to enjoy the sight of a flower in its natural state. The Showy Lady's-slipper should be rigidly protected if it is to remain a member of our native flora. It grows in cool swamps and bogs from Newfoundland to the mountains of North Carolina, west to Tennessee, Missouri, and North Dakota. The flowers appear in June and July, rarely in May or August.

SMALL WHITE LADY'S-SLIPPER — PLATE 42

Cypripedium candidum — *Orchidaceae*

This slender plant of sphagnum bogs and marshy meadows is not as common as the preceding species. Three to five elliptical, pointed leaves clothe the erect stem, which rarely is more than a foot in height. The flowers occur usually singly at the tip of the flowering stalk; they bear slender twisted sepals which taper to a point, and a plump saclike lip. This species flowers in May and June, and can be found mainly in restricted areas from New York to North Dakota.

RAM'S-HEAD LADY'S-SLIPPER

Cypripedium arietinum — *Orchidaceae*

The slender stem is leafy nearly to its tip, with several small elliptical leaves two to four inches long. The flowering stalk, six to twelve inches in height, bears a single flower at its summit. The red-and-white strongly veined lip is prolonged at its tip so that there is a striking resemblance to a ram's head. This is a rare species of cold woods from Quebec and Ontario to New York, west to Michigan and Wisconsin. The flowers appear in May and June.

ROSE POGONIA — PLATE 35

Pogonia ophioglossoides — *Orchidaceae*

Pogonia, or Beard-flower, is a slender and graceful member of the Orchid family, its stem with several oval and pointed leaves growing to a height of eight or ten inches. The flowers are usually single at the top of the stalk, nodding and very fragrant. Five of the sepals and petals are alike in appearance. The sixth, the flattened lip, is crested and fringed, the latter character being responsible for one of its common names. Pogonia thrives in sphagnum bogs, mossy woods, and similar moist secluded habitats from Canada to Florida, west to the Mississippi river and beyond to eastern Texas. The flowers develop from May through August.

SWAMP PINK — PLATE 35

Arethusa bulbosa — *Orchidaceae*

There is a delicate spritelike quality to this beautiful woodland flower which is appropriate to the implication of the scientific name "Arethusa," who was a Greek nymph. Swamp Pink is also known as Arethusa, or Dragon's-mouth. It is a slender plant five to ten inches tall, seemingly leafless because the single grasslike leaf appears only after the flower has withered. The single terminal flower is relatively large, with similar petals and sepals except for the lip, which is ornately fringed or toothed and bears three hairy crests on its upper surface. Arethusa lives in sphagnum bogs and peaty woods, from southeastern Canada and New England to Minnesota, and from Pennsylvania southward in the mountains. The flowers appear in June and July.

PLATE 35

(*left*) **Rose Pogonia,** ***Pogonia ophioglossoides*** (*center*) **Calypso,** ***Calypso bulbosa***
(*right*) **Swamp Pink,** ***Arethusa bulbosa***

PLATE 36

Showy Lady's-slipper, *Cypripedium reginae*

CALYPSO

PLATE 35

Calypso bulbosa — *Orchidaceae*

The goddess Calypso could well be flattered by having this rare and exquisite member of the Orchid family named after her. The orchid Calypso, or Fairy Slipper, is distinctly a cold-climate plant, found in cool mossy woods and cedar swamps from Labrador to the Aleutian Islands and from Maine to Montana and New Mexico, as well as in the west coast states. A slender leafless flowering stalk rises from a tuber which produces also a single basal leaf; the stalk is rarely more than six inches tall. The flower resembles a small lady's-slipper, with its spreading or drooping saclike lip. Calypso generally flowers in May or June.

CORALROOT

PLATE 38

Corallorhiza maculata — *Orchidaceae*

Green is the emblem of the plant kingdom, representing the chlorophyll mechanism which enables plants to live independently of other living things, synthesizing their food from air and water through the utilization of sunlight. In many plant families there are genera and species which have lost this photosynthetic ability and green color, and as a consequence subsist on organic materials absorbed from the environment. In some such cases, where the organic material consists of dead organisms or parts of organisms, the nongreen plant is known as a saprophyte. Coralroot is a saprophyte, living in this way on the humus and other organic debris of plant life found in rich woods. The food is absorbed through corallike underground rhizomes, which give the plant its common name. The aboveground parts of the plant consist of leafless (the leaves are reduced to small scales) purplish or brownish stems which bear terminal clusters of flowers. The lip of the flower is deeply divided into three lobes and bears a yellowish spur. Coralroot flowers appear mostly in July and August, in woods across Canada, throughout the United States, except in warm dry regions, and in Mexico and Guatemala.

CRESTED CORALROOT

Hexalectris spicata *Orchidaceae*

This is another saprophyte in the Orchid family, closely related to the preceding genus, and sometimes called Brunetta. The sepals and petals are nearly equal and spreading; the three-lobed lip lacks the spur of the other coralroots. The purplish stem, sheathed with scalelike leaves, develops flowers from June to August in dry woods of the southern states, from Maryland to Florida and westward to New Mexico.

LADIES'-TRESSES

PLATE 38

Spiranthes cernua *Orchidaceae*

The Ladies'-tresses—also known as Pearl-twists and Screw-augers—are inconspicuous members of the Orchid family, with small fragrant flowers tightly packed in a slender terminal spike which is spirally twisted. Common Ladies'-tresses grows six to twenty-four inches in height, with the narrow pointed leaves grouped in a basal cluster. It is a summer and early autumn flowering species, found in wet woods and meadows from Nova Scotia to Florida and west to beyond the Mississippi River.

SMALL ROUND-LEAVED ORCHIS

Orchis rotundifolia *Orchidaceae*

This is one of the rarest orchids of northeastern United States, living in secluded areas of cool mossy woods from Greenland to Alaska and New England to Minnesota. A single rounded basal leaf grows at the foot of a slender six-inch-tall flowering stalk. Five to ten rose-colored flowers, half the size of those of the showy orchis, terminate the stalk; the lip is white, spotted with purple.

PLATE 37

Yellow Lady's-slipper, *Cypripedium pubescens*

PLATE 38

(*left*) **Coral-root, *Corallorhiza maculata*** (*center*) **Showy Orchis, *Orchis spectabilis***
(*right*) **Ladies' Tresses, *Spiranthes cernua***

SHOWY ORCHIS

PLATE 38

Orchis spectabilis

Orchidaceae

The stems and foliage of this member of the Orchid family lack the delicate grace of many of the species already described. The flowering stalks are fleshy and five-angled, arising between a pair of broadly oval leaves which are clammy to the touch. A terminal spike bears a cluster of three to ten flowers, a foot or less above the ground. The individual flowers, as the name implies, are very showy, about an inch in length; the sepals form a colorful hood, and together with the petals are purple in color; the white lip is prolonged into a spur which is as long as the petals. The Showy Orchis thrives in damp mossy woods from New Brunswick to Georgia and westward to Minnesota and Arkansas. The flowers appear in May and June.

GRASS PINK

PLATE 39

Calopogon pulchellus

Orchidaceae

Also known as Swamp Pink, this species is a slender plant of sphagnum bogs and peaty meadows throughout the entire eastern United States and Canada, its flowers appearing from late spring through summer. A bulblike tuber produces a single elongated leaf which sheathes the erect flowering stalk. Three to fifteen flowers are borne in a loose spike at the summit of the stalk. Each flower has a conspicuous lip with projecting flanges at its base, and a white beard with yellow-and-crimson tips. A closely related, smaller species is restricted to the pine barrens of the southeast, from Virginia to Louisiana.

EPIDENDRUM

PLATE 39

Epidendrum tampensis

Orchidaceae

This epiphytic orchid, also known as Encyclia, is one of several kinds sometimes called Butterfly Orchid. It is found only in peninsular Florida, growing on branches of trees in the subtropical forests of that state. A cluster of bulblike stems bears arching narrow leaves and a branching flowering stem with its cluster of nodding flowers. Each flower has broad spreading sepals and spoon-shaped petals; the lip is three-lobed, with the middle lobe the largest. The flowers appear in spring and on through summer.

SMALL PURPLE FRINGED ORCHIS — PLATE 40

Habenaria psycodes — *Orchidaceae*

The group of wild flowers known as the Fringed Orchids, or Rein Orchises, usually are characterized by many small flowers in a dense terminal cluster; the flowers have distinctive fringed lips in most species. The Small Purple Fringed Orchis is a species whose presence is often indicated by its elusive fragrance before it is actually seen. A slender stem one to two feet high bears elliptical or pointed leaves which become smaller towards the summit. The small flowers are compactly clustered in a terminal raceme which may reach a length of six or eight inches. The fan-shaped segments of the lip are conspicuously fringed. This species frequents wet meadows and low woods from eastern Canada to the Carolinas and west to the Great Lakes region and beyond. The flowers appear in July and August.

RAGGED ORCHIS — PLATE 40

Habenaria lacera — *Orchidaceae*

Another name for this species is Green Fringed Orchis, because of the inconspicuous leafy appearance of the flowering spike. Plants reach a height of two or three feet, clothed with tapering pointed leaves which decrease in size towards the tip of the stem. Each flower bears narrow sepals and petals, and the lip is dissected into threadlike segments which give a ragged appearance to the perianth. The Ragged Orchis grows in a variety of habitats from open fields and clearings to wet woods; it can be found from southeastern Canada to Georgia and west to the Mississippi River. The flowers appear throughout the summer months.

PLATE 39

(*left*) Grass Pink, *Calopogon pulchellus* (*right*) Epidendrum, *Epidendrum tampensis*

PLATE 40

(*left*) **Small Purple Fringed Orchis,** ***Habenaria psycodes*** (*right*) **Ragged Orchis,** ***Habenaria lacera***

YELLOW FRINGED ORCHIS — PLATE 41

Habenaria ciliaris — *Orchidaceae*

Also known as Orange-plume, this showy species is of smaller size than the preceding, being only one to two feet tall. The brilliantly colored flower clusters are conspicuous objects in the meadows and woods where the Yellow Fringed Orchis grows. It shows a strong preference for sandy and dryish habitats. Oval, pointed leaves clothe the stem, as in the other fringed orchises; many flowers are clustered in the terminal spike. Each flower consists of three rounded, reflexed sepals, two narrow petals, and an oblong lip which is conspicuously fringed; the lip projects rearward in a long slender spur. The Yellow Fringed Orchis grows from New England to Florida and Texas, and westward in the north central states to Wisconsin.

PRAIRIE FRINGED ORCHIS — PLATE 41

Habenaria leucophaea — *Orchidaceae*

This is a robust member of the Fringed Orchis group, plants in favorable locations reaching a height of four feet. The flowers, grouped in an open cluster, are very fragrant. The lip is fringed as in the other species of Habenaria already described. The Prairie, or Prairie White, Fringed Orchis is found in wet meadows and open swamps from Nova Scotia to the Dakotas and from Indiana to Arkansas. The flowers appear in July and August.

WHITE ADDER'S-MOUTH

Malaxis brachypoda — *Orchidaceae*

The Adder's-mouths are low-growing plants which produce simple stems bearing one or several rounded or oval leaves, and an erect raceme of small greenish-white flowers. The White Adder's-mouth grows to a height of eight inches and possesses a single sheathing leaf near the base of the stem. Each flower is about half an inch long, with threadlike petals and a triangular or pointed lip. It grows in woods and clearings, mainly in the northeastern states, flowering in midsummer. It also occurs in Alaska.

SNOWY ORCHIS

PLATE 42

Habenaria nivea

Orchidaceae

Because of its stiffly erect appearance, the Snowy Orchis is also appropriately known as Bog-torch. The narrow pointed leaves grow at the base of the stem, which reaches a height of a foot, sometimes slightly more. The flower petals are smaller than the sepals, and unlike the other species in the genus the lip is not fringed. Snowy Orchis is a southeastern coastal plain plant of swampy meadows and bogs, from New Jersey to Florida and Texas. The flowers appear in August and September.

RATTLESNAKE PLANTAIN

PLATE 42

Goodyera tesselata

Orchidaceae

The Rattlesnake Plantains are distinguished by their basal rosette of peculiarly marked leaves, strongly veined and marked with white. Because of this netted pattern they are also known as Lattice-leaf. The leaves sheathe the lower part of the erect leafless flowering stem. In the common Rattlesnake Plantain the stem is six to twelve inches tall, bearing at its summit a loose spiral spike of flowers. The upper sepals are united with the petals to form a hood over the rest of the flower. The saclike lip has a slightly recurved tip. This is essentially a northeastern species, chiefly found from southeastern Canada to New York and west to Michigan and Wisconsin, with flowers appearing in summer.

DOWNY RATTLESNAKE PLANTAIN

Goodyera pubescens

Orchidaceae

This related species can be recognized by its glandular and hairy flowering stalk, growing somewhat taller than the preceding species. The white flowers, tinged with green, form a dense terminal spike. The Downy Rattlesnake Plantain grows in dry woods throughout eastern United States, where its flowers can be found during late summer.

PLATE 41

(*left*) **Yellow Fringed Orchis,** ***Habenaria ciliaris*** (*right*) **Prairie Fringed Orchis,** ***Habenaria leucophaea***

PLATE 42

(*upper left*) **Small White Lady's-slipper, *Cypripedium candidum*** (*right*) **Snowy Orchis, *Habenaria nivea*** (*lower left*) **Rattlesnake Plantain, *Goodyera tesselata***

LARGE TWAYBLADE

PLATE 43

Liparis lilifolia — *Orchidaceae*

The Twayblades are low-growing orchids with bulbs or tubers which produce a pair of basal leaves and a few-flowered cluster of spurless blossoms with entire lips. The Large Twayblade has showy large flowers in a loose raceme. Each flower consists of narrow threadlike petals which give the perianth a spidery appearance. This species grows in woods and clearings from New England to Georgia, west to Minnesota and Missouri; the flowers bloom from May through July.

LOESEL'S TWAYBLADE

Liparis loeselii — *Orchidaceae*

This is a smaller species, sometimes known as Bog Orchis or Fen Orchis. The leaves are yellowish green, and often remain for several seasons. A small cluster of yellowish-green flowers terminates a short flowering stalk; the petals are narrow and occasionally reflexed, and the lip has an incurved tip. The Fen Orchis grows in bogs, swampy meadows and peaty woods from Canada to North Carolina, west to North Dakota and Kansas. The flowers appear in early summer.

SOUTHERN TWAYBLADE

Listera australis — *Orchidaceae*

Also known as Twayblades are the various species of Listera. These are diminutive representatives of the Orchid family, with short flowering stalks, small leaves and inconspicuous flowers. The Southern Twayblade is about five to ten inches tall with a pair of oval, shiny leaves near the middle of the stem. Yellowish-green flowers form an open cluster at the top of the stem. The lip is longer than the sepals or petals, and is split deeply to form two lobes. This species inhabits sphagnum bogs and damp woods from

Virginia southward to Florida and across to Texas; rarely can it be found farther north along the Atlantic coast. The flowers appear up to July.

Other species of Listera grow in the eastern states also. Broad-lipped Twayblade (*Listera convallarioides*) has a glandular and hairy stem, pale green leaves, and whitish green flowers; it can be found in damp mossy woods from Newfoundland to Alaska and from New England to California. Heartleaf Twayblade (*Listera cordata*) is a slender plant with heart-shaped or rounded leaves, smooth stem, and purplish flowers. This is a circumpolar species which inhabits cool mossy woods as far south as North Carolina and New Mexico. It flowers from late May to August.

The Sandalwood Family

Santalaceae

Of the 500 species in this family of temperate and tropical plants only seven are common to eastern United States. The flowers of all are minute, with a colored calyx of four or five lobes comprising the entire perianth.

BASTARD TOADFLAX PLATE 43

Comandra umbellata *Santalaceae*

The horizontal rootstock of the Bastard Toadflax is at times parasitic on the roots of other plants. From it grows a branching stem reaching a height of twelve to eighteen inches and bearing small alternate elliptical leaves. The small white or purplish flowers are grouped in terminal clusters; later they become rounded one-seeded fruits a quarter of an inch in diameter. Bastard Toadflax is found in dry woods and fields from New England to Georgia and west to Michigan. It flowers from April through June. A shrubby relative is the Buffalo Nut (*Pyrularia pubera*) with small greenish flowers, known from Pennsylvania to Alabama as a parasite on the roots of deciduous trees.

PLATE 43

(*left*) **Large Twayblade, *Liparis lilifolia*** (*right*) **Bastard Toadflax, *Comandra umbellata***

PLATE 44

(*left*) Wild Ginger, *Asarum canadense* (*right*) Dutchman's-pipe, *Aristolochia durior*

Dutchman's-Pipe Family

Aristolochiaceae

The members of this family are low-growing herbaceous plants or twining shrubs with alternate simple leaves. It is primarily a tropical family of some 400 species, but represented by only thirteen in the United States. The flowers, solitary or in clusters, have a three-lobed colored calyx and no petals. In some genera the calyx is enlarged into grotesque trumpet or bell shapes.

WILD GINGER

PLATE 44

Asarum canadense — *Aristolochiaceae*

As the name suggests, this plant has the flavor of ginger in its creeping rootstock. In pioneer days it was used as a remedy for whooping cough, and in Canada the rootstocks were dried, pulverized, and used as a spice. Wild Ginger is a stemless plant found in rich woods from New England to the Carolinas and west to Kansas. A pair of large heart-shaped leaves, borne on stout hairy stems, reveal the location of the flower which is inconspicuously hidden at the junction of the leaf stalks. The bell-shaped calyx has three pointed lobes. The flowers appear in April and May. A related species known as Heartleaf (*Asarum virginicum*) with leathery evergreen leaves grows in sandy and rocky woods from Virginia to South Carolina, flowering from March through May.

DUTCHMAN'S-PIPE

PLATE 44

Aristolochia durior — *Aristolochiaceae*

Also known as Pipe Vine, this species is a climbing or twining plant of woodlands from Pennsylvania to Georgia, westward to Kansas. The name is suggested by the enlarged S-shaped calyx of the flower which resembles a curved pipe. Rounded kidney-shaped leaves are alternately arranged on the stem. The flowers, borne laterally, have an irregular three-lobed calyx which resembles a set of petals. Dutchman's-pipe flowers in May and June.

Also found in rich woods and along the banks of streams is a related species, Virginia Snakeroot (*Aristolochia serpentaria*), with slender erect stems and ovate leaves with heart-shaped base. This species is found from New York to Florida, west to Texas. An ornamental novelty grown out of doors in the south is the Pelican Flower (*Aristolochia grandiflora*), a vine with huge grotesque flowers, the S-shaped white calyx resembling a swan or pelican.

The Buckwheat Family

Polygonaceae

In the United States this family consists of herbaceous and shrubby plants with inconspicuous flowers clustered in racemes, spikes or heads; the leaves are alternate and simple. Two members of the family are of some economic importance, buckwheat (*Fagopyrum esculentum*) and rhubarb (*Rheum rhaponticum*). Most of the American members of this family belong to the genus Polygonum.

WATER SMARTWEED — PLATE 45

Polygonum lapathifolia — *Polygonaceae*

Also known as Pale Persicaria, this species is an annual plant some six inches tall, common to riverbanks and low ground throughout all temperate regions. The small flowers lack a corolla, but possess a calyx with five petal-like sepals; they are borne in a slender nodding panicle. Appearing in July they continue to flower until November.

PLATE 45

(*above*) **Water Smartweed, *Polygonum lapathifolia*** (*below*) **Lady's Thumb, *Polygonum persicaria***

PLATE 46

(*left*) **Umbrella-wort, *Mirabilis nyctaginea*** (*right*) **Sand Verbena, *Abronia fragrans***

LADY'S-THUMB

PLATE 45

Polygonum persicaria — *Polygonaceae*

This species is also a slender annual, but grows to a height of two feet; its alternate lanceolate leaves are often spotted with purple on the upper surface. Lady's-thumb, sometimes called Heartweed, is a European plant which has made itself at home as a weed in clearings, waste places and along roadsides. The small flowers, like other species in the genus, have a colored calyx of five sepals, but no petals; the flowers are borne in an erect, rather compact raceme. This weedy plant has established itself throughout the country, flowering from June through October.

ARROW-LEAVED TEARTHUMB

Polygonum sagittatum — *Polygonaceae*

A weak-stemmed annual, Arrow-leaved Tearthumb supports itself by climbing on other plants, taking hold with the prickles which arm the angles of the stem. The rose-colored or greenish flowers are borne in the characteristic dense heads or racemes. This species grows in wet soil, from New England to Florida and west to Texas and Kansas; the flowers can be found from July to September. There are over forty other species of Polygonum, known as Smartweeds and Tearthumbs, throughout the eastern states.

The Four-o'clock Family

Nyctaginaceae

A predominantly tropical family of about 250 species, mostly herbaceous plants but with some vines, this group is represented by less than half a dozen native flowers in the eastern states. The leaves are usually opposite and entire, and the regular flowers are borne in clusters. A feature of some species is the colored bracts which surround the small flower, with a petal-like set of calyx segments. The garden annual, Mirabilis, or marvel-of-Peru, and the flamboyant southern vine, Bougainvillea, are ornamental representatives of the family.

UMBRELLA-WORT — PLATE 46

Mirabilis nyctaginea — *Nyctaginaceae*

Also known as Wild Four-o'clock and Allionia, this plant is a perennial with opposite ovate or triangular leaves. The flowers, borne singly or in small clusters, are developed in an involucre with five lobes. Each flower has a short funnel-shaped calyx with the margin divided also into five lobes. Umbrella-wort grows in prairies and open rich soil, from Wisconsin to Louisiana, Texas and Wyoming; it is rare along the eastern coastal plain. In the prairie states it is a common roadside weed. The flowering period is from June to October.

SAND VERBENA — PLATE 46

Abronia fragrans — *Nyctaginaceae*

This erect perennial of light soil and sunny habitats is also known as White Abronia. Ovate or elliptical leaves are borne opposite each other at swollen nodes on the stem. One or more small but fragrant flowers develop in a bracted head. The calyx of each flower is tubular and four- or five-lobed, resembling a corolla. The flowers open at night, and can be found throughout the summer months. Sand Verbena grows from Iowa and Texas into the western states.

PLATE 47

(*left*) Sweet William Catchfly, *Silene armeria* (*right*) Bouncing Bet, *Saponaria officinalis*

PLATE 48

(*left*) **Starry Campion,** *Silene stellata* (*right*) **Wild Pink,** *Silene caroliniana*

The Pink Family

Caryophyllaceae

This large family (2,100 species) is primarily at home in the north temperate regions, with the center of distribution in the Mediterranean area. A great number of the hardy members of this family have established themselves in the subarctic region. Many species have become favorites as garden and greenhouse ornamentals. One of the most distinguished members is the carnation (*Dianthus caryophyllus*), whose scientific name literally means "Jove's flower"; it was so named by Theophrastus about 300 B.C. The original Carnation had flesh-colored petals, but as a result of centuries of breeding the white and the red varieties are now more common. Gardeners interested in this plant formed the American Carnation Society over sixty years ago. The sweet william, another species of Dianthus, has typical Pink family flowers in flat-topped clusters. The garden pink, still another Dianthus species, has been a favorite with rock gardeners for years. Members of the Pink family usually have stems with swollen nodes, opposite and narrow leaves, and regular flowers with a calyx of five sepals and a corolla of five colored petals.

SWEET WILLIAM CATCHFLY — PLATE 47

Silene armeria — *Caryophyllaceae*

This species is a refugee from the garden, being a European plant which has established itself in fields and roadsides near dwellings. It is an annual with smooth erect stems, twelve to eighteen inches in height and bearing ovate leaves with a clasping base. The flowers are borne in flat clusters, each flower characterized by a prominently ribbed calyx and a corolla of notched petals. The flowers appear in June and continue blossoming until October throughout the eastern states from New England to Virginia west to beyond the Mississippi.

BOUNCING BET

PLATE 47

Saponaria officinalis

Caryophyllaceae

This is a European species which has made itself a weed of roadsides and waste places throughout eastern United States. Its stems, reaching a height of three feet, bear opposite oval leaves and clustered flowers. Each flower consists of a five-toothed calyx and a corolla of five separate colored petals, notched at the apex. The mucilaginous sap of this plant forms a soapy lather with water. For this reason it is also known as Soapwort. The flowers can be found throughout the summer.

STARRY CAMPION

PLATE 48

Silene stellata

Caryophyllaceae

A taller plant than most of the other species of Silene, Starry Campion grows to a height of three feet, with stiff erect stems. The inflated base of the flower is very distinctive, supporting a perianth of five fringed petals. The ovate or pointed leaves are usually borne in whorls of four. Starry Campion prefers rich woods and clearings for its home, where it flowers from July to September. Its range is from southern New England to Georgia and west to the plains states.

WILD PINK

PLATE 48

Silene caroliniana

Caryophyllaceae

This attractive wild flower has a dense and low-growing mass of linear leaves, rising from a stout root. The flowers are large (up to an inch in diameter) and grow in loose clusters. The petals are noticeably wedge-shaped, with toothed margins. Wild Pink thrives in the dry soil of rocky and sandy woods, from New England to Georgia and west to Kentucky. The flowering period is from April to June.

PLATE 49

(*left*) **Fire Pink,** ***Silene virginica*** (*right*) **Great Chickweed,** ***Stellaria pubera***

PLATE 50

Bladder Campion, ***Silene cucubalus***

FIRE PINK

PLATE 49

Silene virginica

Caryophyllaceae

A slender-stemmed plant also known as Catchfly, this perennial member of the Pink family grows to a height of two feet. The leaves are oval or elliptic, and the flowers are borne in an open cluster. Each flower has a cylindrical and elongated calyx, and a corolla of five narrow petals, each two-lobed. Fire Pink is partial to open woods and sandy hillsides, mostly in the southeastern and the central states. Its flowers can be found throughout the summer.

GREAT CHICKWEED

PLATE 49

Stellaria pubera

Caryophyllaceae

This species, usually growing to a height of twelve inches, has conspicuously four-angled stems and elliptic to oblong leaves. The flowers are produced in clusters with large leafy bracts; each flower has four or five colored petals, deeply cut into two lobes. Great Chickweed prefers to grow among rocks in shaded woods and in the rich soil of wooded hillsides, from New Jersey south to Alabama and west to Indiana. The flowers begin to appear in late March and continue through May.

BLADDER CAMPION

PLATE 50

Silene cucubalus

Caryophyllaceae

A European species, also known as Bladder Campion, this flower has become naturalized along roadsides and in fields near towns. Ovate or pointed leaves are oppositely arranged on branching stems which reach a height of twenty inches. Large numbers of nodding flowers are borne in loose clusters. Each flower, two thirds of an inch in diameter, has a conspicuous and strongly veined calyx which forms an inflated sac, edged by five pointed lobes. Projecting from this bulbous calyx is a corolla of five separate, two-lobed petals. Bladder Campion is common from New England to Virginia, west to Missouri and Kansas. It has a long flowering period, from April through August.

RAGGED ROBIN

Lychnis flos-cuculi *Caryophyllaceae*

This is another European immigrant which has become common in many parts of the East as a roadside flower. The slender subdivisions of the petals give the flowers an orchidlike appearance. As its specific name "flos-cuculi" implies, it is also called Cuckoo-flower. Slender erect stems, up to two feet in height, bear opposite narrow leaves and terminal clusters of flowers which may be either pink, white, blue or purple. Each flower, up to an inch in breadth, bears five petals with narrow bases and spreading blades deeply divided into four slender spreading segments. Ragged Robin is a summer-flowering species found from Quebec to Pennsylvania.

The Purslane Family

Portulacaceae

The Purslane family includes 500 species of annual and perennial herbaceous plants, distributed mainly though not exclusively along our Pacific coast and in South America. The leaves, which may be either opposite or alternate, are often fleshy and reduced in size. The showy flowers are regular and either solitary or in small clusters, with a calyx of two green sepals (in some cases several) and a corolla of four to six petals. A garden ornamental in this family is the Rose-moss (*Portulaca grandiflora*).

PLATE 51

Spring-beauty, *Claytonia virginica*

PLATE 52

White Water-lily, *Nymphaea odorata*

SPRING BEAUTY PLATE 51

Claytonia virginica *Portulacaceae*

The spring woods of the northeastern states are enlivened by this demure yet colorful wild flower of the Purslane family. A low-growing, sprawling plant, rarely more than ten inches in height, it thrives in moist rich woods where there is sufficient sunlight to open the delicately tinted flowers. A small, deeply buried tuber gives rise to a pair of narrow, grasslike leaves and a branching cluster of flowers. Each flower has a regular corolla of five separate petals. The flowers first appear in March and can occasionally be found through July. The range of the narrow-leaved Spring Beauty is from New England to Louisiana and Texas.

A broader-leaved species (*Claytonia caroliniana*) is a more erect plant than the preceding, with oval instead of lanceolate leaves. Frequently there are fewer flowers in the cluster. The flowers of the two are similar, both being white or pink with stripes of deeper pink. Broad-leaved Spring Beauty grows in damp woods and upland slopes from southern Canada southward in the mountains to North Carolina, where it flowers from March through May.

The Water-Lily Family

Nymphaeaceae

We expect to find wild flowers in the woods and fields, and even along the swampy margins of ponds and streams. However, a few unusual plants have adapted themselves to an entirely aquatic form of life, and live either as submerged or floating plants in fresh water. The Water-lily family comprises such a group of plants. They are annual or perennial in habit, with horizontal rhizomes which anchor the plants in the mud beneath the water. The leaves when floating develop rounded blades, often attached by the center of the underside to a long stem which extends to the surface of the water from the bottom. Submerged leaves are small and in some cases dissected into threadlike segments. The solitary flowers float on the surface of the water or are borne erect just above the surface. Each flower may have three, four, five, or an indefinite number of sepals (either green or colored) and from three to many petals. The fruit is a nutlet or berrylike structure. The ninety species in the family have a wide distribution. The American Indian is said to have prized the large starchy rhizome of some species as a food.

YELLOW POND-LILY — PLATE 54

Nuphar advena — *Nymphaeaceae*

Also known as Cow-lily and Spatterdock, this common member of the Water-lily family can often be found in great numbers, covering the surface of roadside swamps and boggy streams, as well as coves in ponds and lakes. In deep water the rounded leaves with an open cleft at the base are floating; in shallow water or on mud the leaves are borne erect. The flowers are smaller than in either of the preceding species, reaching a maximum diameter of three inches. The perianth consists of five or six colored sepals, numerous scalelike petals which form a fringe around the base of the flat-topped stigma. At home throughout the eastern and central states and south to Mexico, the Yellow Pond-lily produces its flowers from May to September. Numerous similar species are known throughout Alaska, Canada, and the United States.

Two smaller members of the Water-lily family also occur in eastern United States. Water-shield (*Brasenia schreberi*), also known as Purple Bonnet, has small oval floating leaves centrally attached to the stem, and three inches or less in diameter. The small purple flowers are borne in the axils of the leaves, each perianth consisting of three or four narrow sepals and an equal number of narrow petals. Found from New England to Florida, Water-shield flowers from June to September. Another species, found only south of Virginia but also a summer-flowering plant, is Fanwort or Water-shield (*Cabomba caroliniana*). This plant has two kinds of leaves, oblong floating ones and threadlike dissected submerged leaves. The small solitary flowers are borne on long stems; the perianth is white, spotted with yellow.

PLATE 53

Lotus-lily, *Nelumbo lutea*

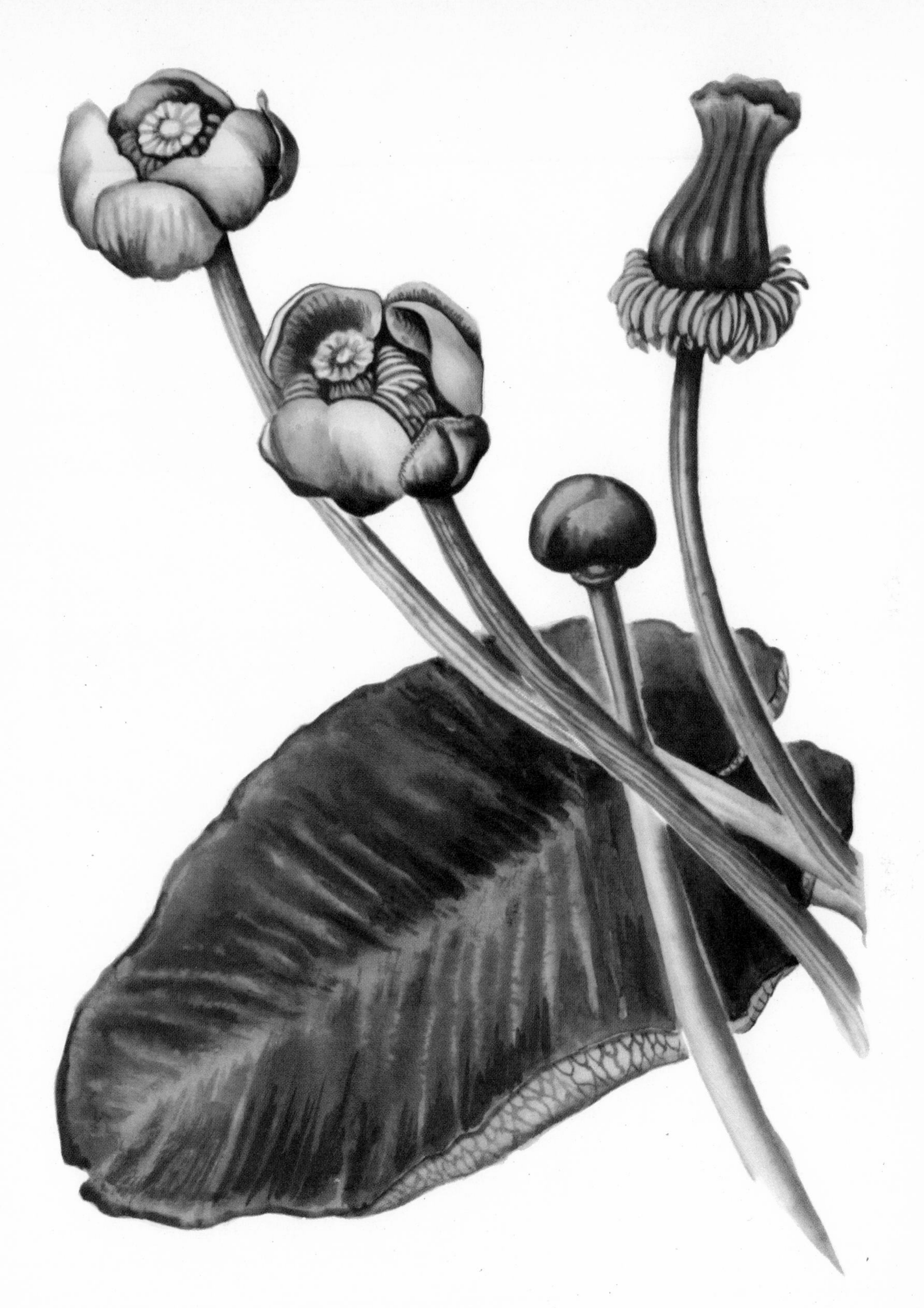

PLATE 54

Yellow Pond-lily, *Nuphar advena*

WHITE WATER LILY

PLATE 52

Nymphaea odorata *Nymphaeaceae*

From July to September many a pond from Canada to Florida and west as far as Texas is given a picturesque beauty by the showy and fragrant flowers of the White Water Lily. The round leaves have a narrow deep cleft near the attachment of the stem and float on the surface of the water. The underside of the leaves, as well as the long ropelike stems, is often purplish or reddish in color. Large flowers, up to eight inches in diameter, almost equal the leaves in size; each flower has four tapering green sepals, several series of petals, and numerous bright yellow stamens surrounding the ovary. An interesting characteristic of this flower is the gradual transition from petals to stamens.

LOTUS LILY

PLATE 53

Nelumbo lutea *Nymphaeaceae*

The genus Nelumbo is best known for its Asiatic member, the sacred lotus, with showy pink flowers. The American Lotus Lily, or Water Chinquapin, differs from the white water lily in having completely circular leaves, with no sinus, each attached to the stem in the center of the undersurface. The leaves are usually raised above the water, rather than floating on it. The flowers, five to ten inches in diameter, are also borne on erect stems above the water; the perianth consists of sepals and petals which grade into each other and surround an enlarged, turnip-shaped receptacle which later becomes an unusual container for the seeds. When in fruit, these flat-topped vessels are studded with pits in which the seeds are embedded. The seeds were eaten by the American Indians. Lotus lilies can be found in ponds and slow streams throughout eastern United States, flowering from July to September.

The Buttercup Family

Ranunculaceae

During the millions of years that plants have been developing and spreading from region to region, some families have retained more of the characteristics of the primitive "first families" than others. The orchids, for example, are considered a most highly specialized and recently evolved group. On the other hand, the Buttercup family is considered by many botanists to represent the most primitive features typical of flowering plants. Although the family includes chiefly herbaceous species, a closely related group with primitive traits combined with the woody habit is the Magnolia family. In the Buttercup family the plants may be either annuals or perennials; the leaves are mostly alternate, and compound with palmate arrangement of the segments of each leaf. Most of the flowers are regular in form —that is, all of the petals or sepals are alike. Some, such as larkspur and monkshood, are irregular, or two-sided in their structure. The regular flowers are of two types: in one group they possess both sepals and petals; in the other group the petals are lacking and the sepals have assumed a color other than green. Both petals and sepals are found in the buttercups, columbine, baneberry, hellebore and goldthread. Petals are lacking in hepatica, meadow-rue, the anemones, marsh marigold, and clematis. The species vary in the number of sepals and petals from two or three to fifteen. The fruit is usually a dry capsule, an achene, or a berry.

This is a fairly large family, with 1,500 species, most of them in north temperate regions. It is represented in the United States by some 200 species, many of which are common as wild flowers throughout the country. A great number of ornamental flowers have also come from the Buttercup family, among them the delphinium and peony.

The Buttercup family is less well known for its poisonous members, such as the western Monkshood (*Aconitum columbianum*) and Larkspurs (Delphinium), which in the West cause considerable loss to cattlemen. The presence of poisonous parts in our native eastern members of this family will be mentioned when the species is described.

PLATE 55

(*left*) **Rue Anemone,** ***Anemonella thalictroides*** (*right*) **Wood Anemone,** ***Anemone quinquefolia***

PLATE 56

(*left*) Thimbleweed, *Anemone virginiana* (*right*) Pasque-flower, *Anemone patens*

RUE ANEMONE

PLATE 55

Anemonella thalictroides

Ranunculaceae

Also known as Windflower, this delicate slender member of the Buttercup family grows to a height of four to ten inches, producing compound leaves divided into gracefully rounded three-lobed leaflets. The flowers, each one-half inch broad, are borne in an umbel; each flower has only a colored calyx of five to ten petallike sepals; there is no corolla. Rue Anemones prefer rich moist woods, where they can be found in blossom from early April until June, throughout eastern United States.

WOOD ANEMONE

PLATE 55

Anemone quinquefolia

Ranunculaceae

There are eleven species of the genus Anemone in eastern United States. Of these, the Wood Anemone is one of the smallest, rarely exceeding ten inches in height. A slender stem bears at its summit a trio of long-stemmed compound leaves, each leaf subdivided into three to five wedge-shaped leaflets. The flowers occur singly, each perianth about an inch in diameter with four to nine white or faintly colored sepals and no petals. Wood Anemones grow in open woods and clearings from New England to North Carolina, west into Ohio. The flowering period is from April to June.

THIMBLEWEED

PLATE 56

Anemone virginiana

Ranunculaceae

In contrast with the preceding species, Thimbleweed is a stout, hairy plant several feet tall, with a group of large compound leaves at the base of the cluster of flower stalks. There are usually three leaves on each stem, forming an involucre beneath the flowers. Each leaf is broader than long, divided into three segments which are in turn edged with sharply pointed lobes. The flowers vary in size from slightly less to slightly more than an inch in diameter; each flower is borne on an elongated stalk which may be eight to ten inches long. As in the other anemones, the perianth consists of colored (whitish) sepals, and no petals. Thimbleweed in fruit forms thimble-like structures containing the achenes. The flowers appear in June and continue developing until August; they can be found in dry or rocky open woods from Maine to Georgia, west to Arkansas and Kansas.

CANADA ANEMONE

PLATE 62

Anemone canadensis — *Ranunculaceae*

This is also known as the Round-leaved Anemone because of the rounded outline of the compound leaf. It is a somewhat stout and moderately hairy-stemmed species found in damp meadows and woods from New England to West Virginia and west to Missouri and Illinois. The plants grow to a height of two feet, producing broad compound leaves with three to five divisions which are lobed or toothed. The flowers are large, reaching a diameter of an inch and a half, with five white sepals, no petals. The fruiting head is spherical, consisting of achenes with stout tips—the remains of the persistent styles. Canada Anemones flower from May through July.

PASQUEFLOWER

PLATE 56

Anemone patens — *Ranunculaceae*

This is a silky-haired plant of prairies and low ground, with compound leaves divided into sharply pointed linear lobes; it is one of the most distinctive plants of the genus Anemone. The erect, solitary flowers reach a breadth of an inch or more, with spreading colored sepals, ranging in number from five to seven. When in fruit the long styles become transformed into silky plumes attached to the hairy achenes. Pasqueflower is a wild flower of our central states, from Illinois and Missouri to Michigan and Texas, where it flowers from April to June.

PLATE 57

(*left*) Meadow Buttercup, *Ranunculus acris* (*right*) Bulbous Buttercup, *Ranunculus bulbosus*

PLATE 58

Wild Columbine, *Aquilegia canadensis*

MEADOW BUTTERCUP

PLATE 57

Ranunculus acris *Ranunculaceae*

The true buttercups, or crowfoots, make up a large group of wild flowers —thirty-six different species being fairly common in the east alone, and many others being known often farther west. They are difficult to identify because the recognition features are based on technical characteristics of the achene and inflorescence. The three species illustrated, however, represent very common members of this genus. Also known as the Tall and the Common Buttercup, the Meadow Buttercup is a European species which has established itself as a weed in fields and along roadsides from New England to Virginia, west to Illinois and Minnesota. The alternate leaves are compound, with five leaflets radiating out from a center like the fingers on one's hand. Each leaflet is toothed and lobed. The flowers, borne in terminal open clusters, each have a calyx of five green sepals and a corolla of usually five colored petals. Buttercup fields reach their height in midsummer, when they gleam with yellow in the sun, but the flowers can be found from May through August.

SWAMP BUTTERCUP

PLATE 60

Ranunculus septentrionalis *Ranunculaceae*

A native species of wet woods and meadows from Canada southward to Georgia and west to Nebraska, the Swamp Buttercup is a robust plant one to two feet tall; it is a perennial, growing from thick fibrous roots, and with stems which become reclining and trailing. Large thick leaves are each divided into three leaflets which in turn are deeply subdivided and lobed. The bright yellow flowers are large for wild buttercups, reaching diameters of an inch or more. The petals are twice as long as the green, spreading sepals. Swamp Buttercups can be found in flower from April through July, often as neighbors to the wild blue flags.

BULBOUS BUTTERCUP

PLATE 57

Ranunculus bulbosus — *Ranunculaceae*

This species, a much smaller plant than the meadow buttercup, grows from a somewhat spherical underground corm which gives it also the name of Turnip Buttercup. It is another European immigrant which has become at home in fields and meadows throughout the coastal states from New England to Alabama. The leaves are compound, with three rounded divisions, each division with three notched leaflets. The flowers appear earlier than those of the meadow buttercup, usually between March and June, when they carpet the ground with their bloom.

WILD COLUMBINE

PLATE 58

Aquilegia canadensis — *Ranunculaceae*

Few wild flowers have the airy grace and ornamental poise of this member of the Buttercup family. Its other name of Rock Bells is suggestive of the rocky wooded banks on which it usually grows. The erect branching stems reach a height of several feet, growing from a perennial root, and producing delicately compound leaves with many small rounded and lobed leaflets. At the summit of the leafy branches grow the nodding flowers, each an inch or two in length. The unusual perianth consists of five cornucopia-like petals which are prolonged backwards into long hollow spurs. The yellow stamens and long styles hang downwards, projecting beyond the corolla like tiny clappers on a bell. Wild Columbine occurs more rarely in salmon-pink and white varieties. The range of the species is from New England to Georgia and Tennessee, west to Wisconsin. It is typically a spring flower of the April woods, but flowers can be found as late as July. Other species with the same and different colors, all with the characteristically spurred petals, occur from Alaska to Florida.

PLATE 59

Marsh Marigold, *Caltha palustris*

PLATE 60

Swamp Buttercup, *Ranunculus septentrionalis*

WHITE WATER CROWFOOT

Ranunculus longirostris *Ranunculaceae*

The Crowfoots are aquatic or amphibious members of the buttercup group, often rooting at the nodes of the stem and producing white rather than yellow flowers. White Water Crowfoot has finely dissected submerged leaves, and bears flowers a half inch in breadth. This species grows in shallow pools and wet depressions from New England to Delaware, westward to Kansas and Texas; the flowers can be found from May through September.

MARSH MARIGOLD

PLATE 59

Caltha palustris *Ranunculaceae*

This common succulent and stout-stemmed plant of swamps, marshes and wet meadows is sometimes known as Cowslip; its golden-yellow flowers brighten the spring landscape, appearing in April and continuing in blossom through June. Branching clumps of Marsh Marigold reach a height of several feet, bearing large heart-shaped or kidney-shaped leaves with an entire or slightly toothed margin. The glossy petallike sepals form a perianth an inch or more in breadth; the flowers grow in branching clusters. In some parts of the East this member of the Buttercup family is eaten as a vegetable "green," the fleshy stems and leaves being cooked in the same fashion as spinach. In addition, the tender unopened flower-buds are pickled and used as capers. Marsh Marigold can be found from Labrador to Alaska, southward to the Carolinas and Tennessee, and west to Iowa and Nebraska. Closely similar species occur in other regions.

ROUND-LEAVED HEPATICA

PLATE 61

Hepatica americana *Ranunculaceae*

Those impatient naturalists who can hardly wait for the winter's snows to melt before they ramble through the still leafless woods in search of the first spring flowers need especially sharp eyes to discover the pale lilac, blue or pinkish-white Hepatica flowers hiding amid the brown leaves and debris. As harbingers of spring in northeastern United States, the Hepaticas have few equals; the flowers appear in March and may continue opening until June. The Round-leaved Hepatica, or Liverleaf, has rounded or kidney-shaped three-lobed leaves borne on hairy stems; the leaves usually persist, discolored, through the winter, new foliage appearing after the flowers. The solitary flowers have a spreading perianth of five to seven colored sepals, no petals, and an involucre of three small leaves. The favorite haunt of this species is dry rocky woods from southern Canada to the southern states, as far as northern Florida, and west to Missouri.

SHARP-LOBED HEPATICA — PLATE 61

Hepatica acutiloba — *Ranunculaceae*

This species is also known as Pointed Liverleaf, indicating an important difference with the preceding species. The three leaf lobes are more pointed and usually longer than broad. Normally blue-flowered, varieties occur with both white and pink flowers. Sharp-lobed Hepatica grows in rich woods, from Maine to Georgia and Minnesota; the flowers appear at the same time as those of the round-leaved hepatica, from March through June.

PURPLE CLEMATIS — PLATE 63

Clematis verticillaris — *Ranunculaceae*

Also known as Purple Virgin's Bower, this species does not develop its flowers in clusters, but as solitary blooms in the axils of the compound leaves. The flowers are large (two to four inches in diameter) and characterized by a perianth of four thin strongly veined and silk-edged sepals; the stamens are numerous, and the styles long and plumelike. Purple Clematis grows in rocky woods from southeastern Canada to Maryland, and west to Wisconsin and Iowa, where the flowers appear from May through June.

PLATE 61

(*left*) **Round-leaved Hepatica,** ***Hepatica americana*** (*right*) **Sharp-lobed Hepatica,** ***Hepatica acutiloba***

PLATE 62

(*left*) Virgin's Bower, *Clematis virginiana* (*right*) Canada Anemone, *Anemone canadensis*

VIRGIN'S BOWER

PLATE 62

Clematis virginiana — *Ranunculaceae*

Commonly known also as Wild Clematis, this member of the Buttercup family is a woody vine which climbs upon other plants by means of a bending or clasping of the leafstalks. The trailing stem bears opposite compound leaves, each leaf made up of three oval leaflets. The flowers, an inch or less in diameter, are borne in large leafy clusters; each flower has four spreading petallike sepals and lacks petals. Wild Clematis is quite as attractive in autumn as when in bloom, for the flower clusters change to masses of silky-haired fruits, the style of each flower becoming an inch-long plume to the tiny achene. Low woods and edges of thickets, especially fence-rows, are the home of Wild Clematis, from southern Canada to the Gulf of Mexico and westward to Kansas; the flowers can be found from July through September.

GOLDENSEAL

Hydrastis canadensis — *Ranunculaceae*

The rhizome of this member of the Buttercup family contains several alkaloid substances which act as poisons, but which also are useful drugs. For this reason the species has been so much sought after that its extinction has been threatened. It is also known as Orangeroot and Yellow Puccoon, "puccoon" being an Indian word applied to numerous plants which yield a red or yellow dye. Goldenseal has a hairy erect stem ten to twelve inches in height, bearing at its summit two deeply lobed and toothed leaves; seated close to the base of one of these leaves is the solitary greenish-white flower about half an inch in breadth, appearing in April and May. The three petal-like sepals wither almost as soon as the flower opens; there are no petals. Goldenseal grows in rich woods from New England to Georgia, westward to Minnesota and Arkansas.

LEATHERFLOWER

PLATE 63

Clematis viorna — *Ranunculaceae*

This Clematis grows in rich woods and thickets from Pennsylvania and Ohio to Georgia and Texas, where it flowers from May to August. The vine bears compound leaves with three to seven leaflets on angular stems. Each flower has a bell-shaped calyx of four or five thick leathery sepals.

AMERICAN GLOBEFLOWER

Trollius laxus — *Ranunculaceae*

Easily mistaken for a marsh marigold, the Globeflower has perennial fibrous roots which give rise to weak stems producing long-stalked leaves which are deeply lobed, being divided into five to seven wedge-shaped segments with toothed margins. The flowers, yellowish-green and an inch or more in diameter, have five to fifteen petallike sepals; petals are present but very small and less conspicuous than the many yellow stamens in the center of the flower. The fruit is a broad structure, made up of several pods tipped with slender beaks. Globeflower is a rare plant of swampy meadows and woods, found from New England to Pennsylvania and ranging westward to Michigan; the flowers appear in early spring, from April to May.

GOLDTHREAD

Coptis groenlandica — *Ranunculaceae*

One of the few evergreen perennials in the Buttercup family, Goldthread (also known as Cankerroot) is a low-growing plant with a slender, bright yellow rootstock. The leaves are basal and compound, with three shiny dark green leaflets. Each erect flowering stalk, four or five inches tall, bears a solitary flower with five to seven white sepals and a set of small club-shaped petals. This species of the family hides in the depths of mossy woods and swamps. Its home is from Greenland and Labrador to the mountains of North Carolina and Tennessee, and somewhat westward. It flowers from May to July.

PLATE 63

Black Snakeroot, *Cimicifuga racemosa*

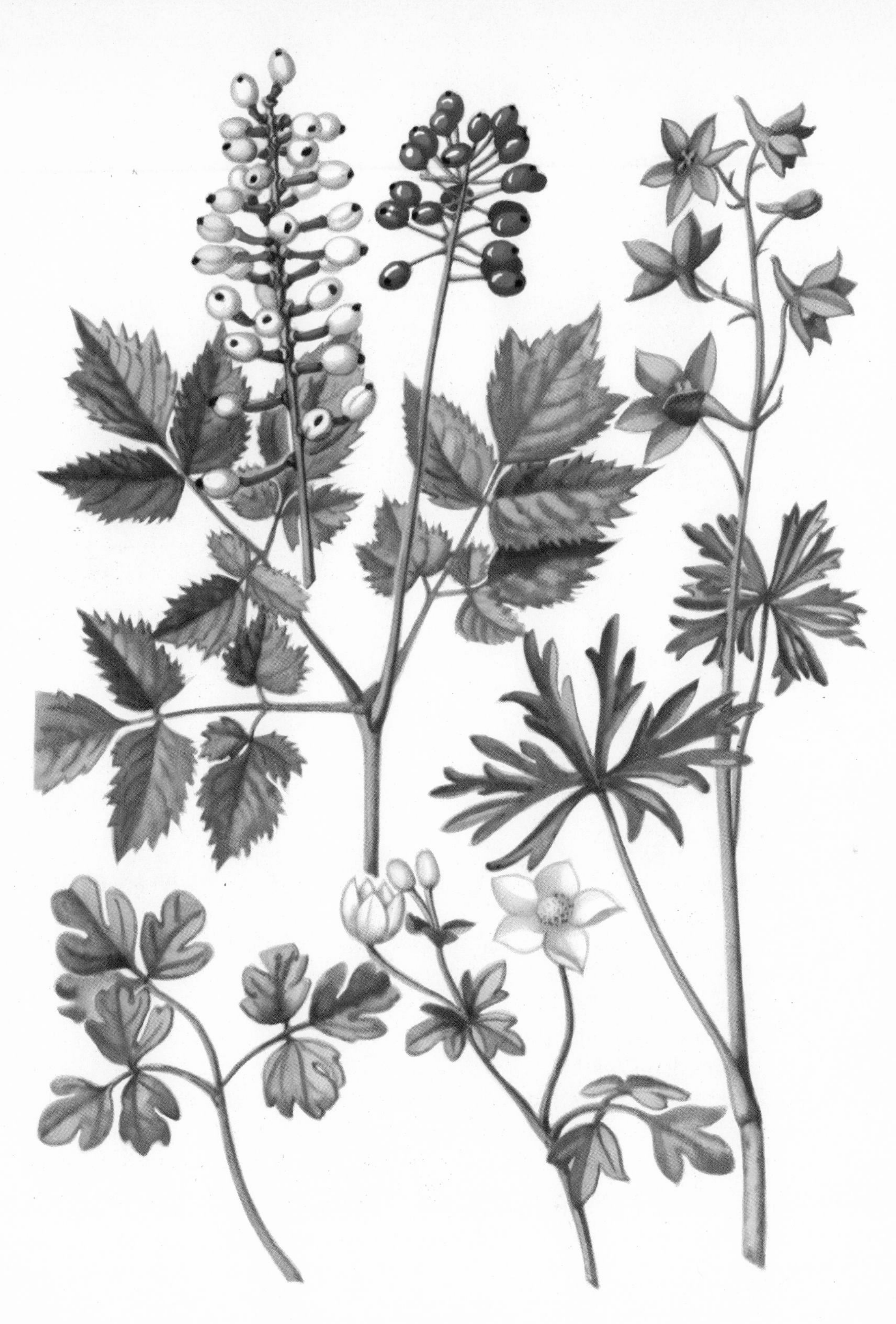

PLATE 64

(*upper left*) White Baneberry, *Actaea pachypoda* (*lower left*) False Rue Anemone, *Isopyrum biternatum* (*center*) Red Baneberry, *Actaea rubra* (*right*) Dwarf Larkspur, *Delphinium tricorne*

WHITE BANEBERRY

PLATE 64

Actaea pachypoda

Ranunculaceae

The Baneberries are erect plants with oval or cylindrical compact flower clusters and conspicuous berries as fruits instead of the small achenes characteristic of many of the buttercup group. White Baneberry, also known as Doll's-eyes, Snakeroot, and White Cohosh, grows to a height of two feet or more; the compound leaves are divided into oval, toothed leaflets. The oblong flower cluster, three to seven inches in length, consists of many small flowers, each with a perianth of three to five short-lived whitish sepals and four to ten short petals. A conspicuous part of each flower is the central mass of projecting white stamens. The fruits are unusual looking berries, all white except for a cap of the remains of the purple or red stigma; one variety has red berries instead of white ones. Flowering in May and June, White Baneberry grows in rich woods, from Canada to Georgia and Oklahoma.

RED BANEBERRY

PLATE 64

Actaea rubra

Ranunculaceae

Also known as Black Cohosh, this species is vegetatively very similar to the white baneberry. The flower clusters, however, are more rounded and less cylindrical; they are characterized by the same conspicuous clusters of white stamens. In fruit, the Red Baneberry produces bright red oval or elliptical berries, each berry reaching a maximum size of half an inch. This species grows in woods from New England to West Virginia and ranges westward to Iowa; the flowers can be found from May through July. The berries are mildly poisonous and the rootstock acts as a strong purgative. The berries of a related European species have caused reported deaths of children.

DWARF LARKSPUR

PLATE 64

Delphinium tricorne

Ranunculaceae

The genus Delphinium is an unusual one for the Buttercup family, because the flowers are irregular, with one sepal and several petals prolonged backwards into long spurs. The leaves are compound, with the segments radiating from the basal end like the fingers on a hand. Six species are found in the eastern states, with these and others farther west. The Dwarf Larkspur has a loose cluster of blue, white, or variegated flowers; some individual flowers attain a length of an inch. Favoring rich wooded slopes, this species grows from Pennsylvania southward to Georgia and Alabama, west to Nebraska and Oklahoma. The flowering period is from April to June.

FALSE RUE ANEMONE

PLATE 64

Isopyrum biternatum

Ranunculaceae

This is a low-growing plant of woods and bluffs throughout the central states from the Great Lakes to Florida and Texas. False Rue Anemone has compound leaves, divided into lobed and toothed segments; the flowers, some of which are terminal and some growing in the axils of the leaves, have a perianth of five petallike sepals. Its general resemblance to an anemone is evident. The flowers appear in late spring, from April through May.

AMERICAN BUGBANE

Cimicifuga americana

Ranunculaceae

Known as Summer Cohosh, this species is a slightly smaller plant with a less rigid elongated flower cluster. It grows in moist woods in mountainous portions of Pennsylvania and West Virginia to Georgia and Tennessee. The flowering period is from August to September.

PLATE 65

(*left*) **Purple Clematis,** ***Clematis verticillaris*** (*right*) **Leather-flower,** ***Clematis viorna***

PLATE 66

Tall Meadow-rue, *Thalictrum polygamum*

BLACK SNAKEROOT

PLATE 63

Cimicifuga racemosa — *Ranunculaceae*

Also commonly known as Bugbane and sometimes as Black Cohosh—"cohosh" being a name applied to numerous plants used medicinally by the American Indians—this species is one of the rank-growing members of the family, vigorous plants often reaching a height of eight feet. The compound leaves have large leaflets which grow to be six or eight inches in length; they are coarsely toothed and lobed. The flowers are grouped in a tall, spire-like cluster one to three feet in length, often surrounded with smaller spires. Each has four or five short-lived sepals; the petallike stamens are two-lobed at their tips. After flowering, the dry dehiscent fruits develop. Black Snakeroot grows in woods from New England to Georgia and Tennessee, and flowers from June to September.

TALL MEADOW RUE

PLATE 66

Thalictrum polygamum — *Ranunculaceae*

Few herbaceous plants reach more lofty stature, in the eastern United States, than the Tall Meadow Rue, also known as Muskrat Weed and King-of-the-Meadow. In its favored habitat of swampy meadows and in fields adjoining shallow ponds, this robust plant may grow taller than a man. It has finely divided compound leaves, the smallest leaflets rounded and bluntly lobed. A great number of small flowers are borne in the spreading flower cluster. The greenish petallike sepals soon drop off and since there are no petals, the flowers are mainly masses of white stamens, even the purplish pistillate flowers generally having a number of stamens present. Tall Meadow Rue is found from southeastern Canada to Georgia and Tennessee; it flowers from June through August.

EARLY MEADOW RUE — PLATE 67

Thalictrum dioicum — *Ranunculaceae*

A smooth-stemmed plant, usually one or two feet in height, this species is found on rocky banks and slopes in the woods of most of the eastern and midwestern states. It ranges, in fact, from Quebec to Georgia and west to Alabama and North Dakota. The delicately compound leaves are subdivided into thin rounded leaflets with rounded lobes. Small flowers appearing in April hang in drooping clusters, the conspicuous portion of each flower being the greenish-yellow stamens. There are no petals, and the four purplish sepals are small and spreading.

The Barberry Family

Berberidaceae

The Barberry family is a relatively small family of 200 species, chiefly herbaceous plants but including a few shrubs, found in north temperate regions. The three herbaceous members of the family described below occur in the eastern and some midwestern states.

TWINLEAF

Jeffersonia diphylla — *Berberidaceae*

When in flower this species is a low-growing plant, six to eight inches in height. Long-stemmed leaves, generally heart-shaped in outline, become lobed into two halves or divisions. White flowers, an inch in breadth, are borne on erect leafless stems; the perianth consists of a petallike calyx and a corolla of eight petals. Twinleaf grows in woods from New York southward to Alabama and westward to Wisconsin; it flowers in April and May.

PLATE 67

Early Meadow-rue, *Thalictrum dioicum*

PLATE 68

May Apple, *Podophyllum peltatum*

MAY APPLE

PLATE 68

Podophyllum peltatum — *Berberidaceae*

This species has several other names, among them Umbrella-leaf and Mandrake, though it is not the same as the mandrake of the Old World. It is a colonizing plant, growing in dense patches in wet meadows and open stretches in the woods. The plants grow up to two feet high. First a single large leaf is usually produced by the horizontal rootstock; this leaf is shield-shaped, five- to nine-lobed, and attached to its supporting stem in the middle of the lower surface. Flowering plants have a pair of three- to seven-parted leaves. A single nodding flower opens beneath the leaves, in the angle of the two leafstalks. Each flower is an inch or two in diameter and consists of a calyx of six short-lived sepals and a corolla of six to nine flat petals. The "apple" is a large yellow juicy berry, edible when ripe; it is egg-shaped with a thick skin and a many-seeded pulp. Its flavor has been compared to that of a strawberry, and it is one of the few wild fruits acclaimed by poets; James Whitcomb Riley has described its qualities in his "Rhymes of Childhood." Rootstocks of May Apple contain a bitter resinous substance harmful to livestock; its effect is that of a purgative. The plant is fairly common from western Quebec to Texas and Florida. The flowering is from April to June.

BLUE COHOSH

Caulophyllum thalictroides — *Berberidaceae*

Also known as Papooseroot, this species has a single compound leaf borne by the same erect stem which terminates in a small cluster of yellowish green flowers. Plants reach a height of a foot to eighteen inches, producing the flowers before the leaves are fully developed. The mature seeds burst through the ovary wall, remaining attached by their seed stalks and resembling blue one-seeded fruits. Blue Cohosh is found in rich woods from New England to the mountainous parts of North Carolina and Tennessee, also westward to North Dakota and Nebraska. It flowers from April through June.

The Poppy Family

Papaveraceae

The Poppy family is a group of herbaceous plants, some annuals and some perennials, with about 250 species distributed chiefly in the temperate and subtropical portions of the northern hemisphere. A fairly reliable characteristic of the family is the presence of milky or colored sap, alternate leaves, regular flowers with a showy corolla, and a capsular fruit splitting open at maturity by pores or valves. Native wild flowers in the family in the East include less than a dozen species, of which the best known are bloodroot, prickly poppy, and celandine poppy. On the Pacific coast perhaps the best known member of the family is the California Poppy (Eschscholzia), famous for its painting of the landscape with acres of golden-yellow flowers.

BLOODROOT

PLATE 69

Sanguinaria canadensis — *Papaveraceae*

The common name of this plant is derived from the fact that the sap of the thick rootstock, as well as the stems, is red. Fortunately the bitter taste makes most animals (and humans) avoid it; the sap contains a toxic alkaloid which affects the heart, nervous system and muscles; there have been reported deaths from this source. The sap was used as a dye by the American Indians. Basal leaves, at first tightly rolled, spear their way through the accumulation of dead leaves and twigs on the woodland floor in late March. Within is the protected flowering stalk with its single terminal flower. Each flower, with two short-lived sepals and eight to twelve delicate petals which fall at a touch, is safely seated just above the notched base of the lobed and rounded leaf. The fruit is a narrow capsule, pointed at both ends. Bloodroot often grows in colonies along the edges of thickets and in open woods, from southern Canada to Florida and west beyond the Mississippi river; the first flowers appear with the hepaticas, in March, and continue through May. The leaves increase in breadth after the flowers are gone.

PLATE 69

(*left*) **Bloodroot,** ***Sanguinaria canadensis*** (*right*) **Prickly Poppy,** ***Argemone mexicana***

PLATE 70

(*left*) **Climbing Fumitory,** ***Adlumia fungosa*** (*right*) **Squirrel-corn,** ***Dicentra canadensis***

CELANDINE

Chelidonium majus *Papaveraceae*

This is a biennial from Europe which has made itself at home along roadsides and in fields near houses. The brittle stems contain a light-yellow sap, and bear compound leaves with numerous lobed and toothed leaflets. Small yellow flowers are borne in an open cluster, each flower with two sepals and four petals. Celandine has spread throughout the northeastern and north central states, where its flowers can be found from March to August.

CELANDINE POPPY

Stylophorum diphyllum *Papaveraceae*

Also known as Wood Poppy, this member of the family inhabits woods from Pennsylvania to Virginia, westward to Missouri and Wisconsin. It is a low-growing perennial with two opposite leaves and one or several flowers at the summit of a naked stem. The leaves are deeply cut into lobed segments. The yellow flower has a perianth of two hairy sepals and four petals. When in bud the flowers are nodding, as are the ovoid capsules. The Celandine Poppy flowers in the period between March and May.

PRICKLY POPPY

PLATE 69

Argemone mexicana *Papaveraceae*

Also called Mexican Poppy and Yellow Thistle, this southwestern species has escaped from cultivation in the eastern states where it inhabits sandy roadsides and waste fields. The prickly character of the foliage gives the plant, which grows to a height of three feet, a thistlelike appearance. The deeply lobed leaves are often blotched with white. Each flower has a spreading perianth of four to six large papery petals. The blossoms first appear in late spring, and continue through the summer.

The Fumitory Family

Fumariaceae

The members of this family, which is closely allied to the Poppy family, have a watery sap and fernlike compound leaves. The four hundred species of this family are chiefly inhabitants of the Old World, among them the bleeding heart of gardens. About a dozen species occur in eastern United States. These are all herbaceous plants of graceful and delicate appearance.

PINK CORYDALIS PLATE 71

Corydalis sempervirens *Fumariaceae*

A delicate plant with branching erect stems, bearing compound leaves divided into small oval-lobed segments, Pink Corydalis (also known as Pale Corydalis) is an inhabitant of rocky ledges and open woods. Its range is from Newfoundland to Tennessee and Georgia, from Alaska to British Columbia, and in intervening regions. The dainty nodding flowers borne in open terminal clusters are well named "Corydalis" for in Greek the word means "crested lark." Each flower is a half or two-thirds of an inch in length, with two small sepals and an irregular corolla of four petals, one of which is prolonged backward as a spur. The fruit is a narrow erect capsule an inch or two in length. Pink Corydalis can be found in flower intermittently from May through September.

There are six other species closely related to the Pink Corydalis; all have yellow flowers and less erect stems. Of these, Golden Corydalis (*Corydalis aurea*) is found over much the same range; its flowers have keeled petals without a crest. Yellow Fumewort (*Corydalis flavula*), with crested petals, occurs between Connecticut and Kansas; it flowers from April to May. The Slender Fumewort (*Corydalis micrantha*) is a tiny-flowered species seen in gravelly fields and rocky woods from the southeastern to the central states.

PLATE 71

(*left*) Pink Corydalis, *Corydalis sempervirens* (*right*) Dutchman's Breeches, *Dicentra cucullaria*

PLATE 72

Pink Cleome, *Cleome serrulata*

CLIMBING FUMITORY

PLATE 70

Adlumia fungosa

Fumariaceae

Known in some localities as Alleghany Vine and Mountain Fringe, this weak-stemmed climbing plant has much subdivided compound leaves with the leaflets about a quarter of an inch in length. The flowers, about the same length as the leaflets, are grouped in drooping clusters. The four petals of each flower are united to form a heart-shaped corolla, of a spongy texture. This remains when the seeds are formed, acting as a sac for the small capsule with its enclosed seeds. Alleghany Vine is especially common in recently burned-over woodlands, as well as in moist woods and shaded riverbanks. It is found from southern Canada south to the mountains of North Carolina and Tennessee, west to Minnesota. The flowering period is from June to October.

SQUIRREL CORN

PLATE 70

Dicentra canadensis

Fumariaceae

The name of this species refers to the cornlike tubers scattered along the subterranean stems; the plants are low-growing, reaching a maximum height of twelve inches. In early spring the underground scaly bulb, which is formed by the cluster of grainlike tubers, sends up fernlike, much divided, compound leaves and erect flowering stalks. The nodding flowers are borne in drooping clusters. Each flower consists of petals which adhere at their base to form a two-spurred corolla; the spurs are short and rounded, and the inner petals have conspicuous crests. Squirrel Corn is found in rich woods from New England to the southern Appalachians, west to Missouri and Minnesota. The flowers, said to have fragrance like hyacinths, appear in April and May.

DUTCHMAN'S BREECHES PLATE 71

Dicentra cucullaria *Fumariaceae*

Very similar to squirrel corn in its habit and foliage, Dutchman's Breeches produces clusters of drooping and fragrant flowers amid a basal tuft of fernlike foliage. Each flower has an obvious resemblance to a pair of baggy breeches, hanging upside down. This effect is produced by the divergent pair of spurs developed by the corolla's outermost two petals. The two inner petals are narrow and minutely crested. Growing in rich woods, Dutchman's Breeches extends across the continent from Quebec to Washington and Oregon, and south to Georgia, Alabama and Kansas. It flowers from April into June. A variety has been found with purple calyx and pink corolla, marked with orange.

The Caper Family

Capparidaceae

Although the Caper family includes about 700 species, at least 550 of them are tropical in distribution. The few which do occur in the United States are chiefly plants of dry arid habitats. The claim to economic importance lies in the use of the dried flower buds of a Mediterranean species (*Capparis spinosa*) as capers for seasoning food. The principal herbaceous plant in the family is often seen in gardens under the name of Spider Flower (*Cleome spinosa*). In some parts of the country it has escaped from gardens to mingle with the wild plants of the roadside.

PLATE 73

(*left*) Trumpets, *Sarracenia flava* (*right*) Common Pitcher-plant, *Sarracenia purpurea*

PLATE 74

(*upper left*) **Round-leaved Sundew, *Drosera rotundifolia*** (*upper right*) **Venus Flytrap, *Dionaea muscipula*** (*below*) **Stonecrop, *Sedum ternatum***

PINK CLEOME PLATE 72

Cleome serrulata *Capparidaceae*

Also known as Stinking Clover or Spider Flower, this representative of the Caper family is an annual of damp prairies and waste places from Illinois and Missouri westward. The alternate compound leaves are divided into three narrow tapering leaflets. The flowers are borne in a dense terminal cluster, mingled with leafy bracts. Each flower has a calyx of four spreading sepals and a corolla of four petals with narrowed basal portions. Projecting beyond the perianth is the long slender receptacle with the stamens attached near its tip; this gives the flower cluster a spidery appearance. Pink Cleome flowers from May through September.

The Pitcher-Plant Family

Sarraceniaceae

When an animal catches and eats a plant it is considered the normal arrangement in nature, but when a plant catches and devours an animal, that is a newsworthy turn of affairs. The members of the Pitcher-plant family, as well as those of the Sundew family, which follows, have this animal-eating habit; for this reason they are known as carnivorous plants. It is true that the animals consumed are tiny insects and other small invertebrates; but even so the special adaptations by which the leaves of these carnivorous plants have become traps for unwary small creatures are surprising. For this reason, the plants in these families are of interest because of their foliage peculiarities, as well as for their flowers. The latter, in fact, are often much less striking than the remarkable leaves.

The Pitcher-plant family is made up of herbaceous perennials which produce a basal rosette of tubular, hollow leaves which arch upward like pitchers or trumpets. Each "pitcher" has a winglike external ridge extending throughout its length. The open end of the pitcher is often protected by an overarching portion of the leaf, reminding us of the jack-in-the-pulpit flower. Each of these colorful pitchers is a death trap for small insects, attracted by a special nectar secreted around the edge of the leaf. The inside of the leaf is lined with downward pointing soft spines which make it easy for the insects to slide down to the bottom of the trap, but difficult to get back up. Rain water accumulates in the pitchers, causing a pool in which the trapped insects drown. Their remains are absorbed by digestive cells lining the inside of the leaf. Thus the plant has an added source of nitrogenous food, in addition to that absorbed from the soil.

COMMON PITCHER-PLANT — PLATE 73

Sarracenia purpurea — *Sarraceniaceae*

This species is also known in various parts of its range as Sidesaddle Flower and Huntsman's Cup. The pitcherlike leaves are swollen and broadly winged, often reclining on the ground. An erect leafless flowering stalk bears a nodding flower with five colored sepals and five incurved petals; these stalks reach a height of twelve to eighteen inches. In the center of each flower is a flat-topped umbrellalike stigma. Pitcher plants are common to sphagnum bogs and wet peaty woods from northern Labrador to Maryland, west to Minnesota and Iowa. The flowers appear in June, and can be found through August.

TRUMPETS — PLATE 73

Sarracenia flava — *Sarraceniaceae*

The tubular insect-catching leaves of this species are longer and more slender, looking more like horns than pitchers. (In fact, another common name is Huntsman's Horn.) The winglike ridge is almost entirely lacking. Trumpets' flowers have a drooping appearance, because the pendent petals are longer than those of the common pitcher-plant. Trumpets grow in colonies on the swampy floor of wet pinelands, as well as in grassy bogs; this species is a southeastern member of the group, being found from Virginia to Florida and westward in the coastal pine belt. The flowering period is in April and May.

PLATE 75

(*upper left*) **Early Saxifrage,** ***Saxifraga virginiensis*** (*upper right*) **Grass-of-Parnassus,** ***Parnassia glauca*** (*below*) **Missouri Currant,** ***Ribes odoratum***

PLATE 76

(*left*) **False Miterwort, *Tiarella cordifolia*** (*right*) **Miterwort, *Mitella diphylla***

The Sundew Family

Droseraceae

In this insectivorous family the plants are either annuals or perennials, usually with the leaves in basal rosettes which are hidden amid the surrounding ground cover. The leaves, instead of being hollow pitchers, are glandular or toothed structures which have their own distinctive method of trapping their prey.

ROUND-LEAVED SUNDEW — PLATE 74

Drosera rotundifolia — *Droseraceae*

The Sundews are a widespread genus of peculiar plants, with more than 80 species scattered throughout the world; seven of them occur in eastern United States. Round-leaved Sundew has a low-growing cluster of flat and rounded leaves with long hairy stems; the leaves seem to cling close to the ground and are often hidden by grasses. Each leaf has a glistening red appearance because of the many red-stalked hairs covering its surface, each hair in reality a gland tipped with mucilage. The resulting glistening effect gives the impression of a dew-covered plant. The leaves, about the size of a small coin, look like little harmless pincushions; but the unwary insect which steps on one is caught by the glandular hairs, eventually dies, and its digestible remains are absorbed by the leaves. Sundew flowers grow in a one-sided terminal cluster. Round-leaved Sundew occurs across the continent from Labrador to Alaska and from Florida to California, wherever there is peaty or moist acid soil. The flowers appear during the summer.

VENUS FLYTRAP — PLATE 74

Dionaea muscipula — *Droseraceae*

This carnivorous plant has a more restricted range than the preceding species, being found only in North and South Carolina, where it grows in wet pinelands and sandy bogs. Venus Flytrap has the most unique insect-catching leaves of all, each prostrate leaf (several inches in length) having a hinged midrib, with the margin of the leaf edged with sharp teeth. The basal part of each leaf is neither hinged nor toothed, but functions as a normal leaf. In the center of the hinged portion are short stiff spines which act as triggers to set off the trap mechanism. When an insect chances to step on one of these spines, an impulse is transmitted to the midrib portion and the two halves of the leaf close over the insect, the marginal teeth interlocking to prevent his escape. Glands on the surface of the leaf secrete digestive juices which prepare the insect's body for absorption. During the flowering season, in spring, stalks up to a foot in height bear clusters of small flowers. Each has a calyx of five sepals and a regular corolla of five separate petals.

The Orpine Family

Crassulaceae

The Orpine family is another family with unusual members; in this case they are succulent annuals and perennials with fleshy leaves, adapted for living in arid, desert habitats. Of the 500 or more species included in the Orpine family, almost all of them inhabit south Asia, south Africa, the Mediterranean region and Mexico. Many novelty plants are found in this family, such as the "life plants," Kalanchoe and Bryophyllum, which sprout new plants from the edges of the leaves; and the cultivated houseleek and hen-and-chickens, which are species of Sempervivum.

STONECROP PLATE 74

Sedum ternatum *Crassulaceae*

This is a species with prostrate or spreading weak stems which bear several pairs of flat succulent leaves and a terminal rosette of crowded leaves. The small flowers are borne in clusters which are often one-sided. Each flower has four or five sepals and an equal number of petals. Stonecrop grows on damp rocks, mossy banks and edges of streams from New York to Georgia, west to Michigan. The flowering period is from April to June.

PLATE 77

Wild Turnip, *Brassica rapa*

PLATE 78

Toothwort, *Dentaria laciniata*

The Saxifrage Family

Saxifragaceae

In this family we find a variety of plant types, from herbs to shrubs and small trees. Among the wild flower members are the various saxifrages, miterwort, grass-of-Parnassus and alumroot. Shrubby members include the currants and gooseberries; the hydrangea grows to be a small tree. Ornamentals in the family include mock orange (Philadelphus) and deutzia. Of the 1,200 species in the family, a great number occur in the United States. The flower of the Saxifrage family typically has five petals, five sepals, and five or ten stamens. Beneath the perianth the stem is enlarged to form a saucer-shaped or bell-shaped base to the flower. The fruit may be a juicy berry or a dry capsule.

EARLY SAXIFRAGE — PLATE 75

Saxifraga virginiensis — *Saxifragaceae*

This is a plant of rocky hillsides, where the basal rosettes of toothed, ovate leaves cling close to the soil. Stout flowering stalks arise from the leaf clusters, bearing groups of small five-parted flowers. Early Saxifrage is variable in its flower colors, some plants producing white blossoms, others green ones, and still another variety with the petals replaced by stamens. Its range is from southeastern Canada to Georgia, west to Missouri; the flowering period is from April to June.

GRASS-OF-PARNASSUS — PLATE 75

Parnassia glauca — *Saxifragaceae*

Like the saxifrages, Grass-of-Parnassus is a stemless plant with a basal rosette of leaves; these are oval or rounded, one to two inches in length. A tall stalk, up to two feet in height, bears erect solitary flowers. Each flower has a calyx of five separate sepals and a regular corolla of five strongly veined petals. The fruit is a small capsule. Grass-of-Parnassus grows in swampy meadows and other low wet habitats, from New England to Pennsylvania and Illinois. The flowering period is from July to October.

MISSOURI CURRANT

PLATE 75

Ribes odoratum — *Saxifragaceae*

The currants are low shrubs, some with prickly and spiny stems, and alternate leaves lobed after the fashion of maple leaves. The flowers grow in pendent clusters, later becoming juicy berries. Missouri Currant is a tall spineless species with golden-yellow flowers which are spicy and fragrant. Native to rocky slopes from Minnesota west to Texas, it has been introduced into the eastern states as an ornamental shrub. The black (sometimes yellow) fruit has an insipid flavor. The Indians used the dried currants in making pemmican, which was a composite of dried buffalo meat, fat, and berries. Like the other currants, the flowers have a five-lobed calyx and a regular corolla of five small petals. The flowers appear from April to June, the berries from June to August.

WILD GOOSEBERRY

Ribes cynosbati — *Saxifragaceae*

The Prickly Gooseberry, or Wild Gooseberry, is a spiny-stemmed plant three or four feet high with drooping branches and rounded three-lobed leaves. There usually is a group of spines at the base of each leaf cluster. One to a few greenish flowers open with the leaves. Plump brownish or purplish-red berries appear in midsummer, sometimes spiny but in some varieties with a smooth skin. Wild Gooseberry is found from southeastern Canada to Alabama in open sunny woods. In northern New England and New York a related smooth-fruited species is found with very flavorsome berries, excellent for eating fresh or in pies and jellies.

PLATE 79

Rocket, ***Hesperis matronalis***

PLATE 80

(*left*) Winter Cress, *Barbarea vulgaris* (*right*) Spring Cress, *Cardamine bulbosa*

FALSE MITERWORT

PLATE 76

Tiarella cordifolia — *Saxifragaceae*

Also known as Foamflower, False Miterwort is a slender plant with maplelike basal leaves on long stalks. Amid these leaves rise stems, up to twelve inches in height, terminated with spirelike clusters of small flowers. Each flower, about a quarter of an inch in breadth, has a bell-shaped calyx with five lobes and a corolla of five oblong petals. False Miterwort grows in rich woods from eastern Canada to North Carolina and Tennessee, and west to Michigan, where it can be found in flower from April to July.

MITERWORT

PLATE 76

Mitella diphylla — *Saxifragaceae*

Another name for this dainty flower is Bishop's-cap, in reference to the form of the young fruiting capsule. Miterwort has several basal heart-shaped leaves, and a pair of opposite leaves near the middle of the erect stem. At the summit of the stem is a slender spire of small flowers, each flower with a corolla of five finely fringed petals. Miterwort prefers rich loamy woods, where it can be found in flower in late spring, until June; its range is from New England to the Carolinas, westward to Minnesota.

ALUMROOT

Heuchera americana — *Saxifragaceae*

This is one of the largest members of the herbaceous group in the Saxifrage family, erect stems reaching a height of three feet. The large rounded leaves have smoothly rounded lobes. Elongated flower clusters bear greenish-yellow blossoms with typical five-lobed calyx and five small petals. Alumroot grows in dry rocky woods from New England to Georgia, Oklahoma, and Michigan, flowering in May and June.

The Mustard Family

Cruciferae

Members of the Mustard family are predominantly either obnoxious weeds or valuable food and ornamental plants. It is a large assemblage, numbering about 2,500 species, most of which are found in the cooler portions of the northern hemisphere. The wild flowers of the Mustard family in the United States include toothwort, rocket, water cress and western wallflower. Cabbage, kale, brussels sprouts, cauliflower, and broccoli are all varieties of *Brassica oleracea.* Turnip (*Brassica rapa*), mustard (*Brassica nigra*), radish (*Raphanus sativus*) and horseradish (*Armoracia rusticana*) are other food and condiment plants in the group. Others have become familiar garden flowers, such as candytuft (*Iberis amara*), stock (*Matthiola incana*), sweet alyssum (*Lobularia maritima*) and wallflower (*Cherianthus cheiri*). Some are annual, others are biennial or perennial herbaceous plants. The flower consists of four petals alternated with the sepals, narrowed at the base and arranged in the form of a cross. This arrangement explains the scientific name of the family, which means "cross-bearer."

TOOTHWORT PLATE 78

Dentaria laciniata *Cruciferae*

This species is also known as Pepper-root because of the pungent taste of the long fleshy rhizomes. From the underground parts rise erect basal leaves which are deeply lobed and toothed. Flowering stems eight to twelve inches high bear several compound leaves which are similar to the basal leaves, and broad clusters of flowers. Each flower, about two-thirds of an inch in diameter, has a regular perianth of four short sepals and four separate white or purplish petals. Toothwort is found throughout the eastern states to Minnesota. It flowers from March to May. A related species (*Dentaria diphylla*) is known as Crinkleroot; it has similar flowers but only one pair of stem-leaves, which are less deeply lobed.

PLATE 81

(*left*) Purple Avens, *Geum rivale* (*right*) Western Wallflower, *Erysimum asperum*

PLATE 82

(*upper left*) **Wild Black Raspberry,** ***Rubus occidentalis*** (*center*) **Wild Strawberry,** ***Fragaria virginiana*** (*below*) **Swamp Dewberry,** ***Rubus hispidus***

WILD TURNIP

PLATE 77

Brassica rapa — *Cruciferae*

The cultivated European turnip has escaped in this country to become a common weed of plowed fields and waste places. Stems one to two feet tall bear alternate lobed leaves; the basal portions of the upper leaves often clasp the stem. Small regular flowers of typical mustard appearance are borne in racemes. Found throughout the United States, the flowers appear in spring and the beaked capsular fruits can be found from June through October.

ROCKET

PLATE 79

Hesperis matronalis — *Cruciferae*

This is a European plant which has escaped to become a flower of roadsides and waste places; other names are Sweet Rocket, Dame's-violet and Mother-of-the-evening. A tall stem, up to four feet in height, bears narrow pointed leaves with toothed margins, and terminal clusters of white and many shades of purple flowers. This is a more showy wild flower than most other species of the Mustard family; the flowers become fragrant toward evening. Flowering from May to August, Rocket can be found from Newfoundland to Georgia and west to Minnesota.

SEA ROCKET

Cakile edentula — *Cruciferae*

Sandy habitats along the seashore make a home for Sea Rocket, a fleshy and sprawling plant whose foliage is said to have the flavor of horseradish. The flowers, produced in ascending clusters, are light purple. Sea Rocket is found from the New England coast to South Carolina; it flowers from July to September.

WINTER CRESS

PLATE 80

Barbarea vulgaris | *Cruciferae*

Also known as Bitter Cress and Yellow Rocket, this is a European species which has become naturalized in wet meadows and along streams, from New England to Virginia. Winter Cress is a smooth-stemmed plant with its lower leaves lyre-shaped and compound; during the winter it persists as clusters or basal rosettes of leaves. The flowers are borne in racemes; each flower has a calyx of four unequal sepals and a regular corolla of four separate petals. After the flowers have appeared (April–June) the inch-long pointed pods are developed.

SPRING CRESS

PLATE 80

Cardamine bulbosa | *Cruciferae*

This is also a plant of wet meadows and woods, and of stream banks. Rising four to twenty inches from a tuberous base, Spring Cress has variable leaves—oval, elliptic, or lanceolate—alternately arranged on the stems. The flowers, borne in racemes, have a calyx of four greenish sepals edged with white, and a regular corolla of four white petals. It is found from New England to Florida and west to the plains, where it flowers from March to June.

WESTERN WALLFLOWER

PLATE 81

Erysimum asperum | *Cruciferae*

This is a stout plant, growing to a height of three feet; it has a strong preference for open sunny habitats and thus is usually found in dry and sandy fields and bluffs. Its range is from Ohio to Texas, westward, where it can be found in blossom from May to June. The upper leaves of the Western Wallflower are lanceolate and entire, while the lower leaves are sometimes compound. Racemes of showy flowers terminate the erect stems, each flower consisting of the characteristic four sepals and four separate petals.

PLATE 83

(*above*) **Prairie Rose,** ***Rosa setigera*** (*below*) **Carolina Rose,** ***Rosa carolina***

PLATE 84

(*left*) **Meadowsweet,** ***Spiraea latifolia*** (*right*) **Steeplebush,** ***Spiraea tomentosa***

The Rose Family

Rosaceae

A great variety of plants are found in the Rose family. Some are herbaceous wild flowers, such as wild strawberry and the cinquefoils. Others are flowering shrubs and vines such as the raspberries, blackberries, and roses. Still others are trees such as the hawthorns, mountain-ash and shadbush. But most significant is the economic importance, in temperate regions, of the fruit-bearing members of the Rose family. The apple (Malus) chiefly is a native of Europe and Asia, with a few wild species of the crab apple in North America. The pear (Pyrus) is a native of Europe and Asia, and has no American species. The cherries, peaches, plums and prunes are all species of the genus Prunus. There are several native American species of wild cherries and wild plums, but the peach is a Chinese tree introduced into Europe two thousand years ago. Other trees of economic importance in the Rose family are the almond, quince, loquat and apricot. In the Rose family there are some 3,200 species, widely distributed but most abundant in North America, eastern Asia and Europe. The members of the family may have simple or compound leaves, borne on stems which are often thorny or spiny. Regular flowers with their parts in five's are situated on a cup-shaped or urnlike enlargement of the flowering stalk, called a receptacle. The stamens are generally numerous. The fruit is often fleshy, in certain groups occurring in the form of a pome or drupe. A pome is a type of fruit formed from stem tissues surrounding the ovary (apple is an example) and a drupe is a fruit with the inner portion forming a hard stony covering to the seed (cherry is an example).

PURPLE AVENS — PLATE 81

Geum rivale — *Rosaceae*

There are more than a dozen kinds of Avens in the United States. All are perennials with pinnate or lyre-shaped leaves, and the flowers are characterized by a bell-shaped or deeply five-cleft calyx and a corolla of five petals. One of the most widespread species, Purple Avens is an erect plant growing to a height of three feet, with a few terminal flowers; each flower is nodding, and about three-quarters of an inch in diameter. Purple Avens is also known as Water Avens. It can be found frequently in low ground and boggy meadows from Labrador to British Columbia and from New Jersey to New Mexico. The flowers appear in April and continue through June.

WILD STRAWBERRY — PLATE 82

Fragaria virginiana — *Rosaceae*

This familiar wild flower and fruit is an inhabitant of dry sunny fields and hillsides from Newfoundland southward and westward to Oklahoma. The plants are stemless, producing horizontal runners from which rise tufts of compound leaves, each leaf with three leaflets. The flowering stems are four to twelve inches high, and bear regular flowers with spreading green sepals and five rounded petals; the flowering period is from April to June. The strawberry fruit is an unusual structure, originating in an enlarged and fleshy receptacle beneath the perianth; this becomes scarlet in color, and in it are embedded the small achene fruits which look like tiny seeds. The fruits ripen in early summer.

SWAMP DEWBERRY — PLATE 82

Rubus hispidus — *Rosaceae*

This is a trailing species with bristly canes and three-parted compound leaves which tend to become thickened and evergreen. In spite of its name, Swamp Dewberry can be found in dry open soil and sunny woods, as well as in ditches and low grounds. It can be found from New England to the Carolinas, where it blossoms from June to early September, the fruits being found as late as October.

PLATE 85

Canadian Burnet, *Sanguisorba canadensis*

PLATE 86

(*left*) **Rough-fruited Cinquefoil,** ***Potentilla recta*** (*right*) **Marsh Cinquefoil,** ***Potentilla palustris***

WILD BLACK RASPBERRY

PLATE 82

Rubus occidentalis

Rosaceae

The genus Rubus is one of the largest among our native plants; in the eighth (1950) edition of *Gray's Manual of Botany* 205 species are described for eastern United States. They are perennial shrubby plants, often with prickly stems, white flowers, and edible fruits. Wild Black Raspberry, or Thimbleberry (also called Black Caps), is found throughout the eastern states, extending from Canada to Georgia, in ravines and wooded edges of fields as well as in thickets. The stems, known as canes, have a habit of arching over and taking root at the tips; they are armed with hooked prickles as anyone knows who has tried to make his way through a tangle of the brambles. Black Raspberry leaves are compound, usually with three ovate leaflets. The regular flowers, with five sepals and five petals, appear in April and continue blossoming until July, the fruits developing accordingly between June and August. Raspberry fruits are an aggregate of small fleshy drupes forming a thimblelike mass over a spongy receptacle which projects into the hollow center of the "thimble."

FLOWERING RASPBERRY

PLATE 89

Rubus odoratus

Rosaceae

An erect branching shrub with large simple maplelike leaves, Flowering Raspberry has canes which are bristly but not prickly. Large brilliant flowers, an inch or more in diameter, are clustered at the ends of the stems. The calyx of the flower has five lobes, each prolonged into a slender tip; the regular corolla consists of five somewhat rounded petals. Flowering Raspberry grows in rocky woods and roadside thickets, from New England to Georgia, west to Michigan. The flowering period is from June through September. The hard fruits are inedible.

BLACKBERRY

PLATE 89

Rubus frondosus

Rosaceae

This species has erect or arching stems, armed with straight prickles. The three to five leaflets of the compound leaves have a velvety undersurface. Clusters of three to ten flowers are borne on spineless stems, and appear in May and June. The range of this species is from southern New England to Virginia and Indiana.

PRAIRIE ROSE

PLATE 83

Rosa setigera

Rosaceae

The genus Rosa is another large one, with twenty-four species in the eastern United States alone. Most of the species are prickly shrubs with pinnately compound leaves. Prairie Rose, or Climbing Rose, is a trailing and climbing perennial of open woods, clearings, and roadside banks from New York to Florida and Texas, west to Kansas. The flowers appear in late May, and continue through July. Each flower has an urn-shaped calyx and a regular corolla of five showy petals. In the Prairie Rose the styles at the summit of the ovary are fused to form a protruding column. The fruit is a red, rounded structure called a "hip," which remains on the bushes until late fall.

CAROLINA ROSE

PLATE 83

Rosa carolina

Rosaceae

This is a more slender and low-growing species, two or three feet in height; the stems have prickles near the base but are usually unarmed in the upper portion. The compound leaves have five to seven elliptic leaflets. The flowers, usually solitary, are characterized by having separate styles attached to each segment of the ovary. The Carolina Rose prefers dry open woods and rocky slopes; its range is from Maine to Florida and westward into the plains states. The flowers appear in May, and can still be found in early summer. The fruit is a spherical red hip.

PLATE 87

(*above*) **Shrubby Cinquefoil,** ***Potentilla fruticosa*** (*below*) **Common Five-finger,** ***Potentilla canadensis***

PLATE 88

(*above*) **Swamp Rose,** ***Rosa palustris*** (*below*) **Cherokee Rose,** ***Rosa laevigata***

SWAMP ROSE

PLATE 88

Rosa palustris — *Rosaceae*

This species is a stout erect plant which grows to a height of six feet, the thick canes bearing large conical prickles near their base. The compound leaves generally have seven elliptical or lanceolate leaflets which are finely toothed. The flowers may be solitary or in open clusters. The usual "hips" produced in autumn are flattened and elliptical rather than globular. As the name implies, the habitat is swampy woods and shores; it can be found from southern Canada to Florida, westward to Minnesota and Arkansas. The flowering period is from June through August.

CHEROKEE ROSE

PLATE 88

Rosa laevigata — *Rosaceae*

Cherokee Rose is an ornamental, originally native of China, which often escapes locally to grow on roadside banks and along fences. It is a high-climbing species with prickly stems; some stems reach a length of fifteen feet. The compound leaves consist of three (rarely five) lanceolate leaflets. The flowers appear throughout the summer months. Cherokee Rose is but one of hundreds of varieties of the rose which have been cultivated since the time of the Greeks. Most of the garden varieties have been derived from a few Oriental and European species. Some become tall shrubs, and even small trees. Rose culture has become a highly specialized pursuit, and has interested laymen to such an extent that societies have been formed for the sole purposes of studying and growing roses.

MEADOWSWEET

PLATE 84

Spiraea latifolia — *Rosaceae*

Meadowsweet, with its close relative, the steeplebush, represents a shrubby group in the Rose family, with simple leaves and minute flowers in dense spirelike terminal clusters. Meadowsweet is a branching shrub ordinarily three or four feet in height but capable of reaching six or seven feet. The foliage consists of small lanceolate leaves, two to three inches in length, with finely toothed margins. The small dainty flowers are characterized by a short five-lobed calyx and a regular corolla of five small petals. Meadowsweet is common in woods and wooded fields, from Newfoundland to North Carolina and west to Illinois and Missouri. It is a summer-flowering shrub, in bloom from June through September.

STEEPLEBUSH — PLATE 84

Spiraea tomentosa — *Rosaceae*

Also known as Hardhack, this species is a smaller shrub which commonly forms compact clumps in abandoned pastures and sterile fields throughout the northeastern states and well up into Canada. Usually two or three feet tall, the stems bear ovate leaves with toothed margins and a woolly undersurface densely covered with white hairs. The pink or purplish flowers grow in elongated terminal spires which are more definitely spikelike than the flower clusters of meadowsweet. Steeplebush is also a summer flowering shrub, blossoming from July through September.

CANADIAN BURNET — PLATE 85

Sanguisorba canadensis — *Rosaceae*

Also known as American Great Burnet, this member of the Rose family is a tall erect plant reaching a height of five feet. The unequally pinnate, compound leaves are divided into seven to fifteen ovate leaflets. Exceedingly small flowers are borne in a dense terminal spike which may reach a length of six inches. Each flower has a four-lobed calyx, and lacks a corolla; a conspicuous part of the flower is the mass of long white stamens. Canadian Burnet grows in peaty, boggy meadows and swampy woods, from Labrador to Georgia and west to Illinois; the flowers first appear in July and continue until October.

PLATE 89

(*above*) Blackberry, *Rubus frondosus* (*below*) Flowering Raspberry, *Rubus odoratus*

PLATE 90

(*left*) **Sampson's Snakeroot,** ***Psoralea psoralioides*** (*right*) **Leadplant,**
Amorpha canescens

ROUGH-FRUITED CINQUEFOIL — PLATE 86

Potentilla recta — *Rosaceae*

The Cinquefoils, or Five-fingers, are common wild flowers of the Rose family, characteristically with compound leaves divided into five leaflets, generally arranged like the fingers of a hand. Rough-fruited Cinquefoil is a stout-stemmed and erect plant, growing to a height of several feet. It is a European species which has become naturalized in the northeastern states, spreading to dry roadsides and waste places. The numerous flowers are about three-quarters of an inch in diameter, and grouped in spreading terminal clusters. They may be seen from late May through August.

MARSH CINQUEFOIL — PLATE 86

Potentilla palustris — *Rosaceae*

This species of cold swamps and peat bogs has creeping stems from which arise erect branches one to two feet tall. The pinnately compound leaves have five to seven oblong, toothed leaflets. Each flower has a dark purple calyx and purplish petals which are shorter than the calyx lobes. Marsh Cinquefoil, or Marsh Five-finger, grows from Canada southward to Pennsylvania and California. Its flowering period is from June through August.

COMMON FIVE-FINGER — PLATE 87

Potentilla canadensis — *Rosaceae*

This familiar low-growing plant of dry roadside banks and sandy fields develops creeping runners, similar to the habit of the wild strawberry; from the runners arise short stems bearing compound leaves with five radiating leaflets. The flowers, about three-quarters of an inch in diameter, are similar to those of the shrubby cinquefoil. Common Five-finger extends from Nova Scotia to the Carolinas and west to Ohio. The flowers appear first in March, and can be found through June.

SHRUBBY CINQUEFOIL PLATE 87

Potentillа fruticosa *Rosaceae*

Called also Shrubby Five-finger, this branching plant forms a shrub three or four feet in height. The pinnately compound leaves are made up of five to seven linear leaflets. Large flowers, up to an inch in diameter, are either solitary or in small terminal clusters. Each flower has a flattened five-lobed calyx, with five bractlets. The regular corolla consists of five rounded petals. Shrubby Cinquefoil grows in wet or dry open ground, from New England to Pennsylvania and westward to Illinois. The flowering period is from June to October.

The Bean Family

Leguminosae

The Bean family is one of the three largest families of flowering plants, with some 13,000 species distributed widely on all the continents. Few families are as easy to recognize either in flower or in fruit. The majority of the species have an irregular flower of the sweet pea type; the corolla consists of five petals, one of which is large and erect, the two lateral petals smaller with narrowed basal portions, and the two lowermost ones united to form an upturned keel. The fruit, known as a legume, is a bilaterally symmetrical structure which splits open along the two sutures, revealing the large seeds usually arranged lengthwise within the pod. The alternate leaves are usually compound. Herbaceous plants, shrubs and trees are found in this family, many of them of considerable economic importance. Best known native wild flowers of the Bean family are the clovers, lupines, vetches, indigos and psoraleas. Alfalfa, peanut, kidney bean, soy bean, and garden pea are some of the fodder and food plants in the family. Ornamental vines and trees include wisteria, redbud, honey locust, mimosa and acacia; a striking subtropical tree, found in Florida particularly, is the royal poinciana (Delonix). And a ubiquitous woody plant of the southwestern states is the mesquite.

PLATE 91

False Indigo, *Amorpha fruticosa*

PLATE 92

(*left*) **Groundnut,** ***Apios americana*** (*right*) **Vetchling,** ***Lathyrus palustris***

SAMPSON'S SNAKEROOT

PLATE 90

Psoralea psoralioides — *Leguminosae*

Also known as Congo Root, because of the tuberous taproot, this species is an erect plant, one to three feet tall, with compound leaves divided into three to five leaflets. Like other species of Psoralea, the plant is usually roughened with glandular dots, which give the name of Scurf Pea to the group. The flowers are borne in a cylindrical spike; each flower has a typical pealike flower with a five-lobed tubular calyx and an irregular corolla of five petals. Sampson's Snakeroot grows in open woods and dry fields, from Virginia to Georgia and west to Kansas and Texas. The flowering period is from May to July.

SILVER-LEAF

PLATE 100

Psoralea argophylla — *Leguminosae*

As the name implies, the foliage of this species is a silvery silky-white; the palmately lobed leaves have three to five leaflets. The pealike flowers are borne in a terminal interrupted spike. Silver-leaf thrives on dry plains in the central states, being found from Minnesota to Texas and Saskatchewan to New Mexico. The flowers appear in June and July.

SAINFOIN

PLATE 101

Psoralea onobrychis — *Leguminosae*

This is a vigorously growing perennial, reaching a height of six feet. The compound leaves each consist of three leaflets. The small flowers are borne in graceful spikes, up to four inches in length. Each flower is structurally similar to the flowers of silver-leaf. The pods, however, are characteristically tough and wrinkled. Sainfoin grows along river banks and in rich woods, from Ohio and West Virginia, west to Illinois and Missouri, where it flowers during the summer. The plant derives its common name from its similarity to a Eurasian perennial called Sainfoin.

BREADROOT

Psoralea esculenta *Leguminosae*

This species of Psoralea was an important food plant to the Indians of the central states, and the early travelers across the prairies. Known also as Prairie Apple, and Pomme Blanche, it has purplish-blue flowers in dense spikes, and compound leaves with five leaflets. The important portion of the plant is the turniplike root, four to eight inches long, whose starchy content has an agreeable flavor. The Sioux often peeled it and ate it raw, but others preferred to boil or roast it. The roots were often gathered in early summer, peeled, and braided in long strips, then hung up to dry. Breadroot grows on the high plains from Wisconsin and Manitoba to Texas, west to the Rocky Mountains. The flowers appear in May and June.

LEADPLANT

PLATE 90

Amorpha canescens *Leguminosae*

This small shrub, two or three feet tall, has pinnately compound leaves divided into fifteen or more small elliptical leaflets. The foliage is densely hairy, with a whitened appearance. Small flowers crowd into a spikelike terminal cluster; each flower has a five-toothed, inversely conical calyx, and a corolla with a single large petal which is wrapped around the stamens and style. Leadplant is found on dry hills and prairies from Indiana and Michigan to Saskatchewan and south to Texas. It flowers from May to August.

FALSE INDIGO

PLATE 91

Amorpha fruticosa *Leguminosae*

A tall shrub—up to fifteen feet in height—with foliage like a sumac, this species inhabits river banks and swampy woods from Pennsylvania to Florida and Texas. Large, long-stemmed leaves are subdivided into eleven to twenty-five tapering leaflets, hoary with a covering of fine hairs. The flowers are borne in dense spirelike clusters, each flower with but a single petal as in the Leadplant. The flowering period is from May to June.

PLATE 93

(*upper left*) **Hop Clover,** ***. Trifolium agrarium*** (*lower left*) **Red Clover,** ***Trifolium pratense*** (*right*) **Alsike Clover,** ***Trifolium hybridum***

PLATE 94

(*above*) **Wild Lupine,** ***Lupinus perennis*** (*below*) **Goat's Rue,** ***Tephrosia virginiana***

VETCHLING

PLATE 92

Lathyrus palustris — *Leguminosae*

Also known as Everlasting Pea, this species has a creeping rhizome from which rise stems two or three feet tall, bearing pinnately compound leaves with three to four pairs of narrow leaflets. The large flowers, up to an inch in length, are borne in clusters of three to five. Vetchling is a cool-climate plant, found in various forms in damp thickets and along lake shores of northern regions the world around. The flowering period is from June to September. One of the several varieties, known as Myrtle-leaved Marsh Pea (var. *myrtifolius*) has angled, smooth stems, but lacks the wings found in the Vetchling itself; it has yellowish flowers which become pale purple when mature. The axis of the compound leaf terminates in a forked tendril which aids the plant in climbing. The Myrtle-leaved Marsh Pea inhabits wet ground and swamps from New England to North Carolina, where it can be found in flower from May through June.

GROUNDNUT

PLATE 92

Apios americana — *Leguminosae*

Known in some localities as Wild Bean and Potato Bean, this species is a twining and climbing perennial with pinnately compound leaves consisting of five to nine oval, pointed leaflets. The rootstocks have tuberous enlargements one to three inches in diameter, connected by fibrous strands, much as beads are strung on a necklace. These tubers are sweet and edible, even when eaten raw, but are better when cooked. A famous botanist stated that if civilization had started in America rather than Europe, this would have been the first edible tuber to have been cultivated. The numerous pealike flowers are clustered in the axils of the leaves. As with other members of the Pea family, the fruit is a beanlike pod, in this case, two or three inches in length. Groundnut grows in moist woods and bottomlands from New Brunswick to Minnesota, south to Florida and west to Texas and Colorado. The flowering period is from July to September.

BEACH PEA

PLATE 97

Lathyrus japonicus

Leguminosae

Beach Pea is a fleshy perennial with stout prostrate stems and pinnately compound leaves consisting of six to twelve oval leaflets. As in the other members of the genus Lathyrus, the axis of the leaf terminates in a tendril. Its favorite habitat is the gravelly beach or sand dune near the water. The irregular flowers, an inch in length, grow in clusters of ten, sometimes less. The Beach Pea is known in Greenland, the Aleutian Islands, and Japan, occurring southward in North America to New Jersey and the Great Lakes states, where it flowers from May to August.

RED CLOVER

PLATE 93

Trifolium pratense

Leguminosae

The true clovers, or trefoils, are familiar to even the most inexperienced naturalist because of the generally three-parted leaves with oval or elliptical leaflets. The minute pealike flowers are clustered in a compact head. The familiar Red Clover is a European species which has established itself along roadsides and in fields. It grows either as a biennial or a short-lived perennial. The small flowers are clustered compactly in a somewhat spherical head about an inch in diameter. Varieties can be found with creamy-white corollas instead of the usual purplish-rose or "red" color. Escaped from cultivation, Red Clover has spread throughout most of the North American continent, flowering from May to September.

HOP CLOVER

PLATE 93

Trifolium agrarium

Leguminosae

Hop Clover, or Yellow Clover, is another European species which has escaped to fields and waste places, occurring from Newfoundland to Georgia and west to Kansas. It is an annual, which blossoms from June through September. The head is cylindrical or oblong in shape.

PLATE 95

(*upper left*) **Old-field Clover, *Trifolium arvense*** (*upper right*) **Bush Tick Trefoil, *Desmodium canadense*** (*below*) **Cow Vetch, *Vicia cracca***

PLATE 96

(*upper left*) **Partridge Pea, *Cassia fasciculata*** (*upper right*) **Violet Bush-clover, *Lespedeza violacea*** (*below*) **Rattlebox, *Crotalaria sagittalis***

ALSIKE CLOVER

PLATE 93

Trifolium hybridum — *Leguminosae*

Also known as Alsatian or Swedish Clover, this European plant has made itself widely at home in fields and cleared ground. It is a vigorous perennial, from one to three feet in height, with soft, hollow stems. The dense, fragrant heads reach a diameter of an inch, flowering in the summer months. Alsike Clover is not a hybrid, but a species escaped from cultivation throughout the United States, southern Canada, and Alaska.

HOG PEANUT

Amphicarpa bracteata — *Leguminosae*

This slender-stemmed twining plant is a vine of rich woods, roadsides and fence-rows, at times reaching a length of eight feet. The compound leaves are subdivided into three broadly ovate leaflets with pointed tips. White to pale purple flowers grow in clusters in the axils of the leaves; they develop between July and September. In autumn the seed pods mature, each pod about an inch in length. Beneath the debris on the surface of the ground, creeping branches develop small flowers without petals, which give rise to unusual pods which each have one large peanutlike seed. These are edible, and were an important food plant among the Indians. Hog Peanut is found from Quebec to Florida and west to the plains states.

WILD BEAN

Strophostyles helvola — *Leguminosae*

This is another trailing and twining species; the stems are hairy, and bear compound leaves with three leaflets. Each leaflet is broadly lobed at the base. Greenish-purple flowers, up to half an inch in length, are grouped in clusters of three to a dozen in the axils of the leaves. The pods are one to three inches long, much larger than those of the Hog Peanut. Wild Bean grows in sandy fields and woods near the shore, from southern Canada to Florida and west to the Mississippi River and Texas. The flowering period is from June to October.

OLD-FIELD CLOVER PLATE 95

Trifolium arvense *Leguminosae*

Other names for this common species are Rabbit's-foot Clover and Stone Clover. It is an erect, branching annual reaching a height of ten or twelve inches, with silky hairy stems and the characteristic three-parted leaves. The flowers are clustered in compact cylindrical or oblong heads up to an inch in length; the heads appear silky because of the silky calyx of each flower, which is longer than the corolla. Old-field Clover thrives in waste places, sandy fields and roadsides. It is another European immigrant, common from Quebec to Florida and west to the Mississippi River; the flowers appear from May to September.

WILD LUPINE PLATE 94

Lupinus perennis *Leguminosae*

The Lupines are attractive wild flowers of the Bean family, strangely named because "Lupinus" is derived from the Latin word for wolf. They were once thought to rob the land of its mineral food. There are at least 300 species, but only one is native to northeastern United States—the Wild or Perennial Lupine. This is an erect branching plant with symmetrical, palmately compound leaves, each leaflet an inch or two in length with a blunt tip and a tapering base. The color of the flowers is usually blue, but may be white or pink; the flowers are borne in erect spirelike clusters. Each flower is borne on a long stalk, and has the characteristic pea shape. The flowers first develop in April, and can be found through July. The eastern Wild Lupine is a plant of open sandy stretches in woods and clearings from Maine to Florida and west to Minnesota and Missouri. The number of kinds of lupine increases as one travels south and west; there are six species along the southern coastal plain, nine on the prairies, and some two dozen west of the Rocky Mountains. Cultivated lupines of our gardens have been introduced from Europe and Asia.

PLATE 97

(*above*) **Beach Pea, *Lathyrus japonicus*** (*below*) **Butterfly Pea, *Clitoria mariana***

PLATE 98

(*left*) **Blue False Indigo,** ***Baptisia australis*** (*right*) **Wild Indigo,** ***Baptisia tinctoria***

BUFFALO CLOVER

Trifolium reflexum *Leguminosae*

This is a native species of clover, found in open woods and prairie country from Virginia to Florida, west to Texas. It is an upright annual or biennial, reaching a foot or two in height, wth oblong leaflets. In rounded flower heads, an inch or more in diameter, the erect petals are rosy but the remaining petals are white. Buffalo Clover flowers between May and August. A related species of similar habitats from West Virginia and Kentucky to Missouri is the Running Buffalo Clover (*Trifolium stoloniferum*). This is a creeping plant with basal runners and white flowers tinged with purple. Virginian Clover (*Trifolium virginicum*) is another white-flowering species native to the United States; its range is from Pennsylvania and Maryland to Virginia. Although an erect plant, it does not reach any great size, the upright stems being rarely more than four inches in height. Virginian Clover is usually through flowering by June. The common White Clover of lawns is *Trifolium repens.*

CAROLINA VETCH

PLATE 100

Vicia caroliniana *Leguminosae*

This is a native vetch, found in woods and along shores from New York to Georgia and Oklahoma where it flowers from April to June. Carolina or Wood Vetch is a trailing and climbing perennial whose compound leaves consist of six to twelve pairs of leaflets. The pealike flowers are grouped in open clusters. There are a dozen other vetches found in the eastern states. Among the native species is American Vetch (*Vicia americana*), a perennial with stems up to three feet long, with only four to nine pairs of leaflets in each compound leaf, and with bluish-purple flowers. American Vetch grows on damp shores and in low meadows from Quebec to Virginia and from Alaska to Arizona. The flowers can be found from May to July.

COW VETCH

PLATE 95

Vicia cracca *Leguminosae*

This European climbing plant, also known as Canada Pea, has made itself at home in fields and waste places from southeastern Canada to Virginia, west to Illinois. It is a perennial with angular stems reaching a length of six feet, and pinnately compound leaves with eight to twelve pairs of leaflets which may be silky white in some varieties. Flowers are crowded into one-sided clusters in the axils of the leaves; each flower is reflexed, and although usually purple may occur in whitish varieties. The flowers appear throughout the summer.

BUSH TICK TREFOIL

PLATE 95

Desmodium canadense *Leguminosae*

The Tick Trefoils form a large genus of the Bean family, being represented in eastern United States alone by twenty-four species. They have prickly fruits which attach tenaciously to our clothing. Many of the species are known as Beggar's-ticks. All are perennials, with erect or trailing stems and compound leaves of three leaflets. The small flowers are usually in axillary or terminal clusters. Bush Tick Trefoil grows to a height of four or five feet, and is common in woods and along streams from southern Canada to Virginia, west to Illinois and Oklahoma. The flowers appear in July and August.

CROWN VETCH

Coronilla varia *Leguminosae*

Also known as Axseed and Axwort, this species is a naturalized European plant found in old fields and along roadsides throughout the northeastern states and west to South Dakota. The ascending or sprawling stems, up to three feet in length, bear pinnately compound leaves with fifteen to twenty-five leaflets and rose-colored flowers in rounded clusters at the ends of long flowering stalks. The flowering period is from June to August.

PLATE 99

(*left*) **Purple Prairie Clover,** ***Petalostemum purpureum*** (*center*) **White Sweet Clover,** ***Melilotus alba*** (*right*) **White Prairie Clover,** ***Petalostemum candidum***

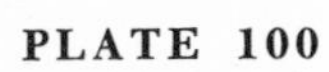

PLATE 100

(*left*) **Silver-leaf,** ***Psoralea argophylla*** (*right*) **Carolina Vetch,** ***Vicia caroliniana***

BLUEBONNET

Lupinus subcarnosus *Leguminosae*

New England may boast of its colorful fields of goldenrod and asters, and California of its spectacular poppies, but a Texan can well be proud of the heavenly blue carpets which appear on his sparsely wooded hillsides in early spring when the Bluebonnets are in bloom. This species of lupine is a low-growing plant, under a foot in height, with the flowers in pyramidal clusters. The erect petal of each flower is deep blue with a white spot at its center.

GOAT'S RUE

PLATE 94

Tephrosia virginiana *Leguminosae*

Also known as Hoary Pea and Rabbit's Pea, this member of the family is an erect plant growing to a height of several feet; both stems and leaves are covered with silky white hairs. The long compound leaves consist of seventeen to twenty-nine narrowly elliptical leaflets. Large flowers, up to three-quarters of an inch in length, are crowded in terminal clusters. Each flower has a rounded conspicuous yellow petal, with lateral petals and keel reddish or purplish. The fruit is a narrow hairy pod, one to two inches in length. Goat's Rue grows in dry sandy soils from southern New England to Florida and southern Ontario to Texas. Its flowering period is from May to August.

PARTRIDGE PEA

PLATE 96

Cassia fasciculata *Leguminosae*

Other names for this plant are Prairie Senna and Golden Cassia. It is a sprawling annual capable of growing to a height of three feet, but more often clinging to the ground, with ten to fifteen pairs of linear leaflets in each compound leaf. The leaflets are somewhat sensitive to touch. Partridge Pea flowers are only slightly irregular, with five spreading petals and a calyx of five sepals barely united at the base. The flowers are borne in two's and four's in the leaf axils. Like many other members of the Bean family, Partridge Pea thrives in sandy open habitats, and can be found in such places from southern New England to Florida and Texas, west to Wisconsin and Minnesota. The flowers develop continuously from July through September.

VIOLET BUSH-CLOVER

PLATE 96

Lespedeza violacea

Leguminosae

The Bush-clovers form another large group of plants, with eighteen species inhabiting eastern United States. They are predominantly erect perennials, although in a few species the stems are trailing. The leaves are compound and, as in the true clovers, consist of three leaflets. The flowers are very small and clover-like, being grouped in axillary heads or panicles. Violet Bush-clover is a plant of dry woods and open clearings from southern New England to Florida, west to Michigan and Kansas. It grows two feet tall and flowers from July to September. This species is more or less characteristic of the purple-flowering members of the genus. A few species have whitish or yellowish flowers. Hairy Bush-clover (*Lespedeza hirta*) is representative of these; it is a stout-stemmed, erect, branching plant, growing to a height of five feet. The Hairy Bush-clover is also found in sandy habitats and extends from southern Ontario throughout eastern United States. Its flowering period is from August to October.

PLATE 101

Sainfoin, ***Psoralea onobrychis***

PLATE 102

(*upper left*) **Common Wood Sorrel, *Oxalis montana*** (*upper right*) **Violet Wood Sorrel, *Oxalis violacea*** (*below*) **Creeping Sorrel, *Oxalis corniculata***

RATTLEBOX

PLATE 96

Crotalaria sagittalis

Leguminosae

The name of this member of the family comes from the inflated dry pod which contains loose seeds. Rattlebox is a hairy annual plant which grows to a height of twelve inches. Unlike its relations, it has simple leaves, the lower ones oval and the upper ones tapering at both base and apex. Two to four flowers are borne in a cluster, each flower with a large heart-shaped erect petal and a scythe-shaped keel. Rattlebox grows in sandy or gravelly soil from southern New England and southern Ontario to South Dakota and southward to Florida and Texas. It flowers from June to September.

BUTTERFLY PEA

PLATE 97

Clitoria mariana

Leguminosae

This species is a low-growing twining perennial of dry banks and pinelands from southern Ontario and New York to Florida and Iowa, west to Arizona. The compound leaves are usually divided into three leaflets. Large showy flowers grow in small clusters; each flower has a very much expanded upper petal, notched at the tip, and the incurved keel is much smaller than the lateral petals. The newly developed seeds are very sticky. Butterfly Pea blossoms from June through August.

WILD INDIGO

PLATE 98

Baptisia tinctoria

Leguminosae

Also known as Horsefly-weed and False Indigo, this plant of dry woods and clearings is a perennial growing to a height of several feet. The palmately compound leaves are made up of three leaflets, resembling clover leaves. Loose clusters of flowers terminate the leafy branches; each flower has an erect petal not much larger than the straight lateral petals and keel. Found from southern New England and New York westward to Minnesota and south to Florida, Wild Indigo flowers from June to September.

BLUE FALSE INDIGO

PLATE 98

Baptisia australis — *Leguminosae*

This species is a smooth, stout-stemmed plant growing to a height of three or four feet; it has larger flowers than the Wild Indigo, and the clusters lack the small bracts characteristic of the leafy inflorescences of that species. Blue False Indigo grows in rich woods from Pennsylvania to Georgia and Indiana. The flowering period is from May to June.

WHITE SWEET CLOVER

PLATE 99

Melilotus alba — *Leguminosae*

The Sweet Clovers have individual flowers much like those of the common clover, but they occur in slender, elongated clusters. All of the species found in the United States are European plants which have escaped and established themselves along roadsides and near dwellings. White Sweet Clover has compound leaves, each with three leaflets; the erect branching stems form tall plants topped with fragrant flowers from May to October. Three other naturalized Sweet Clover species have yellow flowers; these are *Melilotus indica, Melilotus officinalis,* and *Melilotus altissima.*

PURPLE PRAIRIE CLOVER

PLATE 99

Petalostemum purpureum — *Leguminosae*

The Prairie Clovers are upright perennials with glandular-dotted stems and small flowers in dense terminal heads or spikes. Purple Prairie Clover grows to a height of three feet, and is a plant of prairies and dry hillsides throughout the central states from Michigan to Tennessee and New Mexico. The pinnately compound leaves consist of three to five leaflets, linear and about an inch in length. The tiny, almost regular flowers are clustered in a rounded or cylindrical head. Purple Prairie Clover flowers from June to September.

PLATE 103

(*upper left*) Marsh Milkwort, *Polygala cruciata* (*lower left*) Fringed Milkwort, *Polygala paucifolia* (*right*) Orange Milkwort, *Polygala lutea*

PLATE 104

(*left*) **Purple Milkwort, *Polygala sanguinea*** (*center*) **Racemed Milkwort, *Polygala polygama*** (*right*) **Pine-barren Milkwort, *Polygala ramosa***

WHITE PRAIRIE CLOVER

PLATE 99

Petalostemum candidum — *Leguminosae*

This species is a smooth-stemmed plant, smaller than the preceding; the average height is less than two feet. The compound leaves consist of five to seven oblong leaflets, slightly over an inch in length. White Prairie Clover is a prairie inhabitant, found from Canada to Mississippi and Texas; the flowers appear in June and July.

The Wood Sorrel Family

Oxalidaceae

The Wood Sorrel family is a large group in the tropics, but of its 1,000 members, only twenty-five species of the genus Oxalis occur in the United States. These are characterized by palmately compound leaves of three leaflets, and regular flowers with five petals, generally separate but sometimes basally united.

COMMON WOOD SORREL

PLATE 102

Oxalis montana — *Oxalidaceae*

The characteristic three-parted compound leaf is responsible for another common name for this species—Wood Shamrock. Wood Sorrel is a creeping plant with groups of basal compound leaves and flowering stalks as long as, or longer than, the leaves. The delicately tinted flowers have oblong, notched petals; the fruits are small cylindric capsules. Common Wood Sorrel hides in the shade of rich woods, preferring to grow on damp mossy banks in the cooler portions of the eastern states. Its range is from southeastern Canada, farther south in the higher mountains to North Carolina and Tennessee; it also is found westward in Wisconsin and Minnesota. The flowering period is from May to August.

VIOLET WOOD SORREL PLATE 102

Oxalis violacea *Oxalidaceae*

This species is also a stemless perennial, but grows from a scaly bulb instead of the rootstock typical of the common wood sorrel. The leaves are basal and compound, with three broad leaflets. Three or more flowers are borne on erect stalks which rise above the leaves; each flower has five blunt sepals and five longer petals. Violet Wood Sorrel grows in more open, sunny habitats and is found therefore in rocky woods and clearings; its range is from southern New England to Florida, west to New Mexico and North Dakota. The flowers can be found from April to July.

CREEPING SORREL PLATE 102

Oxalis corniculata *Oxalidaceae*

Also known as Ladies' Sorrel and Sourgrass, this species is chiefly a weed of fields and roadsides near dwellings throughout the United States and adjacent Canada. The stems are often prostrate, taking root at the nodes; each compound leaf is divided into three small leaflets often a purple or bronze color. The flowers may be solitary, or in clusters of four or five. Its flowering period is from April to November.

The Milkwort Family

Polygalaceae

In the United States the members of this family are mainly species of Polygala, herbaceous plants with simple leaves and very irregular flowers; two of the five sepals become large and petallike, and the three other petals are connected with each other and with the stamen tube. The fruit is a small capsule. Although the family has 700 species scattered throughout the Old World and the New, the native plants in the group are of little significance.

PLATE 105

(*left*) Snow-on-the-mountain, *Euphorbia marginata* (*right*) Flowering Spurge, *Euphorbia corollata*

PLATE 106

(*left*) Pale Touch-me-not, *Impatiens pallida* (*right*) Spotted Touch-me-not, *Impatiens capensis*

MARSH MILKWORT

PLATE 103

Polygala cruciata — *Polygalaceae*

Known in Florida as Drumheads, this species is a low-growing annual with a maximum height of twenty inches. The simple linear leaves are grouped in whorls of four on the angled or square stems. Marsh Milkwort flowers are borne in compact cylindrical clusters, each flower conspicuous because of the two winglike sepals which may be purplish-green or whitish. Marsh Milkwort grows in wet pinelands, boggy meadows and low ground from New England to Florida and Texas, west to the Mississippi river. The flowers appear in July, and can be found as late as October.

ORANGE MILKWORT

PLATE 103

Polygala lutea — *Polygalaceae*

Another name for this member of the genus is Yellow Bachelor's-button. It is a plant of swamps and wet woods, from Long Island and New Jersey south along the coast to Florida and Louisiana. Its flowers are seen from May to October. Orange Milkwort is also a low-growing biennial, six to twenty inches in height; the simple leaves are alternate and lanceolate. Basal leaves are slightly different in shape, being oblong with a tapering and attenuated base. The many small flowers are clustered in a dense ovoid or cylindrical cluster; they retain their color in drying.

PURPLE MILKWORT

PLATE 104

Polygala sanguinea — *Polygalaceae*

This is an annual species, growing to a height of sixteen inches, with alternate, linear leaves and thick, cylindrical flower clusters. Each flower is structurally similar to the Marsh Milkwort. Purple Milkwort grows in moist and open acid habitats, from southeastern Canada to Louisiana and Oklahoma, flowering from June to October.

FRINGED MILKWORT

PLATE 103

Polygala paucifolia — *Polygalaceae*

This is a very different appearing flower from the others in the genus; it is sometimes known as Flowering Wintergreen or Fringed Polygala. Creeping subterranean stems are perennial, and produce erect stems four to five inches in height. A few crowded simple leaves are borne at the summit of the erect stem, mingling with one to four flowers, each two-thirds to an inch in length. The flowers have conspicuous oval wings, or petaloid sepals, and an attractive fringed corolla. Fringed Polygala is found in rich woods in New England and New York and in higher altitudes southward to Georgia. It flowers from May to early July.

PINE-BARREN MILKWORT

PLATE 104

Polygala ramosa — *Polygalaceae*

A biennial with rosettes of basal elliptic leaves, the Pine-barren Milkwort grows to a height of sixteen or eighteen inches. Erect stems bear alternate lanceolate leaves and loose clusters of long-stemmed flowers. This species is found in damp pinelands from New Jersey to Florida and Texas; the flowering period is from July to September.

RACEMED MILKWORT

PLATE 104

Polygala polygama — *Polygalaceae*

This species has several stems growing from a perennial root to a height of a foot or fifteen inches. The crowded alternate leaves are oblong or broadly lanceolate, about an inch in length. An open terminal cluster of flowers is made up of individual blossoms with large fringed crests on the corolla. Racemed Milkwort grows in dry sandy woods and fields from Canada to Florida, west to Minnesota and Texas. The flowering period is June and July.

PLATE 107

New Jersey Tea, *Ceanothus americanus*

PLATE 108

Poppy Mallow, ***Callirhoë involucrata***

The Spurge Family

Euphorbiaceae

This unique family of herbaceous plants, shrubs and trees is a large one, with about 7,300 species. They are mainly inhabitants of the tropics, although some members have ventured into the south temperate regions. In many species the sap is milky, frequently poisonous, and the flowers often have colored bracts beneath the inflorescence; some species are fleshy and cactuslike. The economic importance of the Spurge family is considerable since it includes the rubber-producing Hevea tree, and in addition the Tung-oil tree (Aleurites) and Castor-oil plant (Ricinus). The most familiar ornamental of the group is the Poinsettia (*Poinsettia pulcherrima*) whose red leaflike floral bracts have made it common as Christmas decorations. The Painted Leaf (*Euphorbia heterophylla*), found in the region from Florida to Texas, most closely resembles the Mexican poinsettia.

SNOW-ON-THE-MOUNTAIN PLATE 105

Euphorbia marginata *Euphorbiaceae*

The uppermost leaves of this plant have white margins, as have the leafy bracts beneath the terminal cluster of small flowers. The flowers are bisexual and of an unusual structure, being borne in a cup-shaped involucre resembling a calyx; there are no petals. Thus the striking appearance of this species is due to the white-marked foliage and not the flowers. Snow-on-the-mountain is a stout-stemmed annual, growing to a height of four feet; its habitat is dry fields and roadsides. Originally native to the central states, from Minnesota southward, it has spread eastward to the Atlantic coast. Flowers are produced from June to October.

FLOWERING SPURGE — PLATE 105

Euphorbia corollata — *Euphorbiaceae*

This species is an erect perennial, one to three feet tall, with entire simple leaves, the uppermost ones whorled or opposite. The floral structure is similar to that of snow-on-the-mountain. Conspicuous white rounded appendages are developed in conjunction with the cup-shaped involucre. Flowering Spurge grows in fields and clearings from southern New York to Florida and Texas, west to Minnesota. The flowering period is from June to October. These are only two of a great many species of Euphorbia found in the United States. The greatest number of kinds is found in the Southeast and Southwest. Technical differences in the structure on which the reduced staminate and pistillate flowers are produced are used to differentiate many of these species.

Touch-Me-Not Family

Balsaminaceae

This small family of less than 500 species of herbaceous plants is most abundant in tropical Asia and Africa. Only two species are native to eastern United States; these have alternate simple leaves and irregular flowers with a spurred calyx and an unusual trigger-mechanism which snaps open the capsule sections quickly and violently when the tip of the fruit is touched. The plants are succulent-stemmed annuals.

PLATE 109

Swamp Rose Mallow, *Hibiscus moscheutos*

PLATE 110

(*left*) Common Mallow, *Malva rotundifolia* (*right*) Musk Mallow, *Malva moschata*

SPOTTED TOUCH-ME-NOT

PLATE 106

Impatiens capensis

Balsaminaceae

Also known as Jewelweed or Snapweed, the Spotted Touch-me-not grows rankly to a height of five or six feet. Flowers up to an inch in length hang by slender pendent stalks. Each flower has a calyx of three sepals, one of which is petallike and prolonged into a conspicuous spur; two of the three petals are divided into dissimilar lobes. Spotted Touch-me-not thrives in roadside ditches and low moist habitats; it is found from Newfoundland to Alaska and southeastward to Florida, flowering from July to September. In many books it is called *Impatiens biflora.*

PALE TOUCH-ME-NOT

PLATE 106

Impatiens pallida

Balsaminaceae

This species is generally similar to the Spotted Touch-me-not but has lighter green foliage and slightly larger flowers which reach a length of an inch and a half. It also grows along stream margins and in low wet ground. Pale Touch-me-not is found from southern Canada to Georgia and Kansas, and flowers from July to September.

The Buckthorn Family

Rhamnaceae

The Buckthorn family includes shrubs and trees with alternate, simple, unlobed leaves and small, regular flowers in spreading clusters; in some genera the branches are thorny. Some species are bitter and astringent, and the fruit or bark may be nauseous or cathartic. The purgative cascara sagrada is obtained from a species of Buckthorn (*Rhamnus purshiana*) found in the Northwest. The family is a small one, of greatest importance in California, where the native species of Ceanothus have been developed as ornamentals.

NEW JERSEY TEA

PLATE 107

Ceanothus americanus

Rhamnaceae

This is a low-growing shrub, under three feet in height, with ovate, pointed leaves up to four inches in length, prominently three-ribbed and gray on the undersurface. Small flowers, each with a calyx of five sepals and a regular corolla of five hooded petals, are borne in umbellike clusters at the tips of leafless flowering stalks. New Jersey Tea has various uses. The fragrant flower clusters attract a variety of insect visitors; the red root makes a usable dye; and the leaves can be used to brew a satisfactory beverage. During the Revolution when it was unpopular to use Oriental tea brought in by English ships, the fresh or dried leaves of this species were used as a tea substitute. New Jersey Tea grows in rocky woods and on gravelly slopes from southern Canada to Florida and westward to Kansas and Texas; its flowers can be found from May to September. A relative known as Wild Lilac (*Ceanothus sanguineus*), growing to a height of twelve feet, is found from Michigan westward to the coast.

The Mallow Family

Malvaceae

The plants of this family are herbs or shrubs with alternate simple leaves, and with regular flowers possessing a calyx of five sepals united at the base, beneath it an involucre of bractlets. The five petals are usually separate, surrounding a conspicuous central structure bearing the stamens. Of the 1,500 species, many of them tropical, some 200 occur in the United States. Many of these have showy flowers and make up an interesting portion of our wild flower population. Some species have become familiar ornamentals, such as the Hollyhock (*Althaea rosea*), Rose of Sharon (*Hibiscus syriacus*), and Chinese Hibiscus (*Hibiscus rosa-sinensis*). Economically the family is important in that it includes Cotton (Gossypium), valuable for the long unicellular hairs or fibers which grow on the seeds.

PLATE 111

(*upper left*) **Early Blue Violet,** ***Viola palmata*** (*upper right*) **Pale Violet,** ***Viola striata*** (*lower left*) **Lance-leaved Violet,** ***Viola lanceolata*** (*lower right*) **Northern Downy Violet,** ***Viola fimbriatula***

PLATE 112

(*upper left*) **Yellow Violet,** ***Viola pensylvanica*** (*upper right*) **Confederate Violet,** ***Viola papilionacea priceana*** (*lower left*) **Common Blue Violet,** ***Viola papilionacea*** (*lower right*) **Birdfoot Violet,** ***Viola pedata***

POPPY MALLOW

PLATE 108

Callirhoë involucrata

Malvaceae

The Poppy Mallows can be recognized by the truncate, sometimes slightly notched petals. As in the other mallows, the fused stamens form a conspicuous central column. Poppy Mallow is a trailing plant with rounded leaves which are deeply cleft into five or seven linear lobes. The flowers may be either red or purplish. Poppy Mallow grows in the dry plains region from North Dakota to Utah, to Texas. It flowers from June to August.

SWAMP ROSE MALLOW

PLATE 109

Hibiscus moscheutos

Malvaceae

Also known as Mallow Rose or Wild Cotton, this species is a tall plant with canelike stems reaching a height of six feet. The large ovate leaves are entire except for the lower ones, which may be lobed. The flowers are unusually large, sometimes reaching a diameter of six inches; in color the petals vary from white to cream, with red or crimson bases. Swamp Rose Mallow thrives in brackish as well as freshwater swamps, where the extensive "meadows" of these beautiful flowers make an arresting sight. Swamp Rose Mallow can be found from southern New England to Michigan, southward to Florida and Alabama; the flowers appear in July, and continue blossoming until September.

COMMON MALLOW

PLATE 110

Malva rotundifolia

Malvaceae

All of the mallows of the genus Malva found in the United States are European plants which have escaped from cultivation and established themselves near dwellings and along roadsides. The Common Mallow, called Cheeses by children, is a trailing or erect annual with heart-shaped but lobed leaves and flowers clustered in the leaf axils. The calyx of each flower is surrounded by an outer cup of three leaflike bracts; the regular corolla consists of five petals. It can be found throughout the United States, and flowers from June to September. The still more common species, *Malva neglecta,* has more rounded lobes on its leaves.

MUSK MALLOW

PLATE 110

Malva moschata

Malvaceae

This is a larger perennial plant, with stems up to two feet in height; its leaves are conspicuously and deeply lobed into narrow segments. The musk-scented flowers are clustered amid the leaves at the top of the plant. Musk Mallow flowers, essentially similar to those of the other mallows, have petals which are distinctly notched at the apex. Its range is from New England to Maryland, west to Nebraska; the flowers appear in June and July.

MARSHMALLOW

Althaea officinalis

Malvaceae

This inhabitant of either freshwater or brackish marshes is also a European immigrant which has made itself at home from Connecticut to Virginia. It is a rank-growing herbaceous perennial with stems up to six feet in height. The ovate leaves are somewhat three-lobed with conspicuous venation. Marshmallow flowers are pink or white, up to two inches in diameter with a number of narrow bracts beneath the calyx. The stamens form the usual column around the pistil and are united with the base of the petals. The flowering period is from July through October. The root of this species was the source of the original mucilaginous material known as marshmallow paste.

PLATE 113

Swamp Loosestrife, *Decodon verticillatus*

PLATE 114

Purple Loosestrife, *Lythrum salicaria*

The Violet Family

Violaceae

The Violet family includes sixteen genera, with over 800 species; but in the United States the family is practically identical with the representative genus Viola—the violets—with fifty-one different species in eastern United States alone. They are all herbaceous plants with alternate and usually simples leaves, and axillary nodding flowers. Each flower is somewhat irregular with five sepals and five petals, one of which is spurred.

EARLY BLUE VIOLET — PLATE 111

Viola palmata — *Violaceae*

This species is a stemless plant with erect leaves, each divided into five to eleven narrow lobes or segments. The solitary flowers are borne on stalks at least as long as the leaves, each flower being about an inch in breadth. Flowering from April to June, this violet grows in dry rich woods throughout the eastern states.

LANCE-LEAVED VIOLET — PLATE 111

Viola lanceolata — *Violaceae*

Also known as Water Violet, this species is a stemless member of the family, like the early blue violet but with white petals, the lower three striped with purple. The lanceolate or elliptical leaves reach a length of six inches and stand erect among the flowering stalks. The Lance-leaved Violet grows in bogs, swamps, and wet meadows throughout the entire eastern United States. It is an early spring flower, being found from late March until July. It resembles the slightly larger Western Water Violet (*Viola occidentalis*).

PALE VIOLET — PLATE 111

Viola striata — *Violaceae*

The Pale, Cream, or Striped Violet is a leafy-stemmed plant reaching a height of six to twelve inches, with axillary flowers striped and bearded in the center. It grows in low woods and fields from New York to Georgia, west to Wisconsin, and flowers from April to June.

NORTHERN DOWNY VIOLET — PLATE 111

Viola fimbriatula — *Violaceae*

The ovate leaves of the small Northern Downy Violet are sometimes deeply incised at the base. With the flowering stalks they arise directly from the long rootstock. This species flowers from April to May in dry fields and clearings from Nova Scotia to Wisconsin and southward in the Appalachians to Georgia.

BIRDFOOT VIOLET — PLATE 112

Viola pedata — *Violaceae*

One of our largest and most attractive violets, the Birdfoot is a stemless species with three-lobed leaves, the lobes again deeply divided, hence the name Birdfoot. The erect stems bear flowers over an inch in breadth. The upper petals are usually a darker color than the lower ones. Birdfoot Violet grows in open, sunny places in sandy fields and edges of woods, where it flowers from late March to early June. It can be found from southern New England to Virginia, inland to Minnesota. The form which occurs in the South has petals all the same color.

PLATE 115

(*upper left*) **Round-fruited St. John's-wort,** ***Hypericum sphaerocarpum*** (*right*) **Prairie Loosestrife,** ***Lythrum alatum*** (*lower left*) **Field Pansy,** ***Viola rafinesquii***

PLATE 116

(*upper left*) **Common St. John's-wort, *Hypericum perforatum*** (*right*) **Golden St. John's-wort, *Hypericum frondosum*** (*lower left*) **Pale St. John's-wort, *Hypericum ellipticum***

YELLOW VIOLET

PLATE 112

Viola pensylvanica

Violaceae

Also known as Smooth Yellow Violet, this species is leafy-stemmed like the pale violet (Plate 111), with axillary flowers. The leaves are long-stemmed, with ovate to kidney-shaped blades. The lateral petals of the flowers are bearded. Yellow Violets grow in moist woods and on shaded rocky slopes, from southern New England to Georgia, west to Minnesota and Oklahoma. The flowers can be found from April to May.

COMMON BLUE VIOLET

PLATE 112

Viola papilionacea

Violaceae

This familiar wild flower, often called the Meadow Violet, is found in moist woods and meadows, but seems especially at home around farm-houses and other dwellings. It is a stemless species, with triangular or heart-shaped leaves which usually overtop the long-stalked flowers. It grows throughout the eastern states and westward to Minnesota and Oklahoma, and can be found in bloom from March to June.

JOHNNY-JUMP-UP

Viola tricolor

Violaceae

This is a European species which often escapes from cultivation into neighboring fields; the soft, brittle stems produce clumps of foliage and flowers four to twelve inches in height. The lower leaves are rounded, the upper ones oblong or heart-shaped. The gaily hued flowers have their petals multicolored yellow, purple and white. The cultivated pansy is a descendant of this species, bred to produce the large flowers we prize as ornamentals. In many cases the broadened petals, with their mixture of colors, look like a little face.

CONFEDERATE VIOLET — PLATE 112

Viola papilionacea priceana — *Violaceae*

This is a variety of the common blue violet, with whitish or pale gray petals marked with blue veins; otherwise the plants are very much alike. Confederate Violet grows in rich soil and partial shade, from Maine to Arkansas and west to Wyoming. It flowers during spring.

FIELD PANSY — PLATE 115

Viola rafinesquii — *Violaceae*

Thought by some to be a European species which has established itself in dry fields and along roadsides, this early-flowering, slender-stemmed annual is also found in remote mountain regions. It has small orbicular leaves; its roots have the fragrance of wintergreen when crushed. The small flowers have bluish-white or creamy petals, appearing in March, April and May. The Field Pansy grows from New York to Georgia and Texas, westward to Kansas and Iowa.

The Loosestrife Family

Lythraceae

This is a family of herbaceous and shrubby plants whose leaves are usually opposite or whorled, and whose flowers are for the most part regular; each flower has a toothed calyx, and may have from four to seven petals. Of the 475 species in the family, the majority live in the American tropics. A few species known as Loosestrifes are the representatives among our eastern wild flowers, although there are four other genera of more restricted distribution. In the southern states an ornamental of the Loosestrife family is widely planted as a flowering shrub or small tree; this is the Crape Myrtle (*Lagerstroemia indica*).

PLATE 117

(*above*) **Apricot-vine, *Passiflora incarnata*** (*below*) **Prickly Pear, *Opuntia compressa***

PLATE 118

(*left*) Virginia Meadow Beauty, *Rhexia virginica* (*center*) Southern Meadow Beauty, *Rhexia lutea* (*right*) Pale Meadow Beauty, *Rhexia mariana*

PRAIRIE LOOSESTRIFE — PLATE 115

Lythrum alatum — *Lythraceae*

This species is also called Winged Loosestrife because the angles of the stem are extended into winglike margins. It is a perennial one to four feet tall, with linear or tapering alternate leaves. Small flowers are scattered among the axils of the upper leaves. Prairie Loosestrife grows in wet meadows and ditches; its range is from Canada southward to Georgia and Texas. The flowers can be found from June to September.

SWAMP LOOSESTRIFE — PLATE 113

Decodon verticillatus — *Lythraceae*

Also known as Water Willow, this rank-growing and angular-stemmed perennial reaches a height of eight feet. The lanceolate leaves are arranged opposite each other in pairs or whorls. The flowers, in axillary clusters, are characterized by a tubular toothed calyx and a regular corolla of six petals: the stamens are conspicuous because they project beyond the corolla. Swamp Loosestrife grows in swamps, shallow pools, and along pond margins from New England to Florida and west to Minnesota. The flowers develop during July and August.

PURPLE LOOSESTRIFE — PLATE 114

Lythrum salicaria — *Lythraceae*

Purple Loosestrife is a stiffly erect plant with four-angled stems two to six feet in height, and lanceolate leaves which occur in pairs or in threes. The flowers, mingled with the leaves, are borne in dense terminal spikes. Each flower has a toothed and cylindrical calyx, with a regular corolla of five separate petals. Purple Loosestrife is a European species which has escaped to the wet habitats of pond and stream margins. It can be found from Newfoundland to Virginia, west to Minnesota; its flowering period is during the summer months.

The St. John's-Wort Family

Guttiferae

The St. John's-wort family includes a small number of herbaceous and shrubby plants with opposite sessile leaves and flowers consisting of four or five separate sepals and four to five separate petals. Most of our native members of this family, in the eastern states, are included in the twenty-five species of St. John's-wort.

ROUND-FRUITED ST. JOHN'S-WORT — PLATE 115

Hypericum sphaerocarpum — *Guttiferae*

This is a herbaceous plant with a somewhat woody base, growing to a height of several feet and bearing linear to elliptical leaves opposite each other on the stem. The flowers, about half an inch in diameter, are borne in open terminal clusters. Each flower has a calyx of five green sepals and a corolla of five separate petals. It grows in rocky woods and on shores, from Ohio, Wisconsin, and Kansas to Alabama. The flowers appear from July to September.

COMMON ST. JOHN'S-WORT — PLATE 116

Hypericum perforatum — *Guttiferae*

This is a tough-stemmed plant growing to a height of three feet, much branched and with linear or oblong leaves. The flowers occur in leafy clusters at the tips of the branching stem. The perianth consists of a regular five-parted calyx and a regular corolla of five separate petals. Common St. John's-wort is a European species which has escaped to become a roadside weed across Canada and throughout all the eastern states. It flowers from June to September.

PLATE 119

(*left*) **Primrose-willow,** ***Jussiaea repens*** (*right*) **Fireweed,** ***Epilobium angustifolium***

PLATE 120

Evening-primrose, *Oenothera biennis*

GOLDEN ST. JOHN'S-WORT PLATE 116

Hypericum frondosum *Guttiferae*

A widely branching shrub growing to a height of three feet, this species of St. John's-wort has showy flowers which are either solitary or several in a small cluster; the leaves are narrow and oblong, up to two inches in length. Golden St. John's-wort grows on limestone barrens and clearings, from Indiana to Alabama and Texas, and flowers from June to August.

PALE ST. JOHN'S-WORT PLATE 116

Hypericum ellipticum *Guttiferae*

This species is a frail plant a foot or two in height, arising from a creeping base. The elliptic or oblong leaves are usually narrower at the basal portion. Small groups of flowers characteristic of the genus are borne in open terminal clusters. Pale St. John's-wort grows on damp shores and wet habitats generally, in some cases even submerged; its range is from southern Canada to Iowa and Virginia. The flowers can be found from June to August.

The Passion-Flower Family

Passifloraceae

Tropical America is the home of the great majority of species in the Passion-flower family; only a few species represent the group in the United States, and they are restricted in range to the southern states, some reaching to Pennsylvania and Illinois. The members of this family are climbing herbs or shrubs, with axillary tendrils and alternate leaves which may be simple or compound.

APRICOT-VINE PLATE 117

Passiflora incarnata *Passifloraceae*

The flower of this plant is perhaps one of the most unusual of any of our native species. It is large—up to three inches in diameter—and very showy. The five sepals are united at the base to form a spreading calyx; the throat is crowned with a fringe of delicate filaments radiating from the center of the flower. Five spreading petals are attached to the inside of the calyx. The stamens form a central column sheathing the style. The various floral parts, in the imaginative minds of some European observers, seemed to resemble the implements used in the crucifixion of Christ; thus the name "passion flower." The yellow berrylike fruit is edible, and is responsible for the common name Apricot-vine, as well as the local name Maypop; it is about the size and shape of a small hen's egg. Its range is from Maryland to Oklahoma and Florida to Texas, inhabiting sandy fields and roadsides. Full-grown vines reach a length of ten to fifteen feet, sometimes covering bushes and fences. The flowering period is from June to September.

The Cactus Family

Cactaceae

Few families of plants have such appeal to the popular imagination as the cacti. The grotesque vegetative bodies afford a striking contrast to the beautiful and showy flowers. And at the same time their abilities to grow in arid and desert areas where few other forms of life can survive arouse our admiration and interest. The family is distinctively American, all the species belonging to the New World. Estimates vary from 1,200 to 1,800 as to the number of cactus species. Except for two genera, all the cacti are leafless plants with cylindrical or flattened green spiny stems; on young plants tiny leaves can be seen, but they disappear as the cactus grows. The center of the cactus country in the United States is Arizona and New Mexico, with a considerable number of species in adjacent California and Texas. As one goes east the species decrease, so that along the Atlantic coast there are only a few kinds, known as Prickly Pears.

PLATE 121

Sundrops, ***Oenothera fruticosa***

PLATE 122

(*left*) Herb Robert, *Geranium robertianum* (*right*) Showy Evening-primrose, *Oenothera speciosa*

PRICKLY PEAR PLATE 117

Opuntia compressa *Cactaceae*

This cactus, which is also known as Indian Fig, is a prostrate or sprawling plant with stems composed of flattened green segments, each segment or "pad" armed with clusters of bristles and spines. The edges of the stem segments bear short-stemmed flowers with numerous rows of sepals and petals and many stamens. The flowers appear in desert regions of the East during June and July; in the following months they give rise to prickly, ovoid, pulpy, dull purple fruits. Prickly Pears can be found on Martha's Vineyard and Nantucket Islands, also on Long Island and inland in dry regions. In Florida and the southwest Prickly Pear often forms a tangle of shrubbery six to ten feet in height. Opuntia is a widespread genus of some 300 species ranging from Canada to the Strait of Magellan.

PINCUSHION CACTUS

Mamillaria vivipara *Cactaceae*

On the western fringe of the central states from Colorado and Kansas to Minnesota and even reaching into Canada, grows another kind of cactus with a compact cylindrical body armed with vertical rows of reddish-brown spines. The flowers are red or purple, the fruits greenish. Pincushion Cactus is a small plant, usually two or three inches in height, and well hidden among the grasses or in crevices of rocks. Many striking species of this genus grow in the country's desert regions.

The Melastome Family

Melastomaceae

Although this is a large family in the tropics, especially in Brazil, there are only a few species in the United States. The leaves are distinctively three- to seven-ribbed, and opposite on the stems, which are often bristly. The flowers have generally four or five sepals and the same number of petals.

VIRGINIA MEADOW BEAUTY

PLATE 118

Rhexia virginica

Melastomaceae

Also known as Deer Grass, this species is a square-stemmed plant often growing to a height of two feet or more. The oval or lanceolate leaves are opposite and sessile; the flowers are borne in a terminal cluster, each flower having an urn-shaped calyx and a corolla of four petals. Virginia Meadow Beauty grows in swamps and wet meadows from southeastern Canada to Georgia and Missouri. It flowers from July to September.

PALE MEADOW BEAUTY

PLATE 118

Rhexia mariana

Melastomaceae

This species has cylindrical stems and linear-oblong leaves; otherwise it is quite similar to deer grass, and grows in similar wet habitats. It can be found from southern Massachusetts to Florida and inland to Kentucky, flowering from late June to early September.

SOUTHERN MEADOW BEAUTY

PLATE 118

Rhexia lutea

Melastomaceae

This is a smaller species than either of the preceding, with elliptic leaves. It prefers the moist pinelands of the coastal plain, where its home is from North Carolina to Florida and Louisiana. The flowering period is spring and summer.

PLATE 123

Spotted Cranesbill, ***Geranium maculatum***

PLATE 124

(*left*) **Dwarf Ginseng,** ***Panax trifolius*** (*right*) **Wild Sarsaparilla,** ***Aralia nudicaulis***

The Evening-Primrose Family

Onagraceae

The symmetrical flowers of the Evening Primrose family have a plan typically based on two or four; they are generally regular in form, and the tube of the calyx adheres to the bottom of the pistil. The members of the family are herbaceous plants with either alternate or opposite leaves. Unlike many of the preceding families which have been mainly tropical or warm temperate in distribution, of the 650 species in the Evening-primrose family some 500 grow in the United States.

FIREWEED PLATE 119

Epilobium angustifolium *Onagraceae*

The special contribution of Fireweed to civilization is its effectiveness in populating burned-over and logged areas with a beautiful cover of orchid-like flowers, thus concealing the scars which man insists upon leaving when he mistreats Nature. A basal perennial crown gives rise to tall leafy stems which stand erect to a height of six feet; the leaves are alternate and simple, with a lanceolate outline. The slightly irregular flowers are borne in a long spikelike cluster which may be a foot in length. Each flower has a short calyx tube with four lobes, and four petals an inch or an inch and a quarter in length. In autumn the spikes are a fluffy mass of wind-dispersed seeds, each seed being provided with whitish hairs. Fireweed is also known as Great Willow-herb; its home is almost everywhere from subarctic regions to the Carolinas and westward to the coast. The flowering period is from July to September.

GREAT WILLOW-HERB

Epilobium hirsutum — *Onagraceae*

This is a European species which has established itself in marshes and roadside ditches throughout eastern United States. It has the same stem features and habit, but the leaves are usually opposite and the purple flowers have a regular corolla rather the slightly irregular corolla of the preceding species. It is said that the young shoots of these Epilobium species are a good substitute for asparagus; the leaves and young stems are cooked for use as a potherb in Canada and parts of northern Europe.

PRIMROSE-WILLOW — PLATE 119

Jussiaea repens — *Onagraceae*

This is a perennial with creeping stems, or stems floating and rooting if in semi-aquatic habitats. The foliage consists of oblong to lanceolate alternate leaves up to three inches in length, borne on long slender stems. Each flower is long-stemmed and axillary, with a calyx of four to six pointed sepals and a regular corolla of four to six petals half an inch in breadth. Primrose-willow grows in wet ditches and other similar muddy habitats from southern New Jersey to Florida, west to Kansas and Texas. The flowers can be found from June to October.

SUNDROPS — PLATE 121

Oenothera fruticosa — *Onagraceae*

This is a slender-stemmed erect plant of the same genus as the evening-primrose, but much smaller and generally more frail in appearance. Usually two or three feet in height, the stems bear alternate oval or tapering leaves an inch to four inches in length. Large bright yellow flowers are borne in a terminal leafy cluster of several to half a dozen blossoms; each flower is an inch to two inches in diameter. Sundrops prefer dry, sandy soil of open woods and clearings; they can be found in flower by day from early to late summer, throughout eastern United States to Oklahoma.

PLATE 125

Hairy Angelica, ***Angelica venenosa***

PLATE 126

(*left*) **Queen Anne's Lace,** ***Daucus carota*** (*right*) **Spotted Cowbane,** ***Cicuta maculata***

EVENING-PRIMROSE

PLATE 120

Oenothera biennis *Onagraceae*

The common Evening-primrose is a stout-stemmed, usually branching plant, often growing to a height of six feet; foliage and stems are somewhat hairy. Narrow pointed leaves grow alternately on the stems, the upper ones sessile. Small clusters of conspicuous flowers with four petals, up to an inch in length, develop among the leaves at the summit of the stem. The four narrow lobes of the calyx are typically bent backward or downward. Evening-primrose flowers, as the name indicates, open in the late afternoon and evening. The species is widely spread throughout the United States, and flowers from June to October. In many localities it is considered a weed, spreading rapidly in dry sandy soil and waste ground.

NORTHERN EVENING-PRIMROSE

Oenothera parviflora *Onagraceae*

This slender edition of the common evening-primrose is a slightly branched biennial with leaves more narrowly lanceolate and stems covered with scattered hairs. The light yellow flowers are one to two inches in diameter, and borne in the axils of the upper leaves. Northern Evening-primrose is a cool climate plant found on sandy shores and in dry clearings only as far south as New York and southern New England; its flowering period is from July to September.

Among the many species of Oenothera which can be found in the United States might be mentioned the Seabeach Evening-primrose (*Oenothera humifusa*) a low-growing hoary-stemmed plant usually a foot or two in height, common to sand dunes and beaches from New Jersey to Florida, with yellow or reddish flowers; Nuttall's Evening-primrose (*Oenothera nuttallii*), an erect plant up to four feet in height, with white or rose-tinted flowers, found in the plains region from Wisconsin to Colorado and northwestward into Canada; the Serrated Evening-primrose (*Oenothera serrulata*), a shrubby and much-branched plant several feet in height, bearing yellow flowers and found in sandy or rocky soil from Manitoba south to Wisconsin, Missouri, and New Mexico; and *Oenothera deltoides,* a showy, low-growing white-flowered species of the southwestern desert regions.

SHOWY EVENING-PRIMROSE

PLATE 122

Oenothera speciosa — *Onagraceae*

Also known as White Evening-primrose, this species is an erect perennial with a creeping rootstock from which grow slender stems with oblong to linear leaves, some of which are pinnately lobed. Each flower has a showy corolla of petals an inch or more in length; the flowers are nodding while in bud, and are borne in small numbers in the axils of the upper leaves. The White Evening-primrose grows on grasslands in the central states, and can be found from Missouri to Texas; sometimes naturalized specimens can be found farther east. The flowers appear in May and July.

GAURA

Gaura biennis — *Onagraceae*

This biennial member of the Evening-primrose family is a slender erect plant with a maximum stature of five feet; the alternate narrow leaves are pointed at both ends. Relatively small flowers (a half inch in diameter) are borne in spikelike clusters at the tips of the stems and main branches. Each flower is white when young, but turns pink with age; the corolla is somewhat irregular, with the four petals not being equal in size and shape. The biennial Gaura grows in moist meadows and along wet shores from Quebec to Virginia and Missouri; the flowers can be found from June to October.

SEEDBOX

Ludwigia alternifolia — *Onagraceae*

Also known as Rattlebox, this member of the family is known for its cup-shaped capsule containing many loose seeds. A perennial root produces stems two or three feet in height, bearing typical, alternate, lanceolate leaves. Flowers appear singly in the axils of the upper leaves. Each flower is about half an inch in breadth, with yellow petals and a short calyx tube. The petals fall off the flowers readily if the plant is handled. Seedbox grows in swampy habitats from Massachusetts to Florida and Texas, west to Kansas; the flowering period is from June to August.

PLATE 127

Water Parsnip, *Sium suave*

PLATE 128

(*above*) **Golden Alexanders,** ***Zizia aurea*** (*below*) **Bunchberry,** ***Cornus canadensis***

The Geranium Family

Geraniaceae

The herbaceous plants which make up most of the Geranium family number about 800 species, widely distributed over temperate and subtropical portions of both hemispheres. The stems, sometimes fleshy, bear opposite or alternate leaves which are either lobed or compound. The flowers have a calyx of five usually separate sepals, and a corolla of a similar number of petals, regular or nearly so. An important feature of the family is the fruit, a capsule of such slender and beaked shape that some species are known as "cranesbills." The capsule splits open in such a fashion that the seeds are forcibly ejected.

HERB ROBERT

PLATE 122

Geranium robertianum — *Geraniaceae*

This is a strongly scented annual with glandular and hairy stems reaching a height of a foot to eighteen inches. The foliage is fernlike, each leaf being deeply divided into three to five leaflets which are further lobed and toothed. Small reddish-purple, sometimes white, flowers are borne in the axils of the upper leaves. Each flower has its sepals prolonged into a hairlike tip, and the petals have a narrowed base. The fruiting capsule is about an inch in length, with a sharp and prolonged tip. Herb Robert is an inhabitant of rocky woods and ravines, over a widespread northern area, south only to Maryland and Illinois. The flowers appear from May to October.

STORKSBILL

Erodium cicutarium — *Geraniaceae*

This related genus is a European plant which is often found as an escaped and naturalized flower of roadsides and waste places throughout most of the United States and across both borders. The leaves are pinnately compound, instead of palmately as in herb robert; the rose-purple flowers are borne on long stems in the axils of the leaves.

SPOTTED CRANESBILL PLATE 123

Geranium maculatum *Geraniaceae*

Also known in many localities as Wild Geranium, this species is a familiar late spring flower of rich open woods and meadows, where the delicately tinted flowers may be found from April to June. The leaves are deeply lobed into three to five toothed segments, but are not compound. Stems reach a height of twenty inches, and bear small terminal clusters of flowers an inch or more in breadth. The fruit illustrates an interesting means of mechanical dispersal of seeds; as the capsule ripens, its longitudinal sections split open in such a way that the recoiling segments, like released watch springs, catapult the seeds outward from the plant. Spotted Cranesbill can be found from Maine to Manitoba, south to Georgia and Kansas.

The Ginseng Family

Araliaceae

Wild Sarsaparilla and Groundnut are native members of the Ginseng family, which has a great number of species (about 800) in the tropics. Herbs, shrubs, vines and trees are found in the group, all closely similar to members of the Parsley family, especially in the umbel type of inflorescence. Each flower has a cup-shaped calyx with a minutely toothed rim, and a corolla of five to ten separate petals. A tree in the Ginseng family, known as Hercules'-club or Prickly Ash (*Aralia spinosa*) is found in moist low woods from New Jersey to Florida and Texas. The Rice-paper plant (*Tetrapanax papyriferus*) of China is the source of rice paper, and is also an ornamental plant. The common English Ivy (*Hedera helix*) has related species in Europe, Africa and Asia; as a vigorous climber it has become a naturalized plant in southeastern United States, where it covers wood and stone surfaces with a blanket of green. The stems are provided with aerial roots which enable it to cling to such surfaces.

PLATE 129

(*above*) **Checkerberry, *Gaultheria procumbens*** (*below*) **Trailing Arbutus, *Epigaea repens***

PLATE 130

(*above*) **Swamp Honeysuckle, *Rhododendron viscosum*** (*below*) **Pinxter-flower, *Rhododendron nudiflorum***

WILD SARSAPARILLA

PLATE 124

Aralia nudicaulis

Araliaceae

This species is a short-stemmed plant bearing a single long-stalked leaf up to sixteen inches in height, with three long-stalked segments, each subdivided into many ovate or oval pointed leaflets. Also rising from the short, hidden stem is an erect flowering stalk, somewhat shorter than the stalk of the leaf and bearing at its summit two to seven spherical umbels of small flowers; each flower has a regular corolla of five petals. The horizontal roots have aromatic properties and are often used as a substitute for the true sarsaparilla flavoring. Wild Sarsaparilla grows in open woods across Canada and south to Georgia and Colorado. It flowers from May to July.

DWARF GINSENG

PLATE 124

Panax trifolius

Araliaceae

This low-growing herb, three to six inches in height, is also known as Groundnut. It has a slender erect stem terminated by a trio of palmately compound leaves, each with from three to five leaflets an inch or two in length. Above the leaf cluster rises a short flowering stalk terminated by a single umbel of minute white flowers, each about an eighth of an inch in diameter. The berrylike fruit is a yellow drupe. Underground one can find a globular root or tuber. Dwarf Ginseng occurs from southeastern Canada southward to Georgia and Nebraska.

GINSENG

Panax quinquefolius

Araliaceae

This is one of the two plants known in medicine as Ginseng, the other being an Asiatic species. The American plant was formerly collected and exported to China, where the root is still prized for its medicinal properties. It grows to a height of twelve inches, and usually has five leaflets. The fruit is bright red in contrast with the yellow berry (in reality a drupe) of the Dwarf Ginseng. True Ginseng grows in cool woods throughout the eastern coastal states to Oklahoma. The flowering period is June and July.

The Parsley Family

Umbelliferae

This group is also called the Parsnip family and the Carrot family. It includes herbaceous plants which are mostly biennial or perennial, many of which are characteristically aromatic and possess small flowers in the umbel type of inflorescence. There are about 2,900 species in the Parsley family, the majority of them occurring in the northern hemisphere; the United States has a fair share of these, with 380 species. Economically the family is important, for many food, condiment and ornamental plants have been developed from this family, such as the carrot (Daucus), parsnip (Pastinaca), celery (Apium), parsley (Petroselinum), anise (Pimpinella), caraway (Carum), dill (Anethum), and fennel (Foeniculum). The family also includes some poisonous herbaceous plants such as water hemlock (Cicuta) and poison hemlock (Conium).

HAIRY ANGELICA — PLATE 125

Angelica venenosa — *Umbelliferae*

This species is a slender perennial, two to four feet tall, found in dry or rocky woods from southern New England to Florida, west to Minnesota and Missouri. The much-divided compound leaves consist of elliptic toothed leaflets two to three inches in length. Small flowers are produced in large terminal umbels; each flower has a regular corolla of five white or greenish petals. The flowers appear between July and September.

PLATE 131

(*left*) **Shinleaf, *Pyrola elliptica*** (*center*) **Spotted Wintergreen, *Chimaphila maculata***
(*right*) **One-flowered Wintergreen, *Moneses uniflora***

PLATE 132

Mountain Laurel, *Kalmia latifolia*

QUEEN ANNE'S LACE

PLATE 126

Daucus carota

Umbelliferae

This common weed of fields and roadsides, also known as Wild Carrot, is a European species which has spread through much of the country; it often forms extensive patches of greenish-white during the summer months in fields where its presence is not appreciated by the farmer. Queen Anne's Lace is a bristly stemmed biennial growing to a height of four feet, with fernlike pinnately compound leaves. The inflorescence is a compound umbel, each flower cluster usually flattened or concave on its upper surface. Each of the many small white flowers has a slightly irregular corolla of five separate petals. In the center of each umbel there is usually a single small dark-red flower.

SPOTTED COWBANE

PLATE 126

Cicuta maculata

Umbelliferae

This poisonous member of the Parsley family is also known as Water Hemlock and Beaver-poison. The roots and rootstocks are the most poisonous parts of the plant, containing a resinlike toxin known as cicutoxin. Children and also adults have been poisoned by mistaking the enlarged roots for parsnips. Horses, sheep and other animals have died from eating Spotted Cowbane. A piece of root the size of a walnut is said to be poisonous enough to kill a cow. Death results from convulsions and inability to breathe. Spotted Cowbane is a stout plant, three to six feet tall, growing in swampy meadows, ditches and other low ground. The pinnately compound leaves have pointed lanceolate leaflets, and the stems are often spotted with purple. Each compound umbel is made up of many small flowers whose petals have incurved tips. Spotted Cowbane occurs from southeastern Canada to North Carolina, west to Manitoba and Texas. It flowers from June to September.

WATER PARSNIP

PLATE 127

Sium suave

Umbelliferae

A rank-growing plant which reaches a height of five or six feet, Water Parsnip grows in marshes and along muddy riverbanks from coast to coast except in the Southwest. A stout and sparingly branched stem bears pinnately compound leaves and terminal umbels of flowers. It can be distinguished from the poisonous Spotted Cowbane by the simple pinnate leaves and the corrugated stems. When growing submerged, the underwater leaves are divided into delicate linear segments. The flowering period is from July to October.

GOLDEN ALEXANDERS

PLATE 128

Zizia aurea

Umbelliferae

This is an erect perennial, one to three feet tall, with compound leaves divided into lanceolate segments. The compound umbels are made up of many small regular flowers, each with five incurved petals. Golden Alexanders grow in wet woods and meadows, from Canada south to Georgia and Texas. The flowers appear between June and September.

POISON HEMLOCK

Conium maculatum

Umbelliferae

This hollow-stemmed and purple-spotted perennial is a European plant which has become naturalized in many parts of eastern United States and Canada. It grows up to a height of six feet, and has fernlike compound leaves similar to the garden parsley; it also has a large white taproot similar to a parsnip. The poisonous substance known as coniine is found in the fruits and leaves. It is considered one of the most generally known poisonous plants to the ancients, and is thought to be the poison used by the Greeks as a death penalty for state prisoners, such as Socrates. It bears no relation to the hemlock tree of North America.

PLATE 133

(*left*) **Sparkleberry,** ***Vaccinium arboreum*** (*right*) **Fetter Bush,** ***Leucothoë racemosa***
(*below*) **Smooth Azalea,** ***Rhododendron arborescens***

PLATE 134

(*left*) **Staggerbush, *Lyonia mariana*** (*center*) **Labrador Tea, *Ledum groenlandicum***
(*right*) **Fetterbush, *Lyonia lucida***

The Dogwood Family

Cornaceae

The Dogwood family is a small one (only ninety species), with the majority of its members shrubs or trees. All of the eastern species belong to the dogwood genus, *Cornus*. The flowers are small and regular, often surrounded by large and conspicuous colored bracts. The familiar Flowering Dogwood (*Cornus florida*) is a tree member of the group.

BUNCHBERRY PLATE 128

Cornus canadensis *Cornaceae*

This is a low-growing plant with a horizontal perennial rootstock from which arises a three- to nine-inch erect stem crowned by five or six whorled leaves similar in appearance to those of the flowering dogwood. Above the whorl of leaves is borne a cluster of tiny yellow flowers surrounded by four to six white bracts which are often mistaken for petals. The fruit is a bright red berry. Bunchberry, also known as Dwarf Cornel or Ground Dogwood, grows in moist open woods from Canada south to California and West Virginia. The flowering period is from May to July.

The Heath Family

Ericaceae

The Heath family comprises about 1,900 species of herbaceous perennials, shrubs and trees, many of them with evergreen foliage. The flowers are regular, or only slightly irregular, and often clustered in showy masses. The corolla in some consists of four to seven free petals; in others the petals may be joined to form an urn-shaped structure. The economic importance of the family lies both in its numerous ornamental shrubs such as the azaleas, rhododendrons, and laurels, and in the food plants of the family—the blueberries and cranberries. Two unusual California shrubs and trees belong to the family: Madroño (*Arbutus menziesii*) and Manzanita (*Arctostaphylos glauca*). The true heaths, with 500 species, are best represented in South Africa and the Mediterranean region; the bell-shaped flowers are either white, rose or yellow. These heaths are more successfully grown in Europe than in the United States, since relatively few of the species can stand the heat of our summers.

TRAILING ARBUTUS — PLATE 129

Epigaea repens — *Ericaceae*

Known also as Mayflower and Ground-laurel, this elusive and fragrant member of the family is a prostrate, slightly woody perennial with thick evergreen leaves, oval in shape and two to four inches in length. The few small flowers, half an inch in size, grow in clusters at the ends of the branches, and are usually hidden by the leaves. The corolla is tubular, expanding at the top with a five-lobed margin. Trailing Arbutus usually grows in shaded woods, on rocky or sandy well-drained banks; it is common in many localities under evergreens. Although its range originally was from New England south to Florida, it is fast becoming rare in most of the eastern states. The flowers appear in March or April, and may continue through May.

PLATE 135

Great Laurel, *Rhododendron maximum*

PLATE 136

(*left*) **Sheep Laurel,** ***Kalmia angustifolia*** (*upper right*) **Indian Pipe,** ***Monotropa uniflora*** (*lower right*) **Pine-sap,** ***Monotropa hypopithys***

CHECKERBERRY — PLATE 129

Gaultheria procumbens — *Ericaceae*

This attractive creeping perennial, also with evergreen oval leaves, goes by a variety of other names: Teaberry, Boxberry, Creeping Wintergreen, Spicy Wintergreen. It grows in open woods, often under evergreen trees from New England to Alabama and Georgia. The flowers are solitary or few in the axils of the leaves; they usually have a nodding habit. Each flower has an urn-shaped corolla formed by the fusion of the petals. The fruit is a spicy edible berry. Checkerberry flowers appear in July and August; the berries can be found in autumn and through the winter. A refreshing tea is made from steeping the leaves in hot water, and the berries can be made into pies. Ruffed grouse and partridge are fond of the berries also; in fact in some localities the plant is known as Partridgeberry, though this name more commonly belongs to *Mitchella repens.*

SWAMP HONEYSUCKLE — PLATE 130

Rhododendron viscosum — *Ericaceae*

The genus Rhododendron, with about twenty species in the United States, includes some of our most showy native shrubs. They all have alternate leaves, which may be entire or toothed, and large flowers in conspicuous clusters. Swamp Honeysuckle is a branching shrub which grows to a height of ten or twelve feet; its leaves, covered with sticky hairs, are deciduous, elliptical to lanceolate, and about two inches in length. The fragrant flowers appear between June and August. Each funnel-shaped flower has a corolla with five spreading lobes. This species grows in swamps and wet thickets in the cooler portions of the northeastern states, to the mountains of South Carolina and Tennessee.

PINXTER-FLOWER

PLATE 130

Rhododendron nudiflorum

Ericaceae

This branching shrub with deciduous elliptical leaves and large showy flower clusters goes by a variety of other names, among them Purple Azalea, Pink Azalea, Wild Honeysuckle. It grows to a height of eight or nine feet, thriving in wet woods and swamps from southern New England and Ohio to the mountains of South Carolina and Tennessee. The flowers appear before or with the opening of the leaf buds; they are usually pink, but whitish varieties occur. The corolla, up to two inches in breadth, is slightly irregular and two-lipped. The flowering period is May and June.

SMOOTH AZALEA

PLATE 133

Rhododendron arborescens

Ericaceae

Smooth Azalea is a tall branching shrub growing to a height of twenty feet; it belongs to the group of deciduous species whose flowers appear after the foliage is fully developed. The ovate leaves, up to three inches in length, are a shiny bright green on the upper surface. The fragrant flowers, with the typical funnel-shaped corollas, have conspicuous red stamens. Smooth Azalea grows in swampy woods and along stream banks, from Pennsylvania and Kentucky to Georgia and Alabama; it blossoms in June and July.

FLAME AZALEA

PLATE 138

Rhododendron calendulaceum

Ericaceae

Also known as Yellow Azalea, this species is a deciduous member of the genus, with its flowers appearing before or with the young leaves. Full-grown specimens reach a height of fifteen feet, being most common in open woods from Pennsylvania to Georgia, where the Flame Azaleas can be found in bloom during May and June.

PLATE 137

(*above*) **Highbush Blueberry,** ***Vaccinium corymbosum*** (*below*) **Cranberry,** ***Vaccinium macrocarpon***

PLATE 138

Flame Azalea, *Rhododendron calendulaceum*

GREAT LAUREL

PLATE 135

Rhododendron maximum — *Ericaceae*

One of the most magnificent flowering shrubs of the eastern states, Great Laurel is also called Rose Bay and Giant Rhododendron. Some specimens grow to a height of thirty feet, and are trees rather than shrubs. The foliage is evergreen, which has added to the ornamental value of this species. Great Laurel is widely used as a landscape shrub, being hardy as far north as Maine. In its native home it thrives in damp woods and swamps. Its range is from southeastern Canada to Georgia and Alabama. Pure white as well as rose-pink varieties occur. Each flower has a corolla up to two inches in breadth, bell-shaped and slightly irregular. The flowering period is in June and July.

MOUNTAIN ROSE BAY

PLATE 139

Rhododendron catawbiense — *Ericaceae*

This evergreen shrub is also known as Purple Laurel; it grows to the height of six feet or more with shiny leaves up to six inches in length. The flower clusters are, if anything, showier than its relative, the great laurel. This species and *Rhododendron carolinianum* populate the spectacular heath balds or open summits in the southern Appalachians, adding an attractive floral feature to Shenandoah and Great Smoky Mountains National Parks. It is found almost exclusively in the rocky uplands, extending from Virginia to Georgia. It blossoms in May and June.

RHODORA

Rhododendron canadense — *Ericaceae*

Frequently hiding in mountains from Newfoundland to northeastern Pennsylvania and New Jersey are the low-growing shrubby plants of Rhodora. This deciduous species has very irregular flowers of a pale to deep rose-purple color, appearing very early in spring. The oblong leaves are usually gray-green, and hairy at least on the under-surface.

SHINLEAF — PLATE 131

Pyrola elliptica — *Ericaceae*

Another name for this low-growing perennial with creeping and hidden shoots is Wild Lily-of-the-valley; deciduous oval or elliptical leaves two to four inches in height form basal clusters for the erect flowering stalks, which are up to ten inches tall. The tip of each stalk bears an open and elongated cluster of small, nodding, fragrant flowers. The corolla consists of five blunt and flat petals beyond which the upcurved pistil projects in a conspicuous fashion. Shinleaf prefers the rich soil of dry woods, where it can be found in flower from June to August. Its range is across southern Canada, south to Pennsylvania and New Mexico.

ROUND-LEAVED WINTERGREEN — PLATE 140

Pyrola rotundifolia — *Ericaceae*

Very similar to the preceding shinleaf, Round-leaved Wintergreen, or American Wintergreen, differs in having more rounded basal leaves which are evergreen rather than deciduous. The flower cluster is also larger and more showy, reaching a height of twenty inches. The nodding fragrant flowers are usually white, but in some localities individuals appear which are tinged with pink. Round-leaved Wintergreen also grows in dry woods, from New England to Minnesota, south to Indiana and North Carolina. It flowers during the same early summer months as shinleaf.

ONE-FLOWERED WINTERGREEN — PLATE 131

Moneses uniflora — *Ericaceae*

This is a small perennial of the family, adapted for living in the cooler northern portions of the eastern states and in the mountains. The basal leaves are only an inch in length, arising from a subterranean shoot. A flowering stalk three or four inches in height bears a solitary fragrant flower at its tip, with waxy white or pinkish petals. One-flowered Wintergreen is generally found far from the paved highways, from Labrador to Alaska, south to Oregon, Colorado, and West Virginia. The flowering period is from June to August.

PLATE 139

(*above*) **Mountain Rose Bay,** ***Rhododendron catawbiense*** (*below*) **Deerberry,** ***Vaccinium stamineum***

PLATE 140

(*left*) **Pipsissewa,** ***Chimaphila umbellata*** (*right*) **Round-leaved Wintergreen,** ***Pyrola rotundifolia***

SPOTTED WINTERGREEN PLATE 131
Chimaphila maculata *Ericaceae*

This low-growing plant with creeping underground shoots and basal clusters of thick leaves can be recognized by the variegated condition of the leaf blades; these are mottled with white along the veins. A few leaves are scattered along the erect stem, which grows from four to a height of eight or ten inches. The small flowers are borne in a cluster at the top of the flowering stalk, each corolla with five rounded spreading petals. Spotted Wintergreen grows in dry woods from New England to Georgia, west to Illinois and Michigan; the flowers can be found from June to August.

PIPSISSEWA PLATE 140
Chimaphila umbellata *Ericaceae*

Also known as Prince's Pine, this is a trailing and somewhat woody perennial with leafy shoots and flowering branches reaching occasionally a height of twelve inches. The narrowly wedge-shaped and toothed leaves are evergreen, and not spotted as are those of the preceding species. The flowers, borne in a small terminal umbel, are white or pinkish with a deep pink ring; the style is conspicuously stout and conical. Pipsissewa is another plant of dry woods, most commonly found in pine groves; its range is from New England to Georgia and west to the Great Lakes region, flowering from June to August. A variety is known farther west.

MOUNTAIN LAUREL PLATE 132
Kalmia latifolia *Ericaceae*

One of the handsomest flowering shrubs of the entire world, Mountain Laurel graces the rocky woodlands and fields of many eastern states. A low shrub in the northern part of its range, Mountain Laurel reaches a height of ten to fifteen feet in the Appalachians. It is also known as Calico-bush,

Spoon-wood, and Ivy-bush. Like other species of Kalmia, it is a shrubby plant with a remarkable flower structure. Each petal of the five-parted, saucer-shaped corolla has a pair of pouches at the base into which the tips of the stamens fit while they are developing; when ripe the stamens spring up forcibly to eject their pollen. Large attractive flower clusters appear in May and in some places may be found through July. The glossy foliage is evergreen.

SHEEP LAUREL

PLATE 136

Kalmia angustifolia — *Ericaceae*

A smaller, compact shrub, usually less than three feet in height, this species is common in old pastures and fields, as well as open woods. It is also known as Lambkill, because of the severely toxic substance in the leaves. Horses, cattle and game animals, however, are rarely poisoned from this source. Sheep Laurel has opposite rather than alternate leaves; they are lanceolate in outline with pale green lower surfaces. The individual flowers are much smaller than those of mountain laurel, and borne in less showy clusters. Sheep Laurel can be found from eastern Canada to the mountains of Georgia, west to Michigan; it flowers from May to August.

LEATHERLEAF

Chamaedaphne calyculata — *Ericaceae*

Swamps and bogs from Labrador to Alaska are the home of a retiring but attractive member of the Heath family known as Leatherleaf because of its tough evergreen foliage. It occurs also in the uplands southward to Iowa and Georgia. Leatherleaf is a small branching shrub, reaching a height of four feet, with oblong or pointed leaves an inch in length and a terminal, leafy, one-sided cluster of nodding flowers. Each flower is white and fragrant, cylindrical in shape, and about a quarter of an inch in length. The shrub blooms from March to July.

PLATE 141

(*above*) **Galax, *Galax aphylla*** (*below*) **Pyxie, *Pyxidanthera barbulata***

PLATE 142

Shooting Star, *Dodecatheon meadia*

WILD ROSEMARY

Andromeda glaucophylla *Ericaceae*

This is another bog species, sometimes known as Bog Rosemary or Marsh Holy Rose. It is a small shrub, several feet in height, partial to sphagnum bogs from Greenland to Manitoba, and from there to West Virginia and New Jersey. The linear evergreen leaves have inrolled margins and whitish undersurfaces. A few small drooping white flowers are borne in terminal clusters. The almost globular corolla is less than a quarter of an inch in diameter.

MINNIE-BUSH

Menziesia pilosa *Ericaceae*

This is a low straggling bush found in upland woods of the Appalachians, from Pennsylvania to Georgia. The branches as well as the leaves are usually hairy and covered with chafflike bristles. Oblong to ovate leaves are alternately arranged on the stems. The small flowers are unusual for the Heath family because their parts are in four's rather than five's. A small flattened calyx is four-toothed, and the corolla is urn-shaped, greenish-white or purplish, and nodding. Minnie-bush flowers in May and June.

HIGHBUSH BLUEBERRY

PLATE 137

Vaccinium corymbosum *Ericaceae*

This is a tall shrub, growing to a height of twelve feet; it is also known as Swamp Blueberry because of its preference for wet woods and swampy margins of ponds. The leaves, two to three inches in length, are ovate and deciduous. Small urn-shaped flowers are borne in dense clusters. The sweet juicy berries are bluish-black, usually covered with a bloom; they can be found as early as June, and as late as September. Highbush Blueberry grows throughout the eastern states and adjacent Canada.

SPARKLEBERRY

PLATE 133

Vaccinium arboreum

Ericaceae

The genus Vaccinium includes, in eastern United States, twenty-one species of woody plants familiar to everyone who has enjoyed an unexpected meal of blueberries, bilberries, or cranberries while exploring on foot. Others occur in the West, and both there and in the Southeast, some of the species are evergreen. The plants may be low and creeping or tall and erect shrubs up to the size of small trees. The leaves are smooth, the flowers may be solitary or clustered in the leaf axils, and the fruit is a small berry with few fine seeds. A closely related genus, the huckleberry (Gaylussacia) has glandular-dotted foliage, small orange-tinted flowers in lateral racemes, and berries with large coarse seeds.

One of the tallest of the Vacciniums is a southerly species, which, growing to a height of twenty feet, may develop a trunk diameter of twelve inches. Farkleberry and Tree Huckleberry are other names for this shrubby tree. The thick leathery leaves are evergreen in the southern part of its range. The Sparkleberry grows in sandy woods and clearings from Virginia to Florida, west to Illinois and Texas. The berry is black and dry, with stonelike seeds such as are more commonly found in the genus Gaylussacia. The fruit develops in August and September.

DEERBERRY

PLATE 139

Vaccinium stamineum

Ericaceae

Deerberry, or Squaw-huckleberry, is a low-growing deciduous shrub, one to three feet in height with oval leaves which are whitish-hairy on the undersurface. The small saucer-shaped flowers are in drooping clusters amid leaflike bracts. The buds are miniature flowers which enlarge, instead of opening from a closed position. The fruits are greenish or yellowish berries, among the few in the genus which are inedible. Deerberry can be found in dry woods and thickets from southern New England south to Florida and Louisiana. The flowers appear in early summer, the fruit from July to September.

PLATE 143

Fringed Loosestrife, *Lysimachia ciliata*

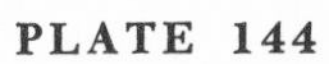

PLATE 144

(*left*) **Whorled Loosestrife,** ***Lysimachia quadrifolia*** (*right*) **Swamp Loosestrife,** ***Lysimachia terrestris***

DWARF BILBERRY

Vaccinium cespitosum *Ericaceae*

One of the smallest members of the genus, the Dwarf Bilberry has branches rarely growing taller than twelve inches. It is a plant of gravelly and rocky openings in the woods of the northeastern states, also from Labrador to Alaska and in mountains elsewhere. Solitary pink flowers are produced in the leaf axils. The light-blue berries which follow them are covered with a bloom. The fruits develop in July and August.

LOW SWEET BLUEBERRY

Vaccinium angustifolium *Ericaceae*

This is also a dwarfed shrubby species, growing to a foot in height. The narrowly lanceolate leaves are shiny green on both surfaces, and reach a length of three-quarters of an inch. The white or pinkish flowers are borne in clusters from tips of branches or old leaf axils. The sweet gray-blue berries, covered with a bloom, are often almost half an inch in diameter. This species is the early market blueberry, ripening in June and July; it is one of the few commercial fruits which is harvested from natural wild sources. In Maine particularly, whose sunny granite ledges provide the open dry habitats ideal for its growth, the Low Sweet Blueberry patches are carefully weeded, burned over, and encouraged to produce a dense low growth which can be "raked" by special hand tools, for mass production of the crop. This species can be found from Labrador to Minnesota, south to Virginia.

CRANBERRY

PLATE 137

Vaccinium macrocarpon *Ericaceae*

Our native Cranberry is a creeping and trailing plant, somewhat woody and with minute, elliptic, evergreen leaves, at home in bogs and peaty swamps from Newfoundland to Minnesota, south to Illinois and North Carolina. Although only a few inches in height the horizontal stems may reach a length of several feet. The nodding flowers are borne on short erect stalks, each corolla divided almost to the base into four separate petals. The large, firm, tart berries ripen in September and October. The majority of the commercial cranberries, so important as an adjunct to Thanksgiving turkey, come from cultivated patches of bogs in the Cape Cod area of Massachusetts, south New Jersey, and Wisconsin.

FETTERBUSH

PLATE 133

Leucothoë racemosa

Ericaceae

Also known as Swamp Leucothoë, this species is a deciduous shrub with simple leaves and flowers in one-sided racemes. Each flower has a calyx of five nearly distinct sepals and an urn-shaped corolla with a five-lobed margin. It grows in moist thickets from southern New England to Florida and Louisiana. In ideal situations the shrubs reach a height of twelve feet. The flowers appear in May and June, a little later than those of *Lyonia lucida,* a shrub of the same region which is also called Fetterbush.

LABRADOR TEA

PLATE 134

Ledum groenlandicum

Ericaceae

This is a small evergreen shrub, one to three feet high, found in cold swamps and on mountain summits across Canada and south to New Jersey, Pennsylvania, and the Great Lakes states. The margins of the simple oblong leaves are rolled backwards, and the undersurface is covered with rusty hairs. The flowers, in terminal clusters, have a calyx of five separate sepals, and a regular corolla of five spreading petals. The flowers appear in May and June. The foliage is fragrant when bruised. It has been said that the leaves served as a tea substitute during the Revolutionary War. The beverage is slightly bitter and astringent.

PLATE 145

(*above*) Moneywort, *Lysimachia nummularia* (*below*) Marsh Rosemary, *Limonium carolinianum*

PLATE 146

(*left*) **Yellow Jessamine,** ***Gelsemium sempervirens*** (*right*) **Indian Pink,** ***Spigelia marilandica***

STAGGERBUSH

PLATE 134

Lyonia mariana

Ericaceae

Staggerbush is a deciduous shrub, two to four feet in height, with some of the flower clusters borne on the leafless portions of the branches below the terminal growth of the current year. It blooms in May and June. Each flower is nodding, and has a cylindrical corolla resulting from the fusion of the five petals. The seed capsule is urn-shaped. Staggerbush lives in pinelands and open woods, from southern New England to Florida and Arkansas. The foliage is said to be poisonous to lambs and young cattle.

FETTERBUSH

PLATE 134

Lyonia lucida

Ericaceae

This species is evergreen in contrast to the deciduous fetterbush, *Leucothoë racemosa.* Its habitat is swamps, pond margins, and moist pinelands from Virginia to Florida and Louisiana. It grows to a height of six feet. The margins of the leaves are inrolled as in Labrador tea, and the urn-shaped flowers are borne in axillary umbels. The flowering period is April and May.

INDIAN PIPE

PLATE 136

Monotropa uniflora

Ericaceae

There are several members of the Heath family which lack chlorophyll, and therefore live as saprophytes or parasites; because of their whitish or yellowish color, they are often mistakenly considered fungi. Indian Pipe, or Corpse-plant, is entirely waxy-white, six to ten inches in height, the erect leafless stems growing from matted roots usually attached to partially decayed organic matter. Each stem is terminated by a nodding flower, half an inch to an inch in length, with a corolla of five separate petals. When fruiting, the tip of the flowering stem becomes erect. Indian Pipes are common in woods over most of the continent, wherever it is damp, shady, and sufficiently well provided with humus. The flowering period is from June to August.

PINE-SAP PLATE 136

Monotropa hypopithys *Ericaceae*

With stems slightly taller than Indian pipe, this species, also known as False Beech-drops, is yellowish and fragrant. Like the Indian pipe the stems lack chlorophyll and leaves. Pine-sap has a terminal cluster of several flowers, drooping at the tip but becoming erect in fruit. It grows in more open sandy habitats in the woods, and is found from southern Canada to Mexico. The flowers appear from June to October.

The Pyxie Family

Diapensiaceae

The Pyxie family is one of the smallest groups of flowering plants, including only ten species common to cool and arctic regions. In the United States these occur only in the eastern highlands. The foliage is evergreen, and the stems are either absent or creeping.

GALAX PLATE 141

Galax aphylla *Diapensiaceae*

Wandflower, or Galax, is a stemless herbaceous plant with a creeping rhizome from which grow erect, long-stemmed, rounded, shining leaves with wavy margins. The flowering stalk, six to twelve inches in length, terminates in a slender spikelike cluster of small flowers. Each flower has a calyx of five partly fused sepals and a corolla of five partly united petals. Galax grows in open woods from Virginia to Georgia and Alabama; the flowers appear in May and continue to July.

PLATE 147

(*left*) **Spreading Dogbane,** ***Apocynum androsaemifolium*** (*right*) **Blue Dogbane,** ***Amsonia ciliata***

PLATE 148

(*left*) **Four-leaved Milkweed,** ***Asclepias quadrifolia*** (*right*) **White Milkweed,** ***Asclepias variegata***

PYXIE — PLATE 141

Pyxidanthera barbulata — *Diapensiaceae*

This flowering plant resembles a prostrate evergreen since its foliage consists of small, narrow, awl-shaped leaves; the matted growth is also mosslike, so it is not surprising that Pyxie is also known as Flowering Moss. Numerous little solitary flowers are borne on short leafy branchlets. The corolla consists of five partly united petals which project as rounded lobes beyond the calyx. Pyxie is found on sandy pine barrens from New Jersey to South Carolina; it flowers from March to May.

The Primrose Family

Primulaceae

The Primrose family is a fairly large one, with 800 species which are most abundant in north temperate regions. Members of the family are annual or perennial herbaceous plants with simple leaves which for the most part are either opposite or whorled. The corolla is tubular or regularly five-parted, and in some of the species very showy. A few ornamentals are derived from this family, including the Primroses (Primula) and Cyclamen (*Cyclamen persica*), the latter originating in the Mediterranean region.

SHOOTING STAR — PLATE 142

Dodecatheon meadia — *Primulaceae*

The leaves of this species form a basal rosette from which rises a flowering stalk six to twenty inches in height. Each leaf is simple and entire; the base is sometimes marked with red. The large terminal umbels bear striking flowers which nod when they bloom. The deeply cleft calyx lobes and the separate petals are all reflexed. The pistil and stamens together form a spear-like tip to each flower. This Shooting Star grows along river banks, in meadows, and in open woods, from Pennsylvania south to Georgia and Texas, flowering from April to June. Other species are found in the western states.

STAR-FLOWER

Trientalis borealis *Primulaceae*

The buried, creeping stems of this plant send up erect slender branches three to nine inches high; each branch bears a whorl of five to ten narrow leaves, pointed at both ends. Above the leaves rises a short flowering stalk which terminates in a white flower with five to nine petals; the corolla is about half an inch in breadth. In some plants two or three flowers may be borne above the leaf whorl. Star-flower is a subalpine plant of cool woods and mountain slopes, found from Canada and south to inland Virginia. It flowers from May to August.

FRINGED LOOSESTRIFE

PLATE 143

Lysimachia ciliata *Primulaceae*

This Loosestrife is a tall species, growing to a height of four feet in its favorite habitats of stream banks and lake shores. Ovate and pointed leaves are produced opposite each other on the slender erect stems. Fairly large flowers, up to an inch in diameter, are borne in the axils of the upper leaves; each flower terminates a long flowering stalk. The calyx is five-lobed, and the regular corolla consists of five separate petals, finely toothed at their tips. Fringed Loosestrife grows throughout all the eastern states; its flowering period is from June to August.

PLATE 149

Butterfly-weed, ***Asclepias tuberosa***

PLATE 150

Common Milkweed, *Asclepias syriaca*

WHORLED LOOSESTRIFE
PLATE 144

Lysimachia quadrifolia — *Primulaceae*

Four-angled stems characterize this species, which is also known as Crosswort. It grows to a height of three feet. Ovate, usually black-dotted leaves are borne in whorls of four or five. The axils of the upper leaf whorls bear four to six flowers, each on a long slender stalks. The corolla of each flower has five petals partly united at their bases. Whorled Loosestrife grows in wet woods and swamps and along pond margins from Maine to Georgia and from Wisconsin to Missouri and Alabama. It flowers from July to August.

SWAMP LOOSESTRIFE
PLATE 144

Lysimachia terrestris — *Primulaceae*

Known in some localities as Swamp Candles, this is a slightly smaller plant than preceding species, one to two feet tall, with opposite lanceolate leaves. The flowers, similar in size and appearance to those of the whorled loosestrife, are borne in a compact terminal cluster instead of in the upper leaf axils. Gravelly shores and low places in the woods are the natural sites for Swamp Candles, whose range is from Newfoundland west to Saskatchewan and south to Georgia. The flowers can be found from June to August.

MONEYWORT
PLATE 145

Lysimachia nummularia — *Primulaceae*

Unlike the preceding species in the Loosestrife genus, Moneywort or Creeping Loosestrife is a low-growing perennial with trailing stems which bear pairs of rounded leaves. It is a European plant which has escaped to become part of our roadside flora in the eastern portion of the United States. Large flowers, an inch in diameter, are produced singly in the axils of the leaves. Moneywort blooms throughout the summer, from June to August.

EUROPEAN COWSLIP

Primula veris *Primulaceae*

This is another European species which has escaped in various parts of the East to become a roadside and field flower. The leaves form a basal rosette from which rises a leafless flowering stalk bearing large purple or yellow flowers. Each flower has a tubular calyx, angular and five-lobed; the lobes of the corolla are typically notched. Like most of the true primroses, it is a boreal or alpine plant.

The Leadwort Family

Plumbaginaceae

The Leadwort family is a relatively small one (300 species) typically found in the semiarid regions of central Asia and the Mediterranean. It contains perennial herbaceous plants and shrubs, with alternate leaves and tubular flowers with a five-lobed corolla. The half-dozen American species are inhabitants of the seashore.

MARSH ROSEMARY

PLATE 145

Limonium carolinianum *Plumbaginaceae*

Another name for this plant of marine habitats is Sea Lavender. The lower portion of the stem is thickened and woody; the leaves are oblong or lanceolate, tipped with a bristly point. From the basal cluster of leaves arise branched flowering stalks several feet in height. The small flowers have a five-lobed calyx and a trumpet-shaped corolla with rounded lobes. Marsh Rosemary is found from southern New England and New York to Mississippi and Florida. It flowers from July to October.

PLATE 151

Swamp Milkweed, ***Asclepias incarnata***

PLATE 152

Hedge Bindweed, *Convolvulus sepium*

The Logania Family

Loganiaceae

The Logania family includes about 800 species of herbaceous plants, vines and shrubs which are predominantly tropical and warm temperate in their distribution. In eastern United States the family is represented by two species, one a vine and the other a herbaceous perennial. The flowers are five-parted, with a funnel-shaped corolla. Two drugs are secured from members of the family; strychnine comes from the seeds of *Strychnos nux-vomica*, and curare from the bark of *Strychnos toxifera*.

YELLOW JESSAMINE

PLATE 146

Gelsemium sempervirens

Loganiaceae

Early in March, while the branches of the swamp maple are still bare of leaves, the roadside woods of the Carolinas are brightened by clusters of golden-yellow flowers twisted among the limbs and over the bushes. Thus Yellow Jessamine, or Evening Trumpet-flower, adds color to the early spring woods, from Virginia to Florida; the flowers continue until May. Yellow Jessamine is a twining or high-climbing vine with opposite, lanceolate leaves which tend to become evergreen in the southern portion of the range. The flowers grow singly or in small groups in the axils of the leaves. Each flower is fragrant, and has a slightly irregular five-lobed corolla with a tapering tubular base.

INDIAN PINK

PLATE 146

Spigelia marilandica

Loganiaceae

One-sided flower clusters mark this southern plant, which is also known as Carolina Pink and Pinkroot. It is an erect perennial one to two feet tall, found in rich woods from Maryland to Florida and Texas. The stems bear ovate opposite leaves united by their stipules. Narrow trumpet-shaped flowers are clustered in terminal one-sided spikes; the outside of the elongated and tubular corolla is red, the inside is yellow. Each corolla has five pointed lobes. The flowering period is from May to June.

The Dogbane Family

Apocynaceae

This predominantly tropical family of some 1,300 species includes herbaceous plants, shrubs, and trees with simple, entire, opposite leaves. The sap is usually milky. The fused base of the petals forms a tubular corolla, arising out of a five-lobed calyx. The North American species are mostly inhabitants of Mexico; only about thirty kinds occur in the United States. Economically the family is important both because of the ornamental varieties and the poisonous properties of some species. The Oleanders (Nerium) are tall shrubs which have been introduced into our southern and southwestern states from the Old World; they have whorled, dark, evergreen leaves and showy clusters of red, white or yellow flowers. Periwinkle or Trailing Myrtle (*Vinca minor*) is a European plant used for ground-cover and escaped to roadside banks; the creeping stems bear glossy evergreen leaves and large blue axillary flowers with five broad corolla lobes. Indian Hemp (*Apocynum cannabinum*), with greenish-white flowers and simple, opposite leaves, is so toxic to horses, cattle and sheep that thirty grams of green leaves will kill a cow. It grows throughout the country. Oleander also contains a toxic substance poisonous to animals; a few cases of human poisoning have been reported.

PLATE 153

(*above*) **Wild Potato-vine,** ***Ipomoea pandurata*** (*below*) **Tall Morning-glory,** ***Ipomoea purpurea***

PLATE 154

(*left*) **Low Bindweed,** ***Convolvulus spithameus*** (*right*) **Downy Gentian,** ***Gentiana puberula***

SPREADING DOGBANE PLATE 147

Apocynum androsaemifolium *Apocynaceae*

This is a wide-branching perennial growing to a height of several feet, with oval, opposite leaves which are dark green above and pale beneath. Numerous small bell-shaped flowers with pink-striped corollas are borne in spreading terminal clusters. The fruit is a long slender beanlike structure known as a follicle; the seeds have long silky hairs. Spreading Dogbane grows along the borders of dry woods, from Canada south to northern Mexico. It flowers from June through August.

BLUE DOGBANE PLATE 147

Amsonia ciliata *Apocynaceae*

Blue Star is another name for this southern member of the Dogbane family. It has erect stems, up to three feet in height, with alternate, lanceolate leaves borne in a crowded fashion up into the terminal inflorescence. Each of the small flowers has a narrow funnel-shaped corolla edged with five long narrow spreading lobes. Blue Dogbane is found from North Caroline and Missouri southward to Mexico, on sand hills and in dry pinelands. The flowering period is from May to June.

The Milkweed Family

Asclepiadaceae

It seems hardly necessary to note that the plants in this family usually have stems with a milky sap, and bear large simple leaves either in pairs or whorls. The familiar fruit is a follicle filled with silky-tufted, wind-dispersed seeds. Most of the 1,800 species in the family are tropical in distribution, many of them found in South America. Some 100 species of Milkweed (*Asclepias*) alone occur in the United States. There are twenty-five species in eastern United States and as many more in the West and South.

FOUR-LEAVED MILKWEED

PLATE 148

Asclepias quadrifolia — *Asclepiadaceae*

All of the species in the genus Asclepias are perennials with milky juice; the flowers have an unusual corolla consisting of five deeply parted lobes, and a crown of five hoods seated on the inside, around the stamen-tube which encloses the pistil. The Four-leaved Milkweed bears its small flowers in the typical umbel, on slender smooth stems which grow to a height of two or three feet. Some of the leaves are in whorls of four, some in pairs. This species grows in dry woods from New England to North Carolina, west to Minnesota and Kansas; it flowers from May to July.

WHITE MILKWEED

PLATE 148

Asclepias variegata — *Asclepiadaceae*

This milkweed has nearly smooth stems, growing to a height of three feet and bearing more or less oval leaves in four to six pairs; the flowers are produced in a compact terminal umbel. White Milkweed prefers dry shaded woods throughout eastern and central United States. The flowering period is during June and July.

BUTTERFLY-WEED

PLATE 149

Asclepias tuberosa — *Asclepiadaceae*

Also known as Pleurisy Root, this species is a hairy-stemmed, stout, branching plant with alternate (occasionally opposite) linear or lanceolate leaves. The stems are very leafy and continue branching up to the summit; the sap is much less milky than that of the other members of the genus. The reflexed petals are very conspicuous, as are the "horns" of the crown inside the corolla. Butterfly-weed is a showy flower of dry open habitats throughout all the eastern and central states. The flowering period is from June to September.

PLATE 155

Prairie Gentian, ***Eustoma russellianum***

PLATE 156

Rose-pink, ***Sabatia angularis***

COMMON MILKWEED

PLATE 150

Asclepias syriaca — *Asclepiadaceae*

The Common Milkweed is a coarse-stemmed, rank-growing plant which reaches a height of five or six feet; it is a common weed of dry fields and thickets, as well as roadsides from New England to Georgia and west to Kansas. The oval or lanceolate leaves reach a length of seven or eight inches, and grow in pairs along the stout stems. The typical milkweed flowers are clustered in umbels in the axils of the upper leaves; they are characterized by a heavy fragrance. Shoots and very young pods are sometimes cooked and eaten as a vegetable. The flowering period is from June to August.

SWAMP MILKWEED

PLATE 151

Asclepias incarnata — *Asclepiadaceae*

This is a tall slender species, growing to a height of five feet, with tapering lanceolate leaves arranged in pairs on the stems. Numerous small flowers are clustered in terminal stalked umbels; each flower has the five-lobed corolla and crown of hooded projections, as in other milkweeds. As its name suggests, Swamp Milkweed prefers wet habitats such as shores of ponds and swampy fields. It occurs from Quebec to Wyoming and Texas, and flowers from June to August.

GREEN MILKWEED

Asclepias viridiflora — *Asclepiadaceae*

This species, found in dry woods and clearings from Pennsylvania to Florida and Texas, is a minutely hairy plant two or three feet in height, with oval or oblong opposite leaves. The flowers are borne in axillary umbels, and are greenish-white in color. Like the other milkweeds, the flowers appear during the summer, between June and August.

The Morning-Glory Family

Convolvulaceae

The Morning-glory family consists of herbaceous perennials, most of them twining and climbing plants. The leaves are alternate and simple; the flowers regular, with a five-parted tubular or funnel-shaped corolla. The majority of the 1,200 species are tropical or subtropical in distribution. The familiar Morning-glory (*Ipomoea purpurea*) of ornamental use is a member of this family, as is the Sweet Potato (*Ipomoea batatas*.).

HEDGE BINDWEED

PLATE 152

Convolvulus sepium — *Convolvulaceae*

Also known as Wild Morning-glory, this is a common roadside flower of all the eastern and central states, where its sprawling vines cover walls, fences and banks. Hedge Bindweed bears alternate, simple leaves with a triangular outline and spreading basal lobes. Showy flowers, rosy-pink to white in color, are borne singly or in small clusters in the leaf axils. Each flower has a small calyx of five sepals enclosed by two large pointed green bracts. The funnel-shaped corolla has a slightly five-lobed margin. Flowering is continuous from May to September.

LOW BINDWEED

PLATE 154

Convolvulus spithameus — *Convolvulaceae*

An erect rather than a twining plant, Low Bindweed grows to a height of twenty inches. The simple or sparingly branched stems bear alternate, oval leaves, the lowest being very small. The funnel-shaped flowers arise singly in the leaf axils. Low Bindweed grows in sandy and rocky woods from New England to Virginia, west to Minnesota. Its flowering period is from May to July.

PLATE 157

(*left*) Fringed Gentian, *Gentiana crinita* (*right*) Closed Gentian, *Gentiana andrewsii*

PLATE 158

(*left*) **Ague-weed,** ***Gentiana quinquefolia*** (*right*) **Large Marsh-pink,** ***Sabatia dodecandra***

WILD POTATO-VINE

PLATE 153

Ipomoea pandurata — *Convolvulaceae*

The stems of this member of the Morning-glory family trail along the ground or climb among the branches of shrubs, sometimes attaining a length of fifteen feet. The long-stalked leaves are heart-shaped and large, and the blossoms are showy, being sometimes three inches in diameter. The vines die each autumn, but beneath the ground hides one of the largest storage roots of any native American plant. Somewhat like a gigantic sweet potato, this root may weigh as much as fifteen or twenty pounds and be several feet in length. When roasted in a campfire it makes a good substitute for a sweet potato, but has a more bitter taste. It was a staple food of the Indians. Wild Potato-vine is found from southern New England and Ontario to Florida and west to Texas.

TALL MORNING-GLORY

PLATE 153

Ipomoea purpurea — *Convolvulaceae*

This is the common ornamental Morning-glory, an immigrant from tropical America which has escaped to become a common weed in the eastern states. It is an annual with heart-shaped or ovate leaves. The flowers show a great variety of colors: purple, red, blue, white, and variegated forms being common. The flowering period is from July to October.

CYPRESS VINE

Impomoea quamoclit — *Convolvulaceae*

Another naturalized wild flower, originally a native of tropical America, Cypress Vine is a thin-stemmed twining annual with unusual threadlike leaves, whose blades are dissected into linear segments. The slender-tubed flowers are a bright scarlet-red. This species has run wild from Virginia to Missouri, flowering from August to October.

The Gentian Family

Gentianaceae

The Gentian family is predominantly made up of herbaceous plants with opposite leaves and regular, showy flowers. The 800 species in the family are of world-wide distribution but are most common in north temperate regions; some 400 species occur in the United States.

DOWNY GENTIAN PLATE 154

Gentiana puberula *Gentianaceae*

There are twenty-three species of gentians in the eastern and central states; their flowers are usually showy and large, with a four- or five-lobed tubular corolla. The Downy Gentian is an erect perennial eight to twenty inches tall, with slender stiff stems covered with a light down. Narrow lanceolate leaves, of which the uppermost reach a length of two inches, occur in pairs. Compact clusters of flowers are borne in the upper leaf axils and at the summit of the stem. Each flower has a tubular corolla, one to two inches in length, with a spreading five-lobed margin. Downy Gentian grows on dry prairies and sand barrens from western New York to Georgia, west to North Dakota and Kansas. Flowering period is September and October.

FRINGED GENTIAN PLATE 157

Gentiana crinita *Gentianaceae*

This attractive wild flower grows in erect clusters from a root which is sometimes biennial; the erect stems have somewhat angular sides and bear ovate, pointed, opposite leaves. Plants reach a height of two or three feet. The flowers are borne singly or in small clusters at the tips of the stems. Each flower has prominently keeled lobes to the calyx, and a cylindrical corolla with spreading lobes, edged with a delicate fringe. From August to November the flowers of the Fringed Gentian can be found in meadows and along stream margins in moist woods, from Maine to Georgia and west to Iowa.

PLATE 159

(*above*) **Wild Blue Phlox,** ***Phlox divaricata*** (*below*) **Moss-pink,** ***Phlox subulata***

PLATE 160

(*left*) **Greek Valerian,** ***Polemonium reptans*** (*right*) **Hairy Phlox,** ***Phlox pilosa***

CLOSED GENTIAN

PLATE 157

Gentiana andrewsii — *Gentianaceae*

This species has stout stems which are usually unbranched, often growing to a height of two feet or more. The stems bear large, opposite leaves which are lanceolate or oblong, with long pointed tips. The uppermost leaves reach a length of four inches. A characteristic of the flowers is their closed position, like buds; for this reason the species is also known as Bottle Gentian or Blind Gentian. The flowers are clustered in a dense terminal group, with one or two also in each of the upper leaf axils. Each perianth is surrounded by two leafy green bracts. Usually blue or purple, the Closed Gentian sometimes is found in pinkish and white varieties. Its range is from New England southward to Georgia and Arkansas. Like the other gentians it is typically an autumn flower, being found in blossom from August to October.

AGUE-WEED

PLATE 158

Gentiana quinquefolia — *Gentianaceae*

This is a slender annual or biennial, two to three feet in height, with the angles of the stems prolonged into wings. Ovate or lanceolate leaves are borne in pairs. Ague-weed, also known as Stiff Gentian and Gall-of-the-earth, has small flowers in dense clusters at the ends of the branches. The four triangular lobes of the corolla are bristle-tipped; the color of the corolla varies from pale blue and lilac to greenish-white. Ague-weed grows in rich, moist woods from New England and New York to the Gulf. The flowering period is from August to November.

PRAIRIE GENTIAN

PLATE 155

Eustoma russellianum

Gentianaceae

The home of this herbaceous annual is on the plains, from South Dakota south to the Mexican border. The stems, which grow to a height of several feet, branch very slightly and bear opposite, ovate or oblong leaves. The flowers, under cultivation becoming as large as tulips, are clustered at the tips of the branches. Each flower has a funnel-shaped corolla with five or six distinctly separated lobes.

ROSE-PINK

PLATE 156

Sabatia angularis

Gentianaceae

Also known as Bitterbloom, this species can be recognized by its square stems, opposite branches, and ovate leaves whose bases clasp the stem. Rose-pink is a biennial averaging one and a half feet in height, with a persistent rosette of oval leaves. The flowers, borne in spreading clusters, are very fragrant; each has a long-lobed calyx and a corolla of five petals, fused at the base. Rose-pink grows in meadows and fields from New England and New York to Florida and Oklahoma. The flowers can be found from July to September.

LARGE MARSH-PINK

PLATE 158

Sabatia dodecandra

Gentianaceae

Another name for this inhabitant of saline and brackish marshes is Sea-pink; it is a slender-stemmed plant growing to a height of two feet. The upper leaves, which are opposite, are lanceolate or linear in outline. Calyx and corolla each consist of eight to twelve segments. The Large Marsh-pink is found along the coastal plain from southern Connecticut to the Gulf; it flowers during July.

PLATE 161

Virginia Waterleaf, *Hydrophyllum virginicum*

PLATE 162

(*left*) **Scorpion-weed,** ***Phacelia purshii*** (*right*) **Wild Comfrey,** ***Cynoglossum virginianum***

SEA-PINK

Sabatia stellaris — *Gentianaceae*

In salt marshes and brackish meadows along the seacoast from Massachusetts to Florida and Louisiana, this slender herbaceous plant raises its colorful flowers a foot to twenty inches above the ground. The slender stems, somewhat four-angled near the base, bear linear, opposite leaves and large terminal flowers up to an inch in breadth. Each corolla has four to seven spreading rounded lobes, crimson-pink with a yellowish center. The flowering period is from July to October.

The Phlox Family

Polemoniaceae

The Phlox family is distinctively American, with most of its 260 species in western United States; it includes annual and perennial herbaceous plants. The leaves may be either alternate or opposite, and are usually simple and entire. Phlox flowers are characterized by a five-lobed calyx and a five-lobed corolla. The importance of the family lies only in the use of many of its species as garden ornamentals, both in borders and in rock gardens.

WILD BLUE PHLOX — PLATE 159

Phlox divaricata — *Polemoniaceae*

This is a matted plant with spreading or ascending stems, rarely more than a foot in height. The opposite leaves are oblong or ovate in shape, and leaflike bracts surround the base of the flowers, which are borne in a dense terminal cluster. Each flower has an angular five-lobed calyx with a plaited appearance. The base of the corolla is an elongated tube, with the margin expanded to form a saucer-shaped structure with a five-parted margin. Wild Blue Phlox grows in open woods and on rocky slopes from New England to the southern coastal plain and west to Nebraska. The flowering period is from April to June.

MOSS-PINK — PLATE 159

Phlox subulata — *Polemoniaceae*

The stems of this species are partly woody and produce horizontal or tufted mats of foliage and flowers. The linear leaves, crowded on the ascending stems, are semi-evergreen. The flowering branches grow upward and bear small clusters of vivid pink, sometimes white, flowers about half an inch in breadth. Each flower has a five-lobed spreading corolla whose segments are sometimes indented at the tips. Moss-pink grows in sandy or gravelly woods from southern New York to North Carolina, and west to Michigan. The flowers can be found from March through May.

HAIRY PHLOX — PLATE 160

Phlox pilosa — *Polemoniaceae*

Also known as Prairie Phlox or Downy Phlox, this tufted plant has slightly hairy, nearly erect stems, a foot or more in height. The opposite leaves are lanceolate or linear, and sharply tipped. The flowers, borne in spreading clusters, are rosy-pink to violet in color. Hairy Phlox prefers sandy slopes and prairies, and is found from New England to Florida, west to Kansas and Texas; it flowers from May to July.

PLATE 163

Virginia Cowslip, *Mertensia virginica*

PLATE 164

Forget-me-not, ***Myosotis scorpioides***

GARDEN PHLOX

Phlox paniculata *Polemoniaceae*

The erect stems of this species frequently reach a stature of five or six feet in favored locations, such as the borders of woods and thickets. The pink, purple, or whitish flowers are borne in a dense terminal cluster; each flower is about an inch in length, with a long tubular base and an expanded tip with five rounded or oblong lobes. The lanceolate leaves, up to six inches in length, grow in pairs along the stems. Native to the region between Pennsylvania and Florida, west to Kansas, Garden Phlox has escaped from cultivation elsewhere to become a common wild flower. It blooms from July to September.

WILD SWEET WILLIAM

Phlox maculata *Polemoniaceae*

This species of meadows and stream banks, from southern New England to upland Virginia west to Missouri, grows to a height of three feet. The stems, arising from the tip of a horizontal rootstock, are usually purple spotted. Numerous flowers are clustered in a terminal inflorescence four to ten inches in length. The flowers are pink or purple, less commonly, white. Wild Sweet William flowers from May to August.

GREEK VALERIAN

PLATE 160

Polemonium reptans *Polemoniaceae*

Also known as Bluebell, this tufted, weak-stemmed plant is usually under two feet in height. It is an unusual member of the family in that it has compound leaves, pinnately divided into eleven to seventeen leaflets. The inflorescence is a cluster of nodding bell-shaped flowers with a tubular five-lobed calyx and a corolla of five segments. Greek Valerian prefers rich woods, and is found from New York to Georgia and Alabama, west to Minnesota. It flowers from April to June.

The Waterleaf Family

Hydrophyllaceae

The Waterleaf family was so named because the original plants described for this group had watery stems and leaves; they are annual and perennial herbaceous plants, closely related to the Morning-glory family. There are only about 260 species in the family, but they are of wide distribution; in this country they are most abundant in the West.

VIRGINIA WATERLEAF PLATE 161
Hydrophyllum virginicum *Hydrophyllaceae*

Another name for this plant is John's-cabbage. It has a perennial rootstock from which arise erect stems, one to three feet in height. The large basal leaves are pinnately compound, with five to seven ovate and toothed leaflets; the upper leaves are smaller, with fewer leaflets. The inflorescence is a long-stalked cyme of white or violet flowers, each with a deeply five-lobed calyx, a bell-shaped corolla with five blunt lobes, and conspicuous projecting stamens. Virginia Waterleaf grows in rich woods and damp clearings from New England to Virginia, west to Manitoba and Kansas. The flowers appear in May, and continue through August.

SCORPION-WEED PLATE 162
Phacelia purshii *Hydrophyllaceae*

Also known as Miami Mist, this sparsely hairy annual (sometimes biennial) has stiff erect stems four to twelve inches in height, bearing pinnately lobed leaves. Open bell-shaped flowers are produced in a raceme which uncoils from the tip downward. The segments of the deeply five-lobed calyx bear long divergent hairs, and the lobes of the corolla are fringed. Scorpion-weed grows in rich woods and clearings from Pennsylvania west to Oklahoma and Wisconsin. Its flowering period is from April to June.

PLATE 165

(*left*) **Viper's Bugloss,** ***Echium vulgare*** (*right*) **Puccoon,** ***Lithospermum canescens***

PLATE 166

(*left*) **Blue Vervain,** ***Verbena hastata*** (*right*) **Hoary Verbena,** ***Verbena stricta***

The Borage Family

Boraginaceae

The Borage family has a world-wide distribution, its 2,000 species including a variey of herbaceous plants, shrubs, and trees. It has but a few representatives in the United States, and these are all herbaceous plants. They are generally rough-hairy, with alternate leaves and a regular, five-lobed corolla. The inflorescence, like that of the Waterleaf family, is peculiar in being a raceme which uncoils from the tip backwards along the stem. Heliotrope and forget-me-not are garden plants belonging to this family.

WILD COMFREY — PLATE 162

Cynoglossum virginianum — *Boraginaceae*

This plant, also known as Hound's-tongue, is a bristly-haired species with perennial roots; its stems grow to a height of several feet. The alternate, lanceolate leaves have heart-shaped bases which clasp the stems. The inflorescence is a raceme or elongated cluster of small flowers, each with a calyx of four or five partly united sepals, and a funnel-shaped corolla with five lobes. Wild Comfrey prefers open deciduous woods and roadsides, and can be found from New England to Florida, west to Missouri and Texas. The flowering period is April and June.

VIRGINIA COWSLIP — PLATE 163

Mertensia virginica — *Boraginaceae*

In many localities known as Bluebells, this is an attractive wild flower with smooth stout stems, often growing to a height of several feet; the oblong leaves are arranged alternately on the stems, with the leaves of the basal shoots on long stalks. Flowers are produced in an uncoiling one-sided raceme, each flower consisting of a short five-parted calyx and a drooping, trumpet-shaped coroila with slightly five-lobed margins. They are pink when young, become blue with age. Virginia Cowslip thrives in rich woods and well-watered meadows, from southern New York to Alabama, west to Minnesota and Kansas. The flowering period is from March to June.

FORGET-ME-NOT — PLATE 164

Myosotis scorpioides — *Boraginaceae*

This favorite and familiar species, which is also known as Mouse-ear and Scorpion-grass, is a European flower which has become naturalized throughout the coastal plains states, wherever there is wet ground or a swampy stream margin. It is a rather succulent-stemmed perennial with lanceolate to linear leaves, usually growing to a stature of twelve to twenty inches. Small delicately-tinted flowers are clustered in curving racemes; each flower has a five-lobed calyx and a corolla of five rounded lobes. The flowers can be found from May to October. Four additional cultivated species of Myosotis can also be found naturalized in the eastern states and adjacent Canada.

VIPER'S BUGLOSS — PLATE 165

Echium vulgare — *Boraginaceae*

Echium is the only genus in the Borage family which has irregular flowers. It is a rough bristly perennial, originally a European immigrant, which has spread rapidly to become a roadside and field weed throughout the eastern states and west to Kansas. Erect, spotted stems grow to a height of two or three feet and bear alternate, oblong or lanceolate, hairy leaves. Showy flowers are clustered in a spirelike inflorescence. Each flower has a calyx of five almost distinct sepals, and a funnel-shaped corolla with five unequal lobes; five reddish stamens are inserted on the inside of the corolla tube. The flowers, which occur from June to September, are pink when in bud, bright blue when mature, and purplish-red when old. The name is not, as many people think, bug-loss, but bu-gloss, meaning ox-tongue. Viper's Bugloss also goes by the name of Blueweed.

PLATE 167

(*left*) Lantana, *Lantana camara* (*right*) Lyre-leaved Sage, *Salvia lyrata*

PLATE 168

(*left*) **Oswego-tea,** ***Monarda didyma*** (*right*) **Wild Bergamot,** ***Monarda fistulosa***

HOUND'S-TONGUE

Cynoglossum officinale — *Boraginaceae*

This is an obnoxious weed with an odor reminiscent of mice, common in pastures and waste places from Quebec to the Pacific and southward to the latitude of Arkansas. It is a naturalized European plant with erect leafy stems reaching a height of three feet. Reddish-purple flowers are clustered in terminal racemes. The fruits are prickly nutlets which attach themselves to the fur of animals, and are an especial nuisance with sheep; hence another name for this species is Sheep-lice.

PUCCOON

PLATE 165

Lithospermum canescens — *Boraginaceae*

This is a densely hairy species, growing to a height of sixteen inches; it is a perennial, with a root which yields a red dye. The leaves are linear to narrowly lanceolate. Sessile flowers are borne in a one-sided raceme, each flower with a deeply five-parted calyx and a funnel-shaped corolla with five broad rounded lobes. Puccoon grows on prairies and in sandy open woods, from southern Canada to Georgia and Texas. The flowering period is from April to June.

SEASIDE HELIOTROPE

Heliotropium curassavicum — *Boraginaceae*

This smooth-stemmed annual is common on sandy shores and marshes along the Atlantic coast, from Delaware to Florida. The plants are creeping, and form matted growths with erect flowering stalks bearing spikes in pairs. Each spike gradually uncoils from the tip, revealing small white or bluish flowers from June to October. A naturalized heliotrope from Europe (*Heliotropium europaeum*) is sometimes found as a roadside wild flower; it is a tall, more erect plant, with both lateral and terminal spikelike inflorescences. The flowers are bluish-white, and appear from June to September.

The Verbena Family

Verbenaceae

The Verbena family is composed of herbaceous plants and shrubs often with quadrangular stems and simple, opposite or whorled leaves. It is a large family of over 2,000 species, most of them restricted to tropical and subtropical regions. The genus Verbena extends into the temperate regions of the New World and by itself includes 230 species. The flower has a five-lobed calyx, also a five-lobed corolla which is sometimes two-lipped. This family is closely allied to the Mint family. Teakwood comes from an East Indian tree in the group; several familiar garden plants also belong to the Verbena family, such as the Beauty-berry (Callicarpa), Lantana, and the various verbenas themselves.

BLUE VERVAIN PLATE 166

Verbena hastata *Verbenaceae*

The tall stems of Blue Vervain are stiff and four-sided, somewhat rough and hairy, and may grow to a height of six feet. The lanceolate and toothed leaves are borne in pairs, the lower leaves with projecting lobes. Small sessile flowers expand their corollas in a slender compact spike which stands upright like a small pencil; this inflorescence may grow to a length of six inches. Each tiny flower has a slightly irregular five-lobed corolla. In spite of its name, Blue Vervain often has purple, pink or whitish flowers. It grows in damp woods and along lake shores from Canada to Florida and California. The flowers appear from July to September.

Related wild species include Rose Vervain (*Verbena canadensis*), a decumbent plant with rose to purple flowers, growing wild from Virginia and Florida to Colorado and northern Mexico; and White Vervain (*Verbena urticifolia*), an erect plant with white flowers, found from southern Canada to Florida and Texas.

PLATE 169

Horse-balm, *Collinsonia canadensis*

PLATE 170

False Dragonhead, *Physostegia virginiana*

HOARY VERBENA

PLATE 166

Verbena stricta — *Verbenaceae*

This species is a downy-haired plant one to three feet tall, with oval or elliptic leaves. The inflorescence is a sessile compact spike of small flowers with the structure of the blue vervain. Hoary Verbena, occasionally seen in the East, grows wild on the prairies and in barren open soil, from the Great Lakes region to Arkansas and west into the plains. The flowering period is from June to September.

FRENCH MULBERRY

Callicarpa americana — *Verbenaceae*

This is a shrubby species, growing to a height of six feet. The oval leaves taper both at the base and the tip, and are finely toothed. Small bluish flowers are borne in clusters, each flower with a four-toothed calyx and a tubular corolla with a flat expanded brim which is four- or five-lobed. The pinkish or violet-colored fruits, which persist into winter, are small one-seeded berries; another common and appropriate name for the shrub is Beauty-berry. It grows from Maryland to Florida and Texas, in rich woods; the flowers first appear in June and continue through August.

LANTANA

PLATE 167

Lantana camara — *Verbenaceae*

A low-growing prickly shrub, Lantana grows to a height of four feet; the foliage consists of thick ovate leaves appearing in pairs on the stems. Small, irregular flowers are borne in a compact flat-topped cluster; each flower has a cup-shaped calyx with two to five lobes, and a funnel-shaped corolla with a similar number of rounded lobes. Lantana grows in sandy soil along the southern coastal plain, from Florida and Texas north to Maryland and Oklahoma south to Florida and Texas. The flowering period is from spring to early autumn.

The Mint Family

Labiatae

The Mint family is a large one, including over 3,000 species of usually aromatic, square-stemmed herbaceous annuals or perennials with opposite or whorled leaves. The flowers are irregular, or two-lipped; the upper lip consists of two lobes of the corolla, the lower lip of three lobes. The flowers are usually in axillary pairs or clusters, although in some cases they are solitary. The Mint family is economically important because it is the source of many aromatic oils from plants such as Lavender (Lavandula), Rosemary (Rosmarinus), Mint (Mentha) and Sage (Salvia). Many of the savory herbs also come from this family, among them basil, thyme, hyssop and pennyroyal.

LYRE-LEAVED SAGE — PLATE 167

Salvia lyrata — *Labiatae*

The genus Salvia is characterized by a two-lipped calyx as well as a two-lipped corolla. The upper lip of the corolla is straight or truncate, the lower lip is broad and spreading, with a large middle lobe. Lyre-leaved Sage, or Cancer-weed, has the characteristic square stems and aromatic foliage; the leaves, which are opposite, are elliptic or oval, usually with a large rounded terminal lobe and smaller lower lobes. The showy flowers grow in clusters near the summit of the stem, which may reach a height of two feet. The range of this species is from southern New England to Florida, Oklahoma, and Texas, west to Missouri, where it can be found in sandy or open woods. The flowers appear in April, May and June.

PLATE 171

(*left*) **Hooded Skullcap,** ***Scutellaria epilobiifolia*** (*center*) **Bluecurls,** ***Trichostema dichotomum*** (*right*) **Basil,** ***Satureja vulgaris***

PLATE 172

(*left*) **Heal-all,** ***Prunella vulgaris*** (*right*) **Wood Mint,** ***Blephilia ciliata***

OSWEGO TEA

PLATE 168

Monarda didyma *Labiatae*

The scarlet heads of this showy member of the Mint family stand out conspicuously amid the lush greenery of stream banks and moist meadows; the flowers are borne in rounded terminal clusters, above green and red bracts. The ovate, sharply-pointed leaves, which occur in pairs, are usually downy on the undersurface. The stout square stems grow to a height of three or four feet. Each flower is an inch or more long. The calyx is tubular and edged with five small teeth prolonged into hairlike tips; the corolla is distinctly two-lipped, with an erect and arching upper lip and a spreading three-lobed lower lip. Two stamens project beyond the lip of the corolla. Oswego Tea, also known as Bee-balm, has a natural range from New York to Michigan, south in the uplands to Georgia and Tennessee; however, it is frequently cultivated as an ornamental, and has escaped to roadsides and fields in the New England states. The flowering period is from June to August.

WILD BERGAMOT

PLATE 168

Monarda fistulosa *Labiatae*

Except for the color of the corolla, this species closely resembles Oswego tea; the stems are similarly square and two to three feet tall, with opposite leaves and a compact terminal head of flowers. The leaves are more lanceolate, however, and the bracts below the flower cluster may be whitish or purple. The tip of the upper lip of the corolla is hairy. In some localities it is known as Horse-mint. Wild Bergamot grows in dry woods and clearings from New England and Quebec to Georgia through the southeastern uplands, also from Minnesota to eastern Texas. The flowers appear in July and August.

HORSE-BALM PLATE 169

Collinsonia canadensis *Labiatae*

Also known as Stoneroot and Richweed, Horse-balm is an erect branching plant with stout stems, up to four feet in height, growing from a thick woody perennial root. Large, coarsely toothed leaves, four to eight inches in length, grow opposite each other. The small flowers form a loosely spreading terminal cluster which is sometimes a foot in length. Each flower is strongly lemon-scented. The bell-shaped calyx is two-lipped and the slightly irregular corolla has four equal lobes with a fifth which is enlarged and fringed. Horse-balm grows in moist woods from southern New England to Florida and Arkansas; it also occurs westward to Ontario and Wisconsin. The flowering period is from July to September.

FALSE DRAGONHEAD PLATE 170

Physostegia virginiana *Labiatae*

This member of the Mint family has slender erect stems, up to four feet in height, with lanceolate, sharply toothed leaves in pairs, varying in length from two to five inches. False Dragonhead flowers are very showy, borne in a spirelike terminal cluster or dense spike up to eight inches in length. The calyx is bell-shaped, with five pointed teeth; each corolla, about an inch in length, is tubular, expanding at the tip into a concave rounded upper lip and a spreading three-lobed lower lip. The behavior of the flowers when handled has given this species also the name of Obedient-plant. False Dragonhead grows in damp woods and along stream margins from southern Canada to inland North Carolina and west to Minnesota and Missouri. It is widely cultivated and frequently escapes to become a roadside flower far from its original range. The flowering period is from June to September.

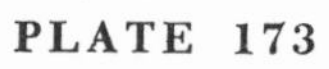

PLATE 173

(*left*) **Common Nightshade,** ***Solanum nigrum*** (*right*) **Bittersweet,** ***Solanum dulcamara***

PLATE 174

Moth Mullein, *Verbascum blattaria*

PURPLE BERGAMOT

Monarda media *Labiatae*

This species resembles the wild bergamot, but the flowers are more reddish-purple than lilac; the bracts of the inflorescence are more conspicuous and darker purple than those of wild bergamot. Purple Bergamot grows naturally from New York to Indiana and southward to the highlands of Tennessee and North Carolina; elsewhere it has escaped from cultivation. It is found in moist thickets, where it flowers from July to September.

HOODED SKULLCAP

PLATE 171

Scutellaria epilobiifolia *Labiatae*

The numerous species of Skullcap can all be recognized by the peculiar shape of the corolla, which becomes an elongated, curved, ascending tube with a dilated throat. Terminating the tube are two lips, the upper short and either entire or slightly notched, the lower lip spreading and three-lobed. These are bitter rather than aromatic plants; they have the Mint family's characteristic opposite leaves and perennial roots. The Hooded Skullcap grows erect, one to three feet in height, with ovate pointed leaves which are often heart-shaped at the base. The flowers, up to an inch in length, grow singly or in small clusters in the upper leaf axils; each corolla has a helmet-shaped upper lip. The usual color is blue-violet with a white throat and tube; however, rose-colored and white varieties occur. Hooded Skullcap prefers gravelly or rocky shores and wet meadows for its home; its range is from Newfoundland across to Alaska and from Delaware west to Arizona and California. The flowers first appear in June and continue through September.

BASIL PLATE 171

Satureja vulgaris *Labiatae*

This is a European perennial which has become naturalized in pastures and along roadsides in some of the eastern states. Basil has a creeping base and ascending stems which grow to a height of several feet; the foliage is densely hairy. The inflorescence is a compact head growing from the upper leaf axils and accompanied by a cluster of leaflike bracts. The tubular calyx, also hairy, is gradually incurved, with bristle-tipped lobes; the corolla is two-lipped, with the lower lip enlarged and notched. The flowering period is from June to September.

HEAL-ALL PLATE 172

Prunella vulgaris *Labiatae*

There are few fields and roadsides in any part of the country which do not have purple patches of this common species, originally from Europe but now practically a native member of our flora. Heal-all, or Selfheal, is a low-growing perennial seldom more than a foot in height, with four-angled, ascending or sprawling stems. The leaves are ovate or tapering, with a margin which is entire or notched with a few blunt teeth. The inflorescence is a compact, flat-topped spike or head. Each flower is accompanied by a bractlike floral leaf, bracts and flowers making up the inflorescence. The two-lipped corolla has an over-arching upper lip and a spreading or reflexed lower lip with three lobes. Heal-all can be found in blossom from late spring to early autumn. White and rose-colored forms are not uncommon.

PLATE 175

(*left*) **Wood Betony,** ***Pedicularis canadensis*** (*right*) **Painted Cup,** ***Castilleja coccinea***

PLATE 176

(*above*) **Common Speedwell,** ***Veronica officinalis*** (*below*) **Culver's-root,**
Veronicastrum virginicum

BLUECURLS

PLATE 171

Trichostema dichotomum

Labiatae

This small annual is also known as Bastard Pennyroyal. Growing usually less than two feet in height, it bears oblong or lanceolate leaves, blunt at the tip, and one to three inches in length. Numerous small flowers appear in a spreading open cluster. Each flower has a deeply five-parted, irregular calyx and a two-lipped corolla whose tubular portion is shorter than the lobed margin. Usually blue, the flowers also occur in pink or whitish varieties. Bluecurls grows in dry open soil of fields and sunny thickets from Maine to North Carolina, west to Michigan; its flowers appear in late summer, from August to October.

WOOD SAGE

Teucrium occidentale

Labiatae

This is a stout-stemmed and hairy plant, growing from one to three feet high; the lanceolate or ovate leaves have sharply-toothed margins. Purplish-pink flowers are borne in dense terminal spikelike clusters, with conspicuously hairy calyx and bracts. Each flower is about half an inch long, with a short tubular portion and an irregular five-lobed margin. Wood Sage is found on alluvial soil from Maine to British Columbia and southward to New Mexico; the flowers appear during July and August. A related species, distinguished as American Wood Sage (*Teucrium canadense*) with less hairy bracts and flower parts, is found south to Florida and Texas.

WOOD MINT

PLATE 172

Blephilia ciliata — *Labiatae*

This is a somewhat downy plant of dry woods and thickets, common in all the eastern states except the Gulf region. It is a perennial growing to a height of two or three feet, with ovate to lanceolate leaves which on the flowering stems are practically sessile. The upper lip of the calyx has three lobes prolonged into hairlike tips; the corolla has an inflated throat and is nearly equally two-lipped with the upper lip erect and the lower one spreading. Wood Mint has a flowering period from June to August.

CATNIP

Nepeta cataria — *Labiatae*

This European species has escaped to become a wild flower and weed over much of the country; it is a pungent-smelling perennial two or three feet in height with long-stemmed ovate leaves and whitish flowers, dotted with purple, crowded near the tips of the stems and branches. Catnip flowers from June to September.

AMERICAN WILD MINT

Mentha arvensis — *Labiatae*

This familiar aromatic perennial has branching stems several feet tall, growing from a perennial root which freely reproduces by suckers. Clusters of small flowers are whorled in the axils of the leaves; each flower has a hairy calyx and a white or pink corolla with a four-lobed margin. Wild Mint thrives in gravelly damp soil, along stream and lake shores, from New England to Virginia and west to the plains states. The flowering period is from July to September.

PLATE 177

(*left*) **Common Mullein,** ***Verbascum thapsus*** (*right*) **Hedge Hyssop,** ***Gratiola aurea***

PLATE 178

(*left*) **Butter-and-eggs,** ***Linaria vulgaris*** (*right*) **Blue Toadflax,** ***Linaria canadensis***

The Nightshade Family

Solanaceae

The Nightshade family is a large one in the tropical portions of Central and South America, where most of its 2,200 species are found; only about a hundred of these occur in the United States. For the most part they are herbaceous plants or woody climbers with a colorless sap and alternate leaves. The family is best known for its poisonous and narcotic members, and for those with edible portions. Among the former can be mentioned belladonna, jimsonweed, deadly nightshade, and tobacco; among the latter, potatoes, eggplants, tomatoes, and the various peppers. The flowers are regular, or only slightly irregular, with tubular or funnel-shaped corollas. The fruit is usually a berry (exemplified by the tomato) or a capsule. From this family comes the ornamental petunia, a native of South America.

COMMON NIGHTSHADE

PLATE 173

Solanum nigrum

Solanaceae

This naturalized European species is a spreading annual with ovate leaves borne alternately on stems which reach a height of four feet. Small flower clusters appear on stout stalks near the tips of the branches. Each flower has a regular, five-lobed calyx and a symmetrically wheel-shaped corolla of five segments. The fruit is a globular, dull black berry. Common Nightshade grows along roadsides and in old fields and pastures along the entire eastern coast; it flowers from May to October.

BITTERSWEET

PLATE 173

Solanum dulcamara — *Solanaceae*

This sprawling, slender, woody vine is another European species which has established itself on fences and hedgerows throughout the eastern states. Its orange-red berries are more familiar than its violet flowers. The vines grow to a length of eight or ten feet, and bear ovate, alternate leaves which taper to a point. Small clusters of flowers grow at the leafy tips of the branches. Each flower has a cup-shaped, toothed calyx and a regular corolla of five spreading petals. The peculiar name "bittersweet" arose from the experiences of early naturalists who claimed the roots tasted bitter when first chewed, later tasted sweet. The berries, if eaten in quantity, are poisonous to cattle and children. Related species include the coarse, weedy Horsenettle (*Solanum carolinense*), a prickly perennial with larger flowers of violet or white, found in waste ground from southern New England to Florida and Texas, west to Nebraska.

GROUND-CHERRY

Physalis heterophylla — *Solanaceae*

There are almost fifty different kinds of Ground-cherry, native and introduced, in the United States. This common member of the group, which grows from one to several feet high, has sticky and hairy stems and leaves. Bell-shaped, drooping, greenish-yellow flowers are usually borne singly in the leaf axils. The fruit is a small, sweet-tasting, yellow berry enclosed in an inflated calyx. Ground-cherries grow in dry open woods from New England to South Carolina, west to Oklahoma and Texas; the flowers appear between June and September.

PLATE 179

(*left*) **Hairy Beardtongue,** ***Penstemon hirsutus*** (*right*) **White Penstemon,** ***Penstemon digitalis***

PLATE 180

(*left*) **False Foxglove, *Gerardia flava* (*right*) Square-stemmed Monkey-flower, *Mimulus ringens***

JIMSONWEED

Datura stramonium *Solanaceae*

This poisonous species introduced from warmer regions has become a dangerous weed throughout the United States; all parts of the plant are poisonous because of the presence of the alkaloid, hyoscyamine. Children are often poisoned by eating the unripe seed pods; the symptoms are dry skin, dilated pupils, temporary loss of vision, and in severe cases, convulsions. Jimsonweed is a stout plant, growing to a height of five feet, with ovate lobed leaves and white or violet, trumpet-shaped flowers up to four inches in length. The fruit, often called Thorn-apple, is a prickly capsule containing large flat seeds. The flowering period is from July to October.

The Figwort Family

Scrophulariaceae

The Figwort family is a large but relatively unimportant one, except ornamentally, with some 3,000 species widely distributed on all the continents. These are mostly herbaceous plants and small shrubs with either alternate or opposite leaves, and irregular flowers with a tubular, four- or five-lobed corolla. One of the petals is sometimes extended into a spur or is saclike. The Figwort family is well represented in eastern United States by thirty-four genera, one of them an ornamental flowering tree introduced from Asia and called the Princess Tree (*Paulownia tomentosa*). Numerous garden plants are included in the family: Foxgloves (Digitalis), Snapdragons (Antirrhinum), Speedwells (Veronica), Beardtongues (Penstemon) and Monkey-flowers (Mimulus).

MOTH MULLEIN

PLATE 174

Verbascum blattaria

Scrophulariaceae

This is an Old World biennial which may be seen all summer long in American fields and along roadsides. Erect, stiff, and smoothish stems grow to a height of three or four feet, bearing alternate, oblong or ovate leaves about two inches in length; the basal leaves are often much larger. The large flowers, about an inch in length, are clustered in an elongated spike-like inflorescence a foot or more in extent. Each flower has a five-lobed, slightly irregular corolla with a short tube and broad rounded lobes.

COMMON MULLEIN

PLATE 177

Verbascum thapsus

Scrophulariaceae

This is another European species which has become a familiar roadside weed. It is so densely woolly on both foliage and stems that it is also known as Flannel-plant. The basal leaves form a large but compact rosette. From this rises a tall, stiff, leafy stem bearing inch-long flowers compactly clustered in a dense spike throughout the summer.

WOOD BETONY

PLATE 175

Pedicularis canadensis

Scrophulariaceae

Wood Betony, or Lousewort, is a tufted plant usually under a foot in height, with fernlike, pinnately lobed leaves. The flowers are borne in dense terminal spikes, intermingled with leafy bracts. Each flower has a minutely toothed calyx and a decidedly two-lipped corolla with a flattened and beaked upper lip, a crested and three-lobed lower lip. Wood Betony grows in woods and clearings from southern Canada to Florida and northern Mexico; the flowering period is from April to June.

PLATE 181

(*above*) **Southern Turtlehead, *Chelone obliqua*** (*below*) **Turtlehead, *Chelone glabra***

PLATE 182

(*left*) **Purple Gerardia, *Gerardia purpurea*** (*right*) **Blue-eyed Mary, *Collinsia verna***

PAINTED CUP

PLATE 175

Castilleja coccinea

Scrophulariaceae

It is the leaflike bracts, tipped with red, and growing at the base of the flowers, which give this plant its unusual aspect and its other name of Indian Paintbrush. The hidden flowers are in a terminal cluster, each with an inconspicuous two-lipped corolla of yellowish green. Painted Cup is an annual with a rosette of ovate or elliptic basal leaves from among which rise stems up to two feet in height. It grows in grassy meadows and wet lowlands from New England and Manitoba to Florida and Texas. The flowers appear from April to August. Similar species are found farther west.

COMMON SPEEDWELL

PLATE 176

Veronica officinalis

Scrophulariaceae

The Speedwells include both ornamental plants and weeds. Though they are of varied appearance, they are mostly low-growing plants with blue or white flowers in terminal or axillary racemes. The Common Speedwell, or Gypsyweed, is a hairy and prostrate plant with creeping stems, considered by some to be so well established that it can be called a native plant, by others a naturalized European species. The ovate to elliptical, toothed leaves, about two inches in length, are thick and short-stemmed. Small flowers are produced in axillary clusters, each flower with a calyx of four sepals and an irregular corolla with four rounded lobes. Common Speedwell grows on dry hillsides and in open woods, from southern Canada southward to the Carolinas and Tennessee. It flowers from May to July.

CULVER'S-ROOT

PLATE 176

Veronicastrum virginicum

Scrophulariaceae

Culver's-root is a stout erect plant growing as tall as a man, unbranched except for the inflorescence. Lanceolate or oblong leaves are borne in whorls or pairs, each leaf three to six inches long and tapering to a sharp tip. Many small flowers are produced in a large branching terminal cluster which reaches a maximum length of nine inches. Each tiny flower has a tubular corolla with four nearly equal lobes, beyond which project the style and stamens. Culver's-root grows in moist woods and meadows from southern New England to northern Florida and Texas. The flowers can be found from June to September.

HEDGE HYSSOP

PLATE 177

Gratiola aurea

Scrophulariaceae

This member of the Figwort family is a low-growing perennial with fleshy rhizomes. The alternate leaves, lanceolate or linear in shape, clasp the four-angled, creeping or ascending stems. Hedge Hyssop rarely grows more than a foot in height. The flowers are borne singly in the axils of the upper leaves; each flower has a narrowly five-lobed calyx and an irregular corolla with a cylindrical tubular base and a two-lipped margin. The upper lip is entire, the lower is three-lobed. Hedge Hyssop grows on sandy or gravelly shores and in open swamps, from Newfoundland southward along the coastal plain to northern Florida, also inland to Illinois and North Dakota. The flowering period is from June to September.

PLATE 183

(*left*) Horned Bladderwort, *Utricularia cornuta* (*center*) Purple Bladderwort, *Utricularia purpurea* (*right*) Tall Bellflower, *Campanula americana*

PLATE 184

(*left*) **Great Lobelia,** ***Lobelia siphilitica*** (*right*) **Cardinal-flower,** ***Lobelia cardinalis***

BUTTER-AND-EGGS — PLATE 178

Linaria vulgaris — *Scrophulariaceae*

Few naturalized European plants have become so familiar in the wild as Butter-and-eggs, found along roadsides and in waste places throughout North America; it has a long flowering period, from May to October. Perennial roots give rise to slender stems one to three feet tall and bearing narrowly linear, alternate leaves. The small but showy flowers, like miniature garden snapdragons, are produced in compact terminal racemes. An inch-long corolla is spurred at the base; the upper lip is erect and two-lobed; the lower lip, which is spreading and three-lobed, has a rounded projection, deep orange in color, which closes the throat of the corolla.

BLUE TOADFLAX — PLATE 178

Linaria canadensis — *Scrophulariaceae*

This is a native species, closely related to butter-and-eggs, with flowers similar in structure. It is a more slender plant, usually two feet or less in height, and may be either an annual or perennial. Basal offshoots have the habit of forming rosettes of linear to oblong leaves which survive the winter. It flowers from April to September. Blue Toadflax grows in sterile dry soil, where it is often a weed; its range is in southern Canada and eastern United States to Texas and the Dakotas.

WHITE PENSTEMON — PLATE 179

Penstemon digitalis — *Scrophulariaceae*

The Penstemons or Beardtongues form a strictly American genus, with a great variety of species native in different parts of the country. The leaves are usually opposite, either entire or toothed; the showy flowers are borne in large terminal clusters. The tubular corolla is dilated at the throat, and is characteristically two-lipped; the upper lip is two-lobed and the lower lip divided into three marginal segments. White Penstemon has purplish stems, two to four feet tall, bearing opposite, lanceolate leaves. The inflorescence is a terminal spreading cluster. This species was originally restricted to meadows and prairies of the Mississippi valley, but has spread from southern Quebec to Texas. The flowering period is from May to July.

HAIRY BEARDTONGUE — PLATE 179

Penstemon hirsutus — *Scrophulariaceae*

This species has whitish hairy stems, as its common name suggests; the plants grow one to three feet high, and bear opposite leaves which are more narrow and tapering than in the accompanying species. The flowers are grouped in an open terminal cluster; each has a five-lobed calyx and an inch-long corolla tube dilated at the opening and edged by the characteristic upper and lower lips. Hairy Beardtongue grows on dry or rocky ground from New England to inland Virginia, west to Wisconsin. The flowers appear in June and July.

FALSE FOXGLOVE — PLATE 180

Gerardia flava — *Scrophulariaceae*

Gerardia, like Penstemon, is a purely American genus of plants. The showy pink, purple or yellow flowers, usually in spikes, appear in late summer or autumn. The yellow-flowered species are known as False Foxgloves. They are rank plants, often growing to a height of five or six feet. The opposite leaves on the stem of *Gerardia flava* are toothed, the basal leaves pinnately lobed. Each funnel-shaped flower has a regular five-lobed calyx and a smooth corolla, broadly expanded at its margin and only obscurely two-lipped. False Foxglove grows in deciduous woods from New England to Maryland, west to Minnesota; it flowers from July to September.

PLATE 185

(*left*) **European Bellflower,** ***Campanula rapunculoides*** (*right*) **Harebell,** ***Campanula rotundifolia***

PLATE 186

(*left*) **Venus's Looking-glass,** ***Specularia perfoliata*** (*right*) **Pale Lobelia,** ***Lobelia spicata***

FERN-LEAVED FALSE FOXGLOVE

Gerardia pedicularia *Scrophulariaceae*

A much-branched erect annual, reaching a height of three feet, this species is distinguished by its fernlike foliage; the opposite leaves, one to three inches long, are deeply lobed and dissected with the appearance of Wood Betony (Pedicularis) leaves. Flowers about an inch long are borne in the upper leaf axils; the yellow corolla is slightly funnel-shaped, hairy on the outside, with five spreading rounded lobes. Fern-leaved False Foxglove grows in dry woods and clearings from Maine to North Carolina, west to the Great Lakes states. It flowers in August and September.

PURPLE GERARDIA

PLATE 182

Gerardia purpurea *Scrophulariaceae*

This is a branching, usually slender-stemmed, annual growing to a height of three feet, with many small, linear, opposite leaves. The flowers, commonly purple but occasionally white, are borne on short stalks at the ends of the branches. Each flower has a bell-shaped calyx with five pointed teeth half as long as the corolla tube; the corolla has a spreading and slightly irregular five-lobed margin. Purple Gerardia thrives in damp meadows, and can be found from southern New England to Florida and Texas, west to the plains states. The flowering period is from July to September.

SQUARE-STEMMED MONKEY-FLOWER

PLATE 180

Mimulus ringens *Scrophulariaceae*

Wet fields, swamps, and stream margins are the habitats of this Monkey-flower, which grows one to three feet tall. Lanceolate leaves with toothed margins are produced in pairs along the stems. Solitary long-stalked flowers are borne in the axils of the upper leaves. Each flower has a five-lobed calyx and a markedly irregular corolla with a two-lipped margin. The Square-stemmed Monkey-flower is common throughout the eastern and central states from Canada to the Gulf. It can be found in bloom from June through September.

SOUTHERN TURTLEHEAD

PLATE 181

Chelone obliqua

Scrophulariaceae

Snakehead is an equally good name for any of the Turtleheads. This one is a plant of wet woods and cypress swamps, from Maryland south to Florida and Mississippi. The stout stems, growing to a height of several feet, bear opposite, elliptic leaves which are a pale green on their undersurface. The flowers are borne in an elongated terminal spike; each flower has a unique appearance because the expanded upper lip arches over and more or less conceals the lower lip. This gives the flower, in profile, a resemblance to a turtle's head. The flowers appear from late August to October.

TURTLEHEAD

PLATE 181

Chelone glabra

Scrophulariaceae

Closely related to the accompanying species, this Turtlehead, or Snake-head, has more definitely stalked leaves. Plants reach a height of three feet, and thrive in wet woods, roadside ditches, and along stream margins. In varying forms this species grows throughout most of the eastern and central states, flowering from July through October. While the flowers are most often white, the corollas sometimes are colored rose or purple.

PLATE 187

Trumpet-creeper, *Campsis radicans*

PLATE 188

(*left*) **Cross-vine, *Bignonia capreolata*** (*right*) **Ruellia, *Ruellia humilis***

BLUE-EYED MARY PLATE 182

Collinsia verna *Scrophulariaceae*

Blue-eyed Mary is a delicate annual, four to twenty inches tall, found in moist woods and on alluvial soil from New York to Kansas and south to Arkansas. The opposite, elliptical or ovate leaves have toothed margins. Flowers half an inch in length are clustered in a loose raceme, each flower with a regular, five-lobed calyx and an irregular two-lipped corolla. The flowering period is from April to June.

The Bladderwort Family

Lentibulariaceae

The members of the Bladderwort family are known as insectivorous or carnivorous plants, for the same reasons as previously described for the Pitcher-plant and related families. Here, however, the plants are aquatic or mud-inhabiting species, with the submerged leaves bearing peculiar bladders which act as traps in catching small aquatic animals. These bladders are very small, appearing as nodules on the threadlike compound leaves. There are less than 300 species in the Bladderwort family, most of them in the one genus Utricularia. The flowers are irregular, with a two-lipped corolla, of which the larger lower lip has a prominent "palate" spurred in the front. The fruit is a capsule.

HORNED BLADDERWORT PLATE 183

Utricularia cornuta *Lentibulariaceae*

This species of Bladderwort is terrestrial, growing in bogs and on sandy shores, with creeping stems and hairlike simple leaves buried in the mud. Spikelike racemes of irregular flowers are borne on wiry leafless flowering stalks ten or twelve inches in height. Horned Bladderwort is found from Newfoundland to northern Ontario, south to Delaware and Texas. The flowers appear in June and continue through September.

PURPLE BLADDERWORT PLATE 183
Utricularia purpurea *Lentibulariaceae*

This is a pond-dwelling species whose submerged stems bear compound floating leaves subdivided into threadlike segments, which develop the bladderlike traps at their tips. The flowers are similar in structure to those of the horned bladderwort. Purple Bladderwort often clogs slow-moving streams and swampy ponds with its tangle of submerged stems; it is a common aquatic plant throughout the East from Canada to the Gulf. The flowers appear during the summer, rising above the water on long slender stalks.

The Bellflower Family

Campanulaceae

The Bellflower family is composed chiefly of herbaceous annuals or perennials, numbering about 1,500 species and widely distributed in temperate and subtropical regions. The leaves are usually alternate and simple; the flowers may occur either singly in the leaf axils or in clusters or heads. The corolla of the flower is tubular or bell-shaped, for the most part symmetrical and regular. The fruit is a capsule.

TALL BELLFLOWER PLATE 183
Campanula americana *Campanulaceae*

This member of the family is a tall annual, growing to a height of five or six feet, with unbranched stems bearing alternate lanceolate and toothed leaves. The showy flowers are clustered in the axils of the upper leaves, or are seated above small leaflike bracts. Each flower has a broadly five-lobed corolla whose segments form a flattened wheel-shaped structure from which projects the upward-curving style. Tall Bellflower thrives in rich moist woods from New York to Florida, west to Minnesota and Missouri; its flowering period is from June to August.

PLATE 189

(*left*) **Northern Bedstraw,** ***Galium boreale*** (*right*) **Yellow Bedstraw,** ***Galium verum***

PLATE 190

(*left*) **Purple Houstonia,** ***Houstonia purpurea*** (*right*) **Bluets,** ***Houstonia caerulea***

EUROPEAN BELLFLOWER — PLATE 185

Campanula rapunculoides — *Campanulaceae*

This species of Bellflower is a European plant which has escaped to roadsides and fields throughout the northeastern and north central states, where it can be found in flower from July to September. It is a slender-stemmed plant growing to a height of three feet, and bears alternate ovate leaves of which the upper ones are sessile or short-stalked. Nodding flowers in the axils of leaflike bracts form spirelike terminal racemes. The showy corollas are an inch in length with gracefully spreading pointed lobes around the margin of the bell-shaped flower.

HAREBELL — PLATE 185

Campanula rotundifolia — *Campanulaceae*

The Harebell, or Bluebell, is a slender perennial with basal leaves which are rounded heart-shaped; the stem leaves are very different, being narrowly linear. Each nodding flower, borne on a long delicate stalk, has a calyx with prominent slender lobes and a regular bell-shaped corolla with five spreading lobes. Known in Europe and Asia as well as North America, the Harebell grows freely on sunny banks, along shores, and in meadows. It flowers continuously from June to September or later.

VENUS'S LOOKING-GLASS — PLATE 186

Specularia perfoliata — *Campanulaceae*

The long, usually unbranched, stems of Venus's Looking-glass bear small rounded leaves whose heart-shaped bases clasp the angled stems. Plants grow to a height of three feet, bearing the showy flowers singly or in small clusters in the upper leaf axils. Each flower has a regular five-lobed calyx and a corolla of five spreading segments. Venus's Looking-glass grows in dry sandy ground throughout the eastern and central states and in adjacent Canada. Its flowers appear throughout the summer months, sometimes as early as May.

GREAT LOBELIA

PLATE 184

Lobelia siphilitica

Campanulaceae

The Lobelias differ from the preceding members of the Bellflower family in having irregular two-lipped flowers. They are, in fact, sometimes put into their own family, the Lobeliaceae. Great Lobelia is a tall and stiffly erect plant with angular stems which produce basal offshoots. Thus the plant survives the winter as a perennial. The leaves are alternate and lanceolate with a toothed margin; in the elongated terminal spikes of showy flowers, each flower is borne in the axil of a leafy bract. The two-lipped corolla has an upper lip of two erect lobes, a lower lip of three spreading segments. Great Lobelia grows in low woods and swamps from southern New England southward to North Carolina and west to South Dakota and Kansas. The flowering period is in August and September.

CARDINAL-FLOWER

PLATE 184

Lobelia cardinalis

Campanulaceae

Like the preceding species, this member of the genus Lobelia is also perennial by basal offshoots. Unbranched coarse stems grow to a height of four feet, bearing numerous alternate, lanceolate leaves. The brilliantly colored flowers form a dense terminal raceme four to twenty inches in length. Each flower is large, up to two inches in length, with a spreading, narrowly-lobed lower lip; the entire flower has the appearance of a brilliant orchid. Cardinal-flower grows in meadows edging small streams, and other moist open habitats; it is common throughout most of the eastern and central states from Canada to the Gulf. The flowers can be found from July through September.

PLATE 191

(*left*) **Yellow Honeysuckle,** ***Lonicera dioica*** (*right*) **Twinflower,** ***Linnaea borealis***
(*below*) **Partridge-berry,** ***Mitchella repens***

PLATE 192

(*left*) **Coral Honeysuckle,** ***Lonicera sempervirens*** (*right*) **Japanese Honeysuckle,** ***Lonicera japonica***

PALE LOBELIA PLATE 186

Lobelia spicata *Campanulaceae*

This is a simple or slightly branched plant, two or three feet in height, with the middle and upper leaves lanceolate and sessile. The flowers are borne in a slender, dense spike; each flower is much smaller than in other members of the group. Pale Lobelia grows in rich meadows and fields, from New England to Georgia and west to Minnesota and Arkansas. The flowers appear in June and continue through August.

The Bignonia Family

Bignoniaceae

Unlike most of the preceding families, the Bignonia family is composed primarily of shrubs, trees and vines. Most of the 750 species are tropical in distribution, occurring in northern South America, tropical Asia and Africa. A familiar tree belonging to this family is the catalpa; here also is the jacaranda, an ornamental tree planted in the southern states. Foliage in this family consists of opposite leaves which are often pinnately compound. The flowers are tubular and irregular; the fruits, capsules with usually winged seeds.

TRUMPET-CREEPER PLATE 187

Campsis radicans *Bignoniaceae*

This vigorous vine of woods, swamps, and fence-rows often becomes a weed as it covers useful trees and shrubs with its mass of foliage. The pinnately compound leaves consist of nine to eleven ovate leaflets, lacking tendrils; the vines climb by means of aerial rootlets. Showy flowers are clustered in a large rounded inflorescence, each flower several inches in length with a conspicuous funnel-shaped corolla, brilliantly colored orange and scarlet. The resemblance to a trumpet is very marked, with an expanded five-lobed margin. Trumpet-creeper is found from New Jersey to Florida and Texas; but it has become naturalized as far north as Connecticut and west to Michigan. It flowers from July to September.

CROSS-VINE PLATE 188

Bignonia capreolata *Bignoniaceae*

This is a tendril-bearing vine with each compound leaf reduced to two ovate or oblong leaflets. It too is a high-climbing woody vine, sometimes reaching the tops of high trees; it becomes an objectionable weed when it encumbers the branches and foliage of trees, especially in the more southern states. The name "Cross-vine" refers to the cross formed in the wood, when seen in transverse section. The flowers are borne singly on long stalks, each flower somewhat bell-shaped with an open mouth, edged with five spreading lobes which form a slightly two-lipped corolla. Cross-vine is found in rich woods and swamps from Maryland to Florida and Louisiana, west to Missouri; it flowers in April and June.

The Acanthus Family

Acanthaceae

The Acanthus family, although a large one in the tropics (2,200 species), has few representatives in the United States. The members are perennial herbaceous plants and shrubs, with opposite simple leaves and irregular tubular flowers. There are only a few species in the United States.

PLATE 193

(*left*) **Yarrow,** ***Achillea millefolium*** (*right*) **Maryland Golden Aster,** ***Chrysopsis mariana***

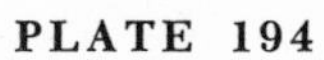

PLATE 194

(*above*) **Beggar-ticks, *Bidens aristosa*** (*lower left*) **Purple-stemmed Aster, *Aster puniceus*** (*lower right*) **Prairie Daisy, *Aphanostephus skirrobasis***

RUELLIA PLATE 188

Ruellia humilis *Acanthaceae*

Ruellia is a hairy plant one to two feet tall, found in open woods and on dry prairies from New Jersey to Florida, west to Michigan and Kansas. Oval or elliptic leaves grow opposite each other, often hairy on the veins and margins. The flowers occur in the axils of the upper leaves, each flower with a regular calyx terminating in five long narrow segments and a funnel-shaped corolla with five notched lobes. The flowering period is from June to August.

The Madder Family

Rubiaceae

The Madder family includes woody and herbaceous plants with opposite entire leaves, or whorls of leaves; the family is closely related to the Honeysuckle family. Like many of the other families represented by a few wild flower species in the United States, the Madder family is a large one (5,000 species) in the tropical and subtropical regions. Economically it is important for the coffee plant (Coffea), quinine (Cinchona), and ipecac (Cephaelis); the gardener has made use of a fragrant member, the gardenia (Gardenia).

NORTHERN BEDSTRAW PLATE 189

Galium boreale *Rubiaceae*

The stems of this plant are four-angled, like those of the mints. They may grow to a height of several feet, but often sprawl, and bear lanceolate or linear leaves in whorls of four. Minute flowers are produced in compact terminal clusters. Each flower has a toothless calyx and a four-lobed wheel-shaped corolla. Northern Bedstraw grows on rocky soil and gravelly beaches from Canada and Alaska southward to West Virginia and New Mexico. The flowering period is from June to August.

YELLOW BEDSTRAW

PLATE 189

Galium verum

Rubiaceae

This is a European species which has become naturalized in dry fields and along roadsides in the northeastern and north central states. Smooth erect stems grow from a perennial creeping base, bearing leaves in whorls of six or eight. The crowded small flowers form a stiff terminal cluster. Yellow Bedstraw flowers from June to August also.

PURPLE HOUSTONIA

PLATE 190

Houstonia purpurea

Rubiaceae

Erect stems, often a foot or more in height, arise in a tuft from a semi-woody crown; the ovate or elliptic leaves along the upper stems occur in pairs. Numerous small flowers are borne in a terminal spreading cluster, each flower with a calyx of four sepals and a regular, tubular corolla with four spreading petals. Purple Houstonia grows in open woods and on rocky slopes from Delaware to Georgia, west to Iowa and Oklahoma. It flowers in May and June.

BLUETS

PLATE 190

Houstonia caerulea

Rubiaceae

This familiar wild flower, also known as Innocence and Quaker-ladies, is a tufted or matted plant whose erect stems rarely exceed eight inches in height. Some leaves grow in a basal rosette; these are oblong to elliptic in shape. The stem leaves are smaller and narrower, and grow opposite each other. The flowers are small and delicately fashioned, each with four sepals and a funnel-shaped corolla expanding into four spreading lobes. Bluets form extensive beds on open grassy slopes and fields from south-eastern Canada to Georgia, west to Wisconsin and Missouri. The flowers appear in April and continue until the first frost.

PLATE 195

(*left*) Blue Lettuce, *Lactuca pulchella* (*right*) Swamp Thistle, *Cirsium muticum*

PLATE 196

(*left*) **Chrysogonum,** ***Chrysogonum virginianum*** (*right*) **Baker's Golden Aster,** ***Chrysopsis bakeri***

BUTTONBUSH

Cephalanthus occidentalis — *Rubiaceae*

Bordering the ponds and streams of the Atlantic coast states from Maine to Florida and in California, Buttonbush is a familiar shrubby member of the Madder family. It is known, in fact, in various regions from Canada to Mexico. The ovate leaves grow in pairs or whorls, and the small white flowers form spherical compact balls an inch or two in diameter. The flowers appear in July and August.

PARTRIDGE-BERRY — PLATE 191

Mitchella repens — *Rubiaceae*

Clinging close to the ground in damp woods and on sandy knolls, the trailing evergreen mat of the Partridge-berry may be seen at any time of year. In winter it is studded with red berries. The stems root at the nodes, and bear pairs of shining oval to heart-shaped leaves. Fragrant waxy-white flowers grow in pairs; the funnel-shaped corolla has four recurved or spreading lobes, hairy on the inner side. The ovaries of the paired flowers are united, so that each fruit is a globular berry formed by two united one-seeded drupes. Partridge-berry is found from southeastern Canada to Florida, west to Minnesota and Texas, being especially abundant in pine forests. The flowers develop during June and July.

The Honeysuckle Family

Caprifoliaceae

Most of the members of the Honeysuckle family are shrubs or vines with opposite leaves, either simple or compound, and funnel-shaped, regular flowers. It is a family of only 275 species, primarily found in the northern hemisphere. Elderberry (Sambucus) is a familiar shrub in the family.

TWINFLOWER PLATE 191

Linnaea borealis *Caprifoliaceae*

This is a rare and beautiful little wild flower of cool northern forests, its slender creeping stems growing on peaty hummocks from Maine to Maryland and in northern California. The small rounded leaves are evergreen. Pairs of short erect stems bear single, nodding, fragrant flowers, each with a bell-like corolla terminating in five lobes. The flowering period is from June to August.

YELLOW HONEYSUCKLE PLATE 191

Lonicera dioica *Caprifoliaceae*

Also known as Mountain Honeysuckle, this shrubby vine has opposite elliptic leaves and axillary clusters of irregular flowers with a minute calyx and a tubular, two-lipped corolla. Each flower grows to be almost an inch in length. Yellow Honeysuckle produces red berries in autumn. Its range is from Maine to Georgia, west to Missouri, growing on rocky banks and in dry woods; the flowering period is from May to July.

CORAL HONEYSUCKLE PLATE 192

Lonicera sempervirens *Caprifoliaceae*

This species is also known as Trumpet Honeysuckle; it is a high-climbing vine with oval leaves whose bases are usually united around the stem. The flowers are clustered at the ends of the branches. Each flower has a trumpet-shaped corolla, about two inches in length, terminating in a slightly two-lipped margin. Coral Honeysuckle grows in woods, especially on low ground, from southern New England to Nebraska, south to Florida and Texas. The flowers can be found March to July.

PLATE 197

(*above*) **Common Tickseed,** ***Coreopsis major*** (*below*) **Haplopappus,** ***Haplopappus spinulosus***

PLATE 198

(*left*) White-topped Aster, *Sericocarpus asteroides* (*right*) Thoroughwort, *Eupatorium hyssopifolium*

JAPANESE HONEYSUCKLE

PLATE 192

Lonicera japonica — *Caprifoliaceae*

Few other naturalized species have established themselves so thoroughly or perniciously as a roadside weed. The destructive tangle of Japanese Honeysuckle vines, semi-evergreen in the southern part of the range, covers the native vegetation with a strangling blanket; the vines even encircle trees and shrubs in their rank growth. The elliptic leaves grow opposite each other, and bear in their axils the fragrant, funnel-shaped flowers with a strongly two-lipped margin. Japanese Honeysuckle is abundant from Maryland south to the Gulf states and west to Kansas. The flowering period is from April to July, occasionally again in late autumn.

BUSH HONEYSUCKLE

Diervilla lonicera — *Caprifoliaceae*

This species is a low-growing shrub, three or four feet in height, with opposite, ovate leaves and small clusters of yellow flowers in the axils of the upper leaves or at the ends of the branches. Each flower, about three-quarters of an inch in length, is narrowly funnel-shaped and regular, with a five-lobed margin. Bush Honeysuckle grows in dry woods and clearings from the mountains of North Carolina, inland to Iowa, and northward to Canada. The flowering period is from June to August.

The Composites

Compositae

The Compositae is the largest family of flowering plants, comprising some 20,000 species distributed widely over the earth. The members of the family are predominantly herbaceous plants; a small number are shrubs such as marsh-elder (Iva), groundsel-tree (Baccharis), and sagebrush (Artemisia). For the size of the family, it has very few plants of economic importance; food plants among the Composites include the artichoke (Cynara), lettuce (Lactuca), endive (Cichorium), and salsify (Tragopogon). On the other hand it has contributed a great number of ornamental plants to our gardens: marigolds (Tagetes), sunflowers (Helianthus), bachelor's buttons (Centaurea), zinnias, chrysanthemums, cosmos, dahlias, and asters.

The Composites represent one of the highest specializations in flower structure. In fact, the flower development has become so complex that special terminology is applied to the floral parts. The individual flowers are very small and clustered in the type of inflorescence known as a head. It is this head which is mistaken for a single flower in the daisy, aster or sunflower. The confusion is heightened by the fact that the head is seated on a receptacle which is surrounded by an involucre of bracts which can easily be mistaken for a calyx. If we take a daisy as an example of a Composite flower, we note that around the rim is a number of strap-shaped segments which are white—and which often are mistaken for petals of the daisy "flower"; and in the center is a compact mass of yellow, erect, tubular structures. The daisy "flower" is actually a head composed of two types of flowers. Around the margin are ray-flowers, each one with a flattened strap-shaped corolla. In the center are the tubular flowers of the disk, each with a five-lobed corolla. The calyx of the minute flower is fused with the ovary. The eventual fruit is a small seedlike structure known as an achene. It is often wind-dispersed, as in the dandelion, the soft bristly hairs which carry it being developed at the summit of the calyx.

The heads of Composites show great variety of specialization. Some heads are composed only of strap-shaped, or ligulate, flowers as in chicory and dandelion. Others are composed only of tubular flowers, as in thistles. Still others, like asters and daisies, have heads which are a combination of ligulate and tubular flowers. In identifying the Composites it is helpful to notice which kind of flowers are found in the head. The heads in turn are sometimes clustered in larger masses, as in the asters and goldenrods. The net result is a concentrated flower mass for attracting insects. At the same time it presents the horticulturist with an opportunity for developing showy ornamental flowers. Many of the garden Composites have escaped to become roadside wild flowers, and in some cases obnoxious weeds.

PLATE 199

(*left*) **Wild Sunflower,** ***Helianthus petiolaris*** (*right*) **Swamp Sunflower,** ***Helianthus angustifolius***

PLATE 200

(*left*) **Prairie Coneflower,** ***Ratibida columnifera*** (*right*) **Gray-headed Coneflower,** ***Ratibida pinnata***

YARROW

PLATE 193

Achillea millefolium

Compositae

Before it blooms, this wild flower, also known as Milfoil, sometimes is mistaken for a fern because of its much-divided leaves. A common weed of roadsides, fields and pastures across Canada and throughout most of the United States, Yarrow is a European perennial which has become as familiar as any of our native plants. The stems and branches grow stiffly erect to a height of several feet, the heads grouped in terminal, flat-topped clusters. Each head consists of tubular disk-flowers surrounded by four to six small whitish ray-flowers. Often local colonies can be found with pink or rosy-purple ray-flowers. Yarrow is in blossom from June to September.

BAKER'S GOLDEN ASTER

PLATE 197

Chrysopsis bakeri

Compositae

The various Golden Asters which occur across the country are characterized by having woolly or hairy stems, alternate simple leaves, and flower-heads with generally both ray- and disk-flowers. Baker's Golden Aster, a perennial, has stems up to twelve inches in height, branching above the middle, with oblong pointed leaves an inch or two in length. It flowers from July to September, each head consisting of a central disk of tubular flowers and a margin of showy ray-flowers. The species is found on dry plains and hillsides from the Great Lakes region west to Idaho, southward to New Mexico.

MARYLAND GOLDEN ASTER

PLATE 193

Chrysopsis mariana

Compositae

The Maryland Golden Aster, also a perennial, has stout silky-hairy stems several feet in height bearing alternate, simple, lanceolate leaves. The flower-heads are large and showy, made up of marginal ray-flowers and central tubular flowers, all with a bristly pappus. Each head is seated on a flat receptacle. This Golden Aster grows in dry woods and clearings, from

New York to Ohio and south to Florida and Texas. The flowering period is from August to October. A related species known as Silkgrass (*Chrysopsis nervosa*), with narrowly linear, silky-hairy foliage and yellow flowers, grows in sandy pine and oak woods from Delaware to Florida and Texas.

PRAIRIE DAISY

PLATE 194

Aphanostephus skirrobasis

Compositae

This asterlike annual or biennial grows to a height of sixteen inches, and is found on dry grasslands in New Mexico and Texas, north to Kansas, and also in Florida. The alternate narrow leaves are sometimes toothed or pinnately lobed. A few flower-heads terminate the branches. Each head consists of tubular yellow flowers and has a margin of ray-flowers which may be white, violet, or purple in color. The flowering period is throughout spring and summer.

BEGGAR-TICKS

PLATE 194

Bidens aristosa

Compositae

The many different species in this genus, variously called Bur-marigolds, Tickseeds and in the Southwest, Spanish Needles, are best known for their persistent, prickly achenes which attach themselves to clothing as one wanders through the fields in early autumn. They are annuals and perennials, with opposite leaves and yellow flowers. The ray-flowers, when present, are only three to eight in number. Beggar-ticks is a much-branched plant one to three feet tall, with opposite, pinnately divided leaves. Each flower-head consists of tubular yellowish disk-flowers and a few yellow ray-flowers, borne within a double involucre. The fruit is the familiar needle-pronged achene. The plant can be found either wild or naturalized in low ground throughout most of the eastern and central states. It flowers from August to October.

PLATE 201

(*left*) Southern Blazing Star, *Liatris elegans* (*right*) Prairie Blazing Star, *Liatris punctata*

PLATE 202

Climbing Hempweed, *Mikania scandens*

NODDING BUR-MARIGOLD

Bidens cernua *Compositae*

This species is also known as Sticktight, because of the persistence of its bristly achene. The nodding Bur-marigold has flower-heads a half-inch to an inch in breadth which have the appearance of drooping after flowering. Six to ten yellow ray-flowers surround the yellowish-brown disk-flowers; often the ray-flowers are absent. The leaves are linear or lanceolate and entire. Nodding Bur-marigold grows in swamps and around springs, across Canada and the United States except in the desert and the extreme south. It flowers from August to October.

BLUE LETTUCE PLATE 195

Lactuca pulchella *Compositae*

Of the numerous wild species of lettuce in the United States, Blue Lettuce can serve as a typical representative. It is a pale or downy perennial with stout stems growing to a height of three feet. The upper leaves are usually slender and lanceolate, with entire margins; the lower leaves are larger and pinnately lobed. The flower-heads are few and large, with a cylindrical involucre a half-inch or more in length; each head consists of ray-flowers only. Blue Lettuce grows along river banks and on prairies from Michigan to Wisconsin south to Oklahoma and Missouri. The flowering period is from July to September. The related Prickly Lettuce (*Lactuca scariola*) with spiny-toothed leaves and small clusters of yellow flower-heads, is a naturalized European species found in waste places throughout the United States and Canada. It flowers from June to October.

SWAMP THISTLE

PLATE 195

Cirsium muticum — *Compositae*

All of the common thistles of the genus Cirsium are characterized by prickly, sessile, alternate leaves, and heads made up entirely of tubular flowers. Swamp Thistle is a robust plant with a flowering stem sometimes exceeding the height of a man. It rises from a basal rosette of ovate, deeply lobed leaves. The smaller stem-leaves are pinnately lobed with prickly margins. The bracts of the spherical or cylindrical involucre have spiny tips, and the receptacle is clothed with soft bristles. Swamp Thistle, as the name suggests, grows in low woods and swamps; it is common in southern Canada and the United States west to the Rockies. It flowers from July to September.

BULL THISTLE

PLATE 229

Cirsium vulgare — *Compositae*

This familiar and unpleasantly prickly weed of pastures and roadsides is a European species which has become established throughout most of the United States and southern Canada. The flowering stems, rising from basal leaf rosettes, grow to a height of six feet and are armed with prickly-lobed wings which extend down the stem from beneath the flower-heads. The involucre is spiny. The flowering period is from June to September.

CANADA THISTLE

Cirsium arvense — *Compositae*

This is another naturalized European species which has become a weed in fields and pastures. The involucres and flower-heads are much smaller than either of the two preceding species; the flowers are pinkish-purple, occasionally white.

PLATE 203

American Feverfew, *Parthenium integrifolium*

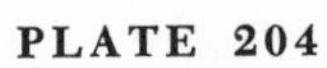

PLATE 204

(*above*) **Sclerolepis,** ***Sclerolepis uniflora*** (*below*) **Coltsfoot,** ***Tussilago farfara***

CHRYSOGONUM

PLATE 196

Chrysogonum virginianum

Compositae

This is a hairy, low-growing perennial, at first almost stemless, later with short stems up to two feet in height, bearing opposite pairs of ovate and pointed leaves with a toothed margin. The solitary flower-heads are borne on long stems, each head seated in an involucre of five or more leaflike bracts. The heads consist of usually five marginal ray-flowers a half-inch in length and a central disk of tubular flowers. Chrysogonum grows in rich woods and shaded rocky banks fom Pennsylvania to Florida and Louisiana; it flowers in April and on into June.

HAPLOPAPPUS

PLATE 197

Haplopappus spinulosus

Compositae

This is a perennial with a woody base and erect leafy stems which grow to a height of several feet. The narrow, pinnately divided leaves are sharply lobed and edged with bristles. Each head has a hemispherical, spiny involucre, a margin of ray-flowers and a central disk of tubular flowers. Haplopappus grows on the plains and central grasslands, from Minnesota to Texas and to California. The flowering period is from June to September.

WHITE-TOPPED ASTER

PLATE 198

Sericocarpus asteroides

Compositae

This perennial asterlike plant has hairy stems a foot to three feet in height, and ovate or lanceolate leaves with toothed margins. The heads are borne in a spreading terminal cluster, each head with five marginal ray-flowers and a central disk of tubular flowers. The involucre is cylindrical, with whitish green-tipped bracts. White-topped Aster grows in dry rocky or sandy woods and clearings from Maine to Michigan and south to Florida and Mississippi. It flowers from June to September.

THOROUGHWORT

PLATE 198

Eupatorium hyssopifolium — *Compositae*

Eupatorium is a large and variable genus, containing many common wild flowers, particularly in the eastern half of the United States. They are typically perennials with opposite or whorled leaves and clusters of heads which consist only of tubular flowers. Many of them are known only as Thoroughwort. The Hyssop-leaved Thoroughwort is a bushy plant a foot or two in height with narrowly linear leaves in crowded whorls. The heads are clustered in a flat-topped panicle; each head is about a third of an inch in height, made up of five tubular flowers on a bell-shaped involucre. This species is found in dry woods and clearings from southern New England to Florida and Texas, flowering from August to October.

BONESET

PLATE 217

Eupatorium perfoliatum — *Compositae*

Boneset is a rank-growing plant with stout hairy stems growing to a height of five feet, from perennial roots. Opposite, lanceolate leaves with a wrinkled surface are often broadened at the base and united so that they surround the stem. On vigorous specimens the leaves may be seven or eight inches in length. The many small heads are compactly grouped in a somewhat flat-topped terminal cluster of dull white. Each individual head, with ten to sixteen tubular flowers, is less than a quarter of an inch in length. In rural sections of the country a tea made from the dried leaves is considered of some medicinal value. Boneset grows in low wet woods and along marshy stream banks from Quebec to Manitoba, south to Florida and Texas. The flowering period is from July to October.

PLATE 205

Compass-plant, *Silphium laciniatum*

PLATE 206

Prairie-dock, *Silphium terebinthinaceum*

JOE-PYE-WEED

PLATE 232

Eupatorium maculatum — *Compositae*

Also known as Purple Boneset, this tall purplish-stemmed perennial sometimes grows to a height of ten feet; it is particularly abundant in low marshy woods and along stream margins. The coarse veiny leaves grow in whorls of three to six, and reach a length of ten or twelve inches. The inflorescence is a large spreading terminal cluster of small flower-heads, each head made up of eight to twenty purple tubular flowers. As in the other species of Eupatorium, there are no ray-flowers. Joe-Pye-weed is found from New England south to North Carolina and New Mexico, flowering from July to September. A closely related species (*Eupatorium purpureum*) is a vanilla-scented plant with creamy-white to pale pink flower-heads, with three to seven tubular flowers per head.

WHITE SNAKEROOT

Eupatorium rugosum — *Compositae*

The erect smooth stems of White Snakeroot grow to a height of three or four feet, and bear pairs of ovate, toothed leaves with heart-shaped base and slender tip. The inflorescence is an open terminal cluster of white heads, each with ten to thirty tubular flowers. White Snakeroot grows in rich woods from New England and New York to upland Georgia and west to Texas. The flowers can be found from July to October. Cows which graze on this plant are capable of transmitting the sometimes fatal "milk disease" to human beings.

The Blue Mistflower (*Eupatorium coelestinum*) of the central and southeastern states is similar in form to White Snakeroot. It is often cultivated under the name of "hardy ageratum."

ROUGH THOROUGHWORT

Eupatorium pilosum *Compositae*

This roughly hairy species is a tall-stemmed plant reaching six or seven feet in height. Opposite, stemless leaves have a margin of rounded teeth. Small white flower-heads are borne in a small flat-topped cluster, each head consisting of five tubular flowers. Rough Thoroughwort grows in wet sandy soil from southern New England to Florida and Louisiana, and flowers in August and September.

WILD SUNFLOWER

PLATE 199

Helianthus petiolaris *Compositae*

Sunflowers, in the wild, are exclusively American plants. Some species are annuals, but the majority are perennials. The stout stems of either kind are often seen growing to heights of ten or twelve feet. The first leaves are opposite, but the succeeding ones become alternate. The flower-heads are usually large and showy, with a margin of few to many ray-flowers and a central disk of tubular flowers. The ray-flowers are always yellow, but the disk-flowers vary from yellowish-brown to reddish-purple. The fruits are laterally compressed, smooth achenes. This species of Wild Sunflower is a tall annual with pale green, triangular-ovate leaves up to six inches in length. The rays are an inch in length, the disk about three-quarters of an inch in diameter. The plant grows in sandy soil and along river bottoms throughout the Middle West and West, is naturalized farther east. The flowers mature from June to October.

PLATE 207

(*left*) **Canada Goldenrod,** ***Solidago canadensis*** (*right*) **Sharp-toothed Goldenrod,** ***Solidago juncea***

PLATE 208

(*left*) **Seaside Goldenrod,** ***Solidago sempervirens*** (*right*) **Grass-leaved Goldenrod,** ***Solidago graminifolia***

COMMON SUNFLOWER

Helianthus annuus *Compositae*

This species, very common in Kansas and adjacent states, is native to the plains region from Minnesota to Texas and is adventive eastward. It has been under cultivation for a long time, and as a garden plant produces heavy heads a foot in diameter. Where it has escaped it has reverted to its original form. The disk is brown or dark purple, and only several inches broad in wild specimens. The seeds were used by the American Indians for food, but the plant is cultivated for this purpose today chiefly in Russia. The seeds yield an oil which is used for cooking, soap-making, and as a cake for cattle food. This species is an annual, closely related to the preceding Wild Sunflower.

SWAMP SUNFLOWER

PLATE 199

Helianthus angustifolius *Compositae*

Also known as Narrow-leaved Sunflower, this perennial is distinguished from other kinds of sunflower by the narrow linear leaves and the purplish disk-flowers. Slender, rough stems, branching near the summit, grow to a height of six or seven feet; the tough leaves are two to seven inches in length. The rim of each head consists of twelve to twenty ray-flowers; the entire head is about three inches in diameter. Swamp Sunflower grows in bogs, swamps, and wet pinelands from Long Island to Florida and west to Texas and Missouri. The flowering period is from August to October.

TEN-RAYED SUNFLOWER

Helianthus decapetulus *Compositae*

A smooth-stemmed species, the Ten-rayed Sunflower grows three to five feet tall and is sparingly branched. The lower and middle leaves are opposite, the upper ones alternate. All are three to six inches long, triple-nerved, pointed, ovate, and coarsely toothed; the petioles are slightly winged. The flower-heads, about two inches in diameter, terminate long slender stalks; both disk and rays are yellow, the rays around ten in number. It is widespread in the northeastern states and west to Nebraska in open woods and clearings.

JERUSALEM ARTICHOKE

Helianthus tuberosus *Compositae*

This perennial species, growing six to ten feet high with ovate tapering leaves and numerous yellow flower-heads, two to three inches in diameter, is best known for the nutritious potatolike tubers produced on its creeping roots. These were cooked and eaten by the Indians and early explorers of the West. Jerusalem Artichoke, whose name has nothing to do with Jerusalem, is native from north of the Great Lakes to Georgia and westward; also widespread from cultivation. The wild tubers are ripe for eating in autumn.

PRAIRIE CONEFLOWER

PLATE 200

Ratibida columnifera *Compositae*

Prairie Coneflower is a branching plant one to three feet tall, rising from a perennial root; the compound leaves, pinnately divided into five to nine leaflets, grow alternately on the stems. Usually a single showy head terminates a stem or branch. The head bears a marginal series of a few drooping ray-flowers, and a striking columnar or cone-shaped disk made up of minute grayish flowers. The Prairie Coneflower grows on dry plains from Canada to Mexico, through the prairie states, and flowers from June to September. It is sometimes naturalized farther east.

PLATE 209

Ironweed, *Vernonia noveboracensis*

PLATE 210

(*left*) Smooth Aster, *Aster laevis* (*right*) Large-flowered Aster, *Aster grandiflorus*

TALL SUNFLOWER

Helianthus giganteus *Compositae*

The hairy, rough stems of the Tall Sunflower, a perennial species, grow stiffly to a height of nine feet or more, and are much branched near the summit. The lanceolate toothed leaves may be either opposite or alternate, and reach a length of six inches. The outward-facing, lemon-yellow flowers two inches in diameter are borne in a long panicle. They appear from July to October in the northeastern and prairie states and into Canada.

WOODLAND SUNFLOWER

Helianthus divaricatus *Compositae*

This species is also known as Rough Sunflower because of the rough upper surface of the lanceolate leaves. It is a slender yellow-flowered perennial, seldom growing over thirty inches high with few flower-heads and these under two inches in breadth. The Woodland Sunflower is found in dry woods and along roadsides from New England to Georgia and Arkansas; it flowers from July to October.

GRAY-HEADED CONEFLOWER

PLATE 200

Ratibida pinnata *Compositae*

This is a more slender and hoary plant, whose pinnately compound leaves consist of three to seven leaflets; stems reach a height of four feet. The heads are similar to those of the preceding species, but the ray-flowers are longer (up to two inches in length) and the disk-flowers form a more hemispherical cone. The Gray-headed Coneflower is found in dry soil from New York to Florida, west to Minnesota and Texas. The flowering period is from June to September.

BLAZING STAR

PLATE 227

Liatris pycnostachya

Compositae

This is a coarse and stiffly erect plant, up to four feet in height, with crowded linear leaves. The heads are also crowded into an elongated spire-like inflorescence terminating the stems. Each head is cylindric, with the involucral bracts recurved and colored at the tip. The accompanying leafy bracts are only occasionally longer than the heads. The range of this Blazing Star is from Wisconsin to South Dakota and south to Texas, on damp prairies; the flowers can be found from July to October.

PRAIRIE BLAZING STAR

PLATE 201

Liatris punctata

Compositae

The erect stems of this species grow to a height of three feet from the crown of an elongated vertical underground corm; numerous narrow and upward-reaching leaves clothe the stems with foliage. At the summit of the stem is a dense spikelike cluster of the flower-heads, each head similar to those of the southern blazing star but with less conspicuous tips to the bracts of the involucre. Prairie Blazing Star prefers the dry plains of the central states, from Canada to Iowa and western Texas. The flowering period includes the summer months.

SOUTHERN BLAZING STAR

PLATE 201

Liatris elegans

Compositae

The Blazing Stars are a widespread group. Typically the plants are perennials with underground corms or tubers from which rise simple stems with alternate, narrowly linear leaves. The heads contain only tubular disk-flowers. The Southern Blazing Star is a finely hairy plant growing to a height of four feet, with the heads clustered in a spire. Each head is surrounded by a cylindric involucre of overlapping bracts, some of which have petallike tips, as long as the individual flowers. Southern Blazing Star grows in pinelands and dry sandy woods, from Virginia to Florida and Texas; it flowers through the summer, into early autumn.

PLATE 211

(*left*) **New England Aster,** *Aster novae-angliae* (*right*) **Heath Aster,** *Aster ericoides*

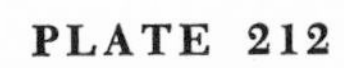

PLATE 212

(*left*) **White Aster,** ***Aster divaricatus*** (*right*) **Late Purple Aster,** ***Aster patens***

SCARIOUS BLAZING STAR

PLATE 227

Liatris scariosa

Compositae

The foliage of this species is dry and scaly; plants reach a height of three or four feet, and bear lanceolate, tapering leaves. Terminating the stems are racemes or panicles of the rounded or hemispherical heads, each head consisting of two dozen or more densely crowded tubular disk-flowers. The involucre is vase-shaped, with spreading, sharply tipped bracts. This species is found in dry woods and clearings from Pennsylvania to the Carolinas, flowering in August and September.

CLIMBING HEMPWEED

PLATE 202

Mikania scandens

Compositae

Climbing Hempweed is one of the few twining vines of the Composite family. The triangular or heart-shaped leaves grow in pairs along the stems, which may reach a length of fifteen feet. Heads are found in compound clusters at the ends of the branches; each head has four tubular flowers, set in an involucre of four narrow bracts. The corollas may be either pink or white. Climbing Hempweed grows in swampy thickets and along streams from New England to Florida and Texas; it flowers from July to October.

AMERICAN FEVERFEW

PLATE 203

Parthenium integrifolium

Compositae

A perennial growing to a height of four feet, American Feverfew is also known as Wild Quinine; it is a plant of open woods and prairies from New York to Georgia, west to Minnesota and Texas. The leaves, alternately arranged on the stems, are elliptic or ovate and simple, with toothed margins; they range from three to twelve inches long. The inflorescence is a flat-topped cluster of many closely-packed small heads. Each head has five ray-flowers which do not project beyond the disk-flowers; the lobes of the tubular disk-flowers have woolly tips. American Feverfew flowers from June to September.

COLTSFOOT

PLATE 204

Tussilago farfara

Compositae

Coltsfoot is a European species which has made itself at home in damp soil, along ditches and stream margins, in the northeastern states and westward to Minnesota. It is a low-growing perennial with creeping rootstocks from which scaly flowering stalks grow, each terminated by a single flower-head; the rounded or heart-shaped leaves, woolly when young, appear later in the season. Coltsfoot has distinctive flower-heads, with several rows of ray-flowers and a central disk of tubular flowers. The plant has a reputation in local folklore as a cure for coughs. The flowers first appear in March, and can be found through June.

COMPASS-PLANT

PLATE 205

Silphium laciniatum

Compositae

This coarse and tall perennial has a resinous sap, hence another common name is Rosinweed. It is a rough-bristly plant, growing to a height of ten feet, having large leaves with deeply-cut pinnate lobes, arranged alternately on the stem. The lower leaves are vertically disposed, with the edges often oriented to the north and south, this position accounting for the name of "compass-plant." A few large showy heads are borne at the ends of the stems, each head about four inches in diameter; the ray-flowers are numerous, surrounding a relatively small disk of tubular flowers. Compass-plant grows on prairies from Michigan to North Dakota, south to Alabama and Texas. It flowers from July to September.

PLATE 213

(*left*) Silverrod, *Solidago bicolor* (*right*) Wreath Goldenrod, *Solidago caesia*

PLATE 214

(*left*) Rabbit-tobacco, *Gnaphalium obtusifolium* (*right*) Ladies'-tobacco, *Antennaria plantaginifòlia*

SCLEROLEPIS

PLATE 204

Sclerolepis uniflora

Compositae

This is a creeping plant of swamps, pond shores, and shallow water from scattered locations in New England, down the coast to Florida and Alabama. The flowering stems grow erect, about a foot in height. The narrow linear leaves grow in whorls of four to six; at the ends of the branches are borne single flower-heads composed entirely of tubular disk-flowers. The flowering period is from July to November.

PRAIRIE-DOCK

PLATE 206

Silphium terebinthinaceum

Compositae

This is a slender and smooth-stemmed plant attaining a height of eight or nine feet with terminal panicles of large heads. The ovate or slightly heart-shaped leaves are thick and rough on the undersurface; they occasionally reach the huge size of twenty-four inches. The heads are composed of flowers much as in the compass-plant with many ray-flowers around the periphery and tubular disk-flowers in the center. Prairie-dock is a plant of prairies and open grasslands, from the Great Lakes region to Missouri and Tennessee. The flowering period is from August to October.

CUP-PLANT

PLATE 231

Silphium perfoliatum

Compositae

Cup-plant, or Indian Cup, a perennial growing four to eight feet high, can be recognized by its square stems and pairs of ovate, coarsely-toothed leaves which are joined by their bases, surrounding the stem and forming a leafy cup. Each head is two to three inches in diameter, with a fringe of narrow, stringy ray-flowers and a central disk of tubular flowers. Cup-plant is found along river banks and in rich woods, from the Great Lakes to South Dakota, south to Georgia and Oklahoma; it has become naturalized as far east as New England. The flowers appear between July and September.

CANADA GOLDENROD

PLATE 207

Solidago canadensis

Compositae

Goldenrods are typically a North American genus, represented in the eastern and central states alone by seventy-five species. They are erect perennials, usually unbranched, bearing alternate leaves, with numerous very small heads containing both tubular and ray-flowers. Each head is seated in an involucre which is bell-shaped or oblong, composed of overlapping bracts. The heads are grouped in compact branching clusters. Canada Goldenrod or Rock Goldenrod is a slender-stemmed plant one to four feet tall, with thin linear-lanceolate leaves up to five inches in length. The many small flower-heads are arranged on only one side of the spreading branches, thus forming an arching terminal panicle. Each flower-head has a cylindric involucre of overlapping bracts, a few ray-flowers, and five-lobed disk-flowers. Canada Goldenrod is a stately flower of hillsides, stream margins and roadsides from New England south to the Carolinas and west to Colorado. Like most of the goldenrods, it is a late summer and autumn species, flowering from July to September.

SHARP-TOOTHED GOLDENROD

PLATE 207

Solidago juncea

Compositae

This is a smooth-stemmed species two to four feet tall with erect solitary stems, or a few stems in a cluster. The basal leaves are narrowly oval with sharply toothed margins. The flower-heads are structurally similar to those of the Canada goldenrod and grouped in a pyramidal, usually gracefully arching, terminal cluster. Sharp-toothed Goldenrod is found in open woods and dry fields from southeastern Canada to Georgia west to Missouri. The flowers appear in late June, and continue until October.

PLATE 215

(*left*) **Orange Hawkweed,** ***Hieracium aurantiacum*** (*right*) **King Devil,** ***Hieracium pratense***

PLATE 216

Noble Goldenrod, ***Solidago speciosa***

SEASIDE GOLDENROD

PLATE 208

Solidago sempervirens — *Compositae*

This goldenrod of salt marshes, sea beaches and rocky shores of the ocean is a stout and usually unbranched plant two to six feet in height. The thick, somewhat fleshy leaves are lanceolate with pointed tips, the lower leaves clasping the stem. Small heads, about a quarter of an inch in height, each have eight to ten showy ray-flowers; the heads are clustered in elongated one-sided racemes. Seaside Goldenrod is found from New England to New Jersey, and flowers from July to November.

GRASS-LEAVED GOLDENROD

PLATE 208

Solidago graminifolia — *Compositae*

Grass-leaved Goldenrod, as the name implies, has narrow tapering grass-like leaves; they are borne alternately on unbranching stems two to four feet tall. The small flower-heads are borne in a flat-topped and spreading terminal cluster; each head has twenty to thirty ray-flowers which are larger than the disk-flowers. This species is also known as Bushy Goldenrod and Fragrant Goldenrod. It is found along roadsides, clearings and shores across Canada and southward to the Carolinas and Missouri. The flowering period is from July to October.

SILVERROD

PLATE 213

Solidago bicolor — *Compositae*

Also known as Pale or White Goldenrod, this species has slender erect stems which are often ashy with a downy covering; they grow from one to several feet high and bear ovate, alternate leaves. The ray-flowers are white, an unusual color in the genus. The heads are arranged in a slender, elongated, leafy, terminal cluster. A few heads are also grouped in the upper leaf axils. Silverrod grows in open sterile soil, and is found from southeastern Canada to Georgia, west to Minnesota and Arkansas. It flowers from July to October.

WREATH GOLDENROD

PLATE 213

Solidago caesia — *Compositae*

Because of the purplish-green stems, this species is also known as Blue-stem Goldenrod. It is a slender, unbranched plant one to three feet tall, with sessile, lanceolate leaves. The small flower-heads are clustered in the open leaf axils or in a terminal raceme; each head has only three or four ray-flowers. Wreath Goldenrod grows in rich or open woods from Maine to Florida, west to Wisconsin and Texas. It flowers from August to October.

NOBLE GOLDENROD

PLATE 216

Solidago speciosa — *Compositae*

This stout-stemmed species with oblong to lanceolate stem-leaves grows to a height of six feet. Each head has five large ray-flowers; the heads are grouped in dense pyramidal racemes which are very showy. Noble Goldenrod grows in open woods and on the prairies from southern New England to the Carolinas, west to Minnesota and Louisiana. It flowers from August to October.

ZIGZAG GOLDENROD

Solidago flexicaulis — *Compositae*

The slender stem of this species grows in a zigzag fashion to a height of several feet, with broad ovate leaves which taper to a point. The margins of the leaves are sharply toothed. Small clusters of flower-heads grow in the leaf axils and at the ends of the stems, each head yellow and less than a quarter of an inch in height. Zigzag Goldenrod grows in woods and thickets from New England to North Dakota and south to the Carolinas; it flowers from July to October.

PLATE 217

Boneset, ***Eupatorium perfoliatum***

PLATE 218

(*left*) **Common White Daisy,** ***Chrysanthemum leucanthemum*** (*right*) **Black-eyed Susan,** ***Rudbeckia hirta***

DOWNY GOLDENROD

Solidago puberula *Compositae*

The stems of this goldenrod are minutely downy and often purplish; they grow to a height of two or three feet. The lanceolate, pointed leaves are an inch or two in length, and either entire or slightly toothed. The yellow flower-heads are grouped in a cylindrical, compact, leafy cluster. Downy Goldenrod grows in dry sandy soil from New England to Florida and Mississippi. The flowering period is from July to October.

IRONWEED

PLATE 209

Vernonia noveboracensis *Compositae*

This is a stiffly erect plant with coarse stems growing three to six feet high, occasionally branching near the summit; the alternate leaves, four to ten inches long, are slender and lanceolate with tapering tips and finely toothed margins. The flower-heads form a loose and open cluster at the summit of the stems and branches. There are only tubular flowers in the heads; their five-lobed corollas give a fringed effect. The involucre of each head consists of greenish or brownish-purple bracts with spreading slender tips. Ironweed grows on low ground, along the margins of streams and ponds, as well as becoming a weed in roadside ditches. It is found from southern New England to Mississippi and Ohio; the flowering period is from August to October.

SMOOTH ASTER

PLATE 210

Aster laevis

Compositae

The genus Aster in North America is about as large as Solidago, containing the goldenrods. The asters are familiar in many parts of the country as the flowers which contribute the rich purples, the lavenders and whites to America's pageant of autumn coloration. They often grow in combination with the goldenrods and thus give the purple-and-gold colors which characterize Eastern fields and roadsides in September and October. Asters are mostly perennial plants (only a few species are annual or biennial) with alternate, simple leaves and flower-heads made up of slender marginal ray-flowers and tubular disk-flowers. The ray-flowers may be white, blue, purple, or pink; the disk-flowers are a golden-yellow, sometimes changing to brown. Smooth Aster is an erect, smooth-stemmed plant growing to a height of four feet. The lanceolate leaves, of which the upper ones clasp the stem with their heart-shaped bases, have an entire or slightly rough margin, and reach a length of four inches. The flower-heads form a large spreading terminal cluster, each head about an inch in diameter with a bell-shaped involucre of green-tipped bracts. Smooth Aster grows in dry fields and pastures and in sandy open woods, from Maine to Louisiana and Kansas. It flowers from August to October.

LARGE-FLOWERED ASTER

PLATE 210

Aster grandiflorus

Compositae

This rare, hairy-stemmed species has long ascending branches reaching a height of three or four feet. The upper leaves, which are oblong to linear in shape, are numerous and small. The showy flower-heads are borne singly at the tips of the upper branches; each head is an inch or two in diameter. The involucre is hemispherical, a half-inch in height. Large-flowered Aster grows in dry open woods and clearings from Virginia to Florida, only along the Atlantic coastal plain. The flowers can be found from early September to early November.

PLATE 219

(*left*) **Ox-eye, *Heliopsis helianthoides*** (*right*) **Dog-fennel, *Anthemis cotula***

PLATE 220

(*left*) **Daisy Fleabane,** ***Erigeron philadelphicus*** (*right*) **Robin's-plantain,**
Erigeron pulchellus

PURPLE-STEMMED ASTER

PLATE 194

Aster puniceus

Compositae

The purplish color of the stems gives this aster one of its common names. It is also known as Swamp Aster. Individuals sometimes grow to a height of eight feet in favored locations, such as swamps and roadside ditches, where they are common over a wide range in the eastern and central states. The leaves are lanceolate and alternate. Each head, rising from an involucre of overlapping bracts, has twenty to forty ray-flowers surrounding the smaller disk-flowers. The blossoms appear from September to November.

NEW ENGLAND ASTER

PLATE 211

Aster novae-angliae

Compositae

New England Aster is a stout, hairy-stemmed plant with crowded lanceolate leaves which clasp the stems; like many of the other asters, it grows vigorously, sometimes becoming taller than a man. The showy flower-heads, an inch or two in diameter, cluster at the ends of the branches. The hemispherical involucres have green and hairy bracts. Each head has forty to fifty ray-flowers, each a half-inch to three-quarters of an inch in length. New England Aster inhabits moist woods and fields from eastern Canada south to Alabama. Occasionally plants are found with rose-colored or whitish rays. The flowering period is from August to October.

HEATH ASTER

PLATE 211

Aster ericoides

Compositae

This species is a prostrate or erect plant, one to three feet tall, with a bushy habit. The leaves are rigid and linear, the upper ones becoming smaller and smaller until they approach the size of the bracts. The flower-heads, each about half an inch in breadth, are clustered in dense one-sided racemes which form a spreading terminal inflorescence. Heath Aster grows in dry open habitats from Maine to Minnesota, south to Florida and Mississippi. The flowers appear in July and continue until October.

WHITE ASTER

PLATE 212

Aster divaricatus

Compositae

This is a more low-growing species than most of the preceding, the slender, often zigzag stems forming tufted plants a foot or two in height. The coarse lower leaves have a heart-shaped base and toothed margins; the upper leaves are smaller and have shorter stalks. The inflorescence is a flattish-topped cluster of many flower-heads, each head with a short cylindric involucre and six to nine ray-flowers. White Aster grows in dry woods and clearings from Maine to Georgia, west to Ohio; it can be found in flower from July to October.

LATE PURPLE ASTER

PLATE 212

Aster patens

Compositae

Late Purple Aster has stiff and slender stems and spreading branches, growing two or three feet tall. The ovate to lanceolate leaves, with entire margins, clasp the stem with a deep heart-shaped base. The flower-heads, solitary at the ends of the upper branches, are an inch or more in diameter; there are twenty to thirty ray-flowers. The Late Purple Aster grows in dry open fields and thickets throughout the eastern and central states; its flowering period is from August to October.

LARGE-LEAVED ASTER

Aster macrophyllus

Compositae

The stems of this species are stout, rough, and angled, and grow to a height of two or three feet. Broad, heart-shaped leaves grow in a basal cluster; the upper leaves have long stalks edged with wings. The heads are grouped in a somewhat flat-topped terminal cluster, each head about half an inch in size, with lavender, violet or pale blue ray-flowers. The Large-leaved Aster is found in dry or moist woods and clearings from New England to Minnesota, south to North Carolina and Illinois; it flowers in August and September.

PLATE 221

Purple Coneflower, *Echinacea purpurea*

PLATE 222

(*left*) Lance-leaved Tickseed, *Coreopsis lanceolata* (*right*) Tall Coreopsis, *Coreopsis tripteris*

CALICO ASTER

Aster lateriflorus *Compositae*

The slender branching stems of this species, which is also known as Starved Aster, form plants four to five feet in height; the basal leaves are ovate, the stem-leaves more lanceolate in outline. The small flower-heads, a half-inch or less in diameter, are grouped in one-sided racemes in a crowded fashion. The ray-flowers are white or pale lilac, the disk-flowers are purplish. Calico Aster grows in a variety of dry and moist habitats from New England to Minnesota, south to Georgia and Arkansas. It flowers from August to October.

RABBIT-TOBACCO

PLATE 214

Gnaphalium obtusifolium *Compositae*

In contrast to the showier pearly everlasting, which is described below but not illustrated here, the small flower-heads of Rabbit-tobacco have the appearance of flowers that never open. They are composed solely of whitish or pale straw-colored, slender tubular flowers. The dry, strawlike involucres give them the quality of everlastings. The foliage is woolly and has a slight lemon scent when bruised. The plant is a weedy biennial growing in dry fields and woodland edges from southeastern Canada and south to the Gulf. Catfoot and Cudweed are other names for Rabbit-tobacco.

PEARLY EVERLASTING

Anaphalis margaritacea *Compositae*

This is a white, woolly perennial one to three feet tall, with alternate lanceolate leaves which are green on the upper surface and whitish underneath. The small flower-heads are clustered in terminal corymbs two to eight inches in breadth. Each flower-head has a large pearly-white involucre surrounding the inconspicuous flowers. Pearly Everlasting is seen in July and August as a common weed of fields and roadsides from Canada south to North Carolina, Colorado and California. The dry chaffy nature of the involucres suggests the name "everlasting."

LADIES'-TOBACCO

PLATE 214

Antennaria plantaginifolia

Compositae

Ladies'-tobacco is similar to rabbit-tobacco, except in its lower stature and its smaller more compact heads of flowers. The species also is locally known as Everlasting and as Pussy-toes. The basal ovate or rounded leaves form a rosette from which rises a flowering stem only a few inches high. Minute lanceolate leaves grow alternately along this stem. The foliage and stems are white and woolly. Ladies'-tobacco is found in open woods, fields and pastures from Maine to Georgia west to Minnesota and Missouri. It flowers from April to June. There are over thirty other similar species.

ORANGE HAWKWEED

PLATE 215

Hieracium aurantiacum

Compositae

Also known as Devil's Paintbrush, Orange Hawkweed has a basal cluster of hairy, oblong or elliptic leaves six to eight inches in length. From the rosette of foliage rises a hairy leafless flower-stalk, six to twenty inches tall, terminated by a few flower-heads each about an inch in diameter. Each head consists only of ray-flowers, whose strap-shaped corollas are five-toothed at the tip. Orange Hawkweed, like many of the related species of Hieracium, is a European plant which has established itself as a colorful weed in fields, from Maine to Minnesota, south to Virginia, west to Iowa. It flowers from June to August.

KING DEVIL

PLATE 215

Hieracium pratense

Compositae

This is another European species which has spread widely from southeastern Canada to North Carolina, becoming a serious weed in fields and pastures. The basal rosette consists of fewer and longer leaves than in Orange Hawkweed. The flowering stalk rises from six inches to an occasional height of three feet. In the small terminal cluster of flower-heads there are only ray-flowers, which appear from May to August.

PLATE 223

(*left*) **Rattlesnake-weed,** ***Hieracium venosum*** (*right*) **Common Tansy,** ***Tanacetum vulgare***

PLATE 224

(*left*) **Golden Ragwort,** ***Senecio aureus*** (*right*) **Squaw-weed,** ***Senecio obovatus***

RATTLESNAKE-WEED

PLATE 223

Hieracium venosum — *Compositae*

A native species among the hawkweeds, Rattlesnake-weed has a basal cluster of elliptic leaves which are purple-veined or -mottled. The slender leafless flowering stalk, branching near its summit, averages one to two feet in height and bears an open cluster of flower-heads. Each head, about two-thirds of an inch in diameter, consists entirely of ray-flowers, toothed at the tip. Rattlesnake-weed thrives in poor and sandy soils and therefore is a common weed in waste places and pastures. It is found from southern New England to Florida, west to Missouri; the flowering period is from May to September.

TALL CONEFLOWER

Rudbeckia laciniata — *Compositae*

Sometimes known as Green-headed Coneflower, this Composite can be recognized by the conical or cylindrical receptacle which rises in the middle of the flower, covered with the tubular disk-flowers. These are often a greenish-yellow color. The ray-flowers are an inch or two in length and very showy; the entire flower-head may be three to four inches in diameter. The lower leaves are deeply lobed into three to seven segments. The upper ones are more or less ovate. Tall Coneflower is a robust, branching plant often growing to a height of eight or nine feet. It is at home in moist woods and along stream margins from Quebec to Florida and west to Montana and Arizona. The flowering period is from July to September. This native species is the origin of the cultivated variety known as Golden Glow, in which the disk-flowers have been reduced in numbers and the ray-flowers increased to produce the "double" head.

BLACK-EYED SUSAN

PLATE 218

Rudbeckia hirta

Compositae

This familiar Composite, also known as Yellow Daisy, is a perennial with rough and hairy stems and leaves; the plants grow to a height of three feet. The basal leaves are broadly ovate, three inches across and twice as long; the upper stem-leaves are narrower and sessile. A few showy flower-heads, each two or three inches in diameter, are borne on stout terminal or axillary flowering stalks. Each flower-head has an involucre of spreading green bracts, ten to twenty ray-flowers, and a cone-shaped mass of dark brown disk-flowers. Closely resembling this plant is the biennial *Rudbeckia serotina* (called *Rudbeckia hirta* in most books), originally a native of the prairie states. The biennial species can now be found over even a wider range in the East than the perennial species shown here, which grows between western Massachusetts and Illinois and southward to Georgia and Alabama. Also similar is *Rudbeckia speciosa*, a less hairy plant with long-stalked leaves, found in eastern woodlands, blossoming in August and September. The others flower over a longer period.

COMMON WHITE DAISY

PLATE 218

Chrysanthemum leucanthemum

Compositae

This European flower has established itself in fields and pastures and throughout most of the United States and Canada. It is an annual or perennial with erect stems up to three feet high. The basal leaves are rounded or oblong; the stem-leaves are more lanceolate in shape, with a toothed or lobed margin, or deeply pinnately lobed. A few heads are borne at the tips of the stems. Each head has a saucer-shaped involucre, ten to twenty ray-flowers and a compact mass of disk-flowers. It flowers from June to August.

PLATE 225

(*above*) **Dandelion, *Taraxacum officinale*** (*below*) **Cynthia, *Krigia biflora***

PLATE 226

(*left*) European Star-thistle, *Centaurea maculosa* (*right*) American Star-thistle, *Centaurea americana*

OX-EYE

PLATE 219

Heliopsis helianthoides

Compositae

This is a robust plant, two to five feet tall, with opposite, ovate leaves and terminal flower-heads on long stalks. Each flower-head is supported by a flattened involucre, and consists of ten to twenty ray-flowers and a rounded mass of disk-flowers. Ox-eye grows in open woods and on dry banks from Canada to the Carolinas, west to Minnesota; it flowers from July to September.

DOG-FENNEL

PLATE 219

Anthemis cotula

Compositae

This strongly scented plant is also known as Chamomile. The alternate, finely divided, pinnately lobed leaves give it a fernlike aspect, though it is usually branched in bushy fashion. It is an annual which originally came from Europe but has escaped to become a roadside weed throughout the United States and Canada. The flower-heads are solitary at the ends of the branches; each head has from ten to fifteen white ray-flowers and numerous greenish-yellow disk-flowers. It flowers from June to October.

DAISY FLEABANE

PLATE 220

Erigeron philadelphicus

Compositae

This Composite is a slender-stemmed plant usually one to three feet in height, slightly downy, and unbranched. The basal leaves are ovate and toothed, up to three inches in length; the upper stem-leaves are more heart-shaped and clasp the stems. The flattish flower-heads, an inch or less in diameter, are borne in a terminal cluster. The margin of each is composed of 100 or more slender ray-flowers and the center of tubular disk-flowers. Daisy Fleabane grows in rich woods and moist meadows throughout Canada and the United States. It flowers from April to August.

ROBIN'S-PLANTAIN

PLATE 220

Erigeron pulchellus — *Compositae*

This is a smaller plant than daisy fleabane, rarely growing more than two feet in height; it has hairy stems which usually are unbranched, and most of its foliage is in a hairy basal rosette. The flower-heads are also smaller, with only fifty to sixty ray-flowers. Robin's-plantain grows in open woods and along roadsides throughout the eastern and central states; its flowering period is from April to July.

PURPLE CONEFLOWER

PLATE 221

Echinacea purpurea — *Compositae*

The conical receptacle which projects from the center of the Purple Coneflower bears disk-flowers which are purplish in color. The long narrow ray-flowers are usually drooping. The stems, which are terminated by solitary showy flower-heads, are smooth, stout, and almost unbranched. The ovate leaves have five distinct veins and a toothed margin. Purple Coneflower grows wild in open woods and on prairies from Virginia to Louisiana, west to Michigan and Iowa. The flowers develop during the summer months, from June to October.

COMMON TICKSEED

PLATE 197

Coreopsis major — *Compositae*

The genus Coreopsis can be recognized by the showy flower-heads with a double involucre, the outer circle of bracts being leaflike and spreading; by the few broad ray-flowers (usually eight); and by the flat receptacle with its disk of tubular flowers. Common Tickseed is an erect plant, growing to a height of three feet, with slender stems and branches bearing sessile, palmately compound leaves. Each flower-head has rays almost an inch in length. Common Tickseed grows in open woods and clearings, from Virginia to Florida, west to Mississippi and north to Ohio. It flowers in June and July.

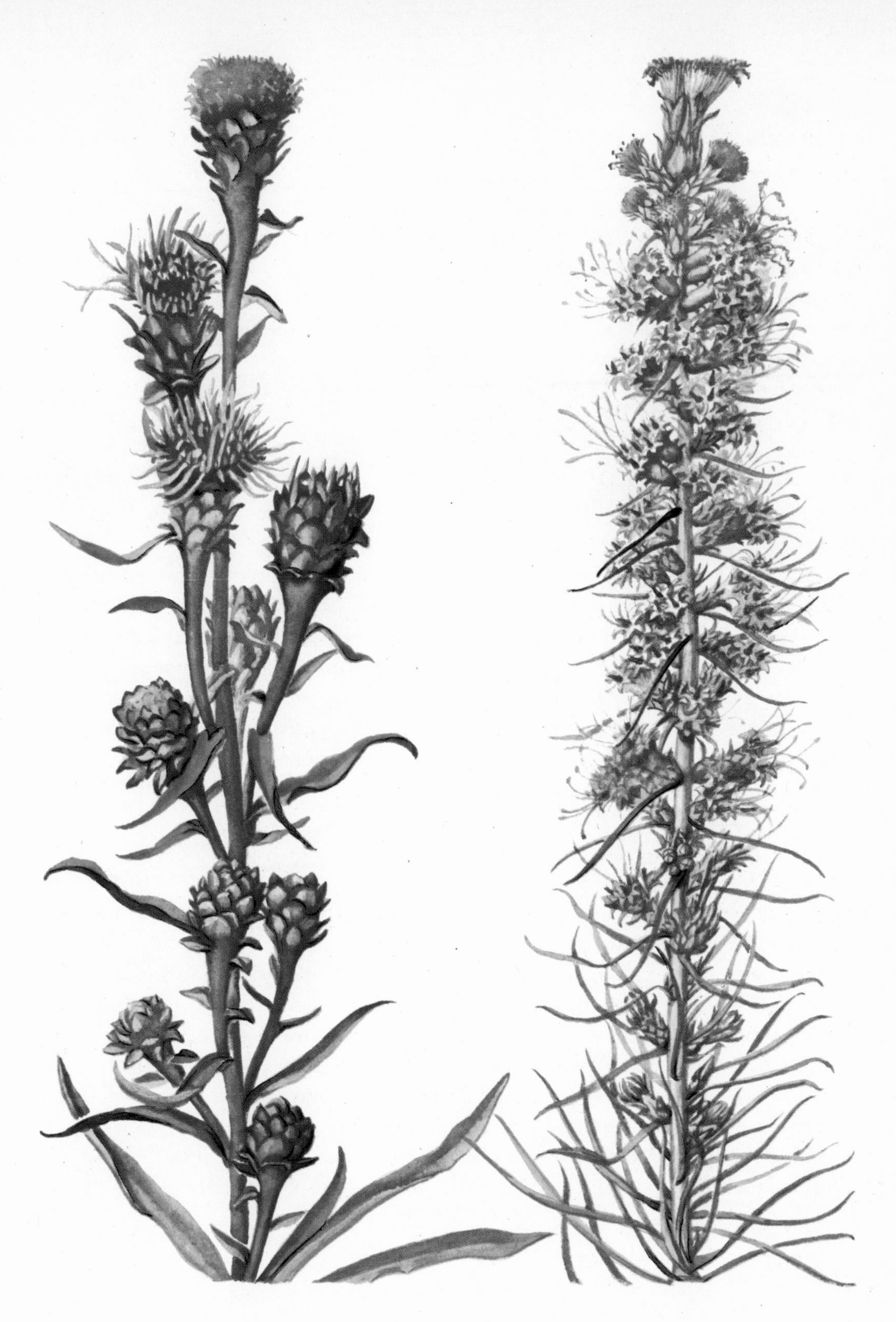

PLATE 227

(*left*) Scarious Blazing Star, *Liatris scariosa* (*right*) Blazing Star, *Liatris pycnostachya*

PLATE 228

(*left*) **Spanish Daisy,** ***Helenium tenuifolium*** (*right*) **Gumweed,** ***Grindelia lanceolata***

LANCE-LEAVED TICKSEED

PLATE 222

Coreopsis lanceolata — *Compositae*

This species of Tickseed is an erect and slender plant one to three feet tall, with opposite, lanceolate leaves, which are sessile or nearly so. The flower-heads occur in groups of two or three, on long slender stalks. Each head, about two inches in diameter, has a flattened involucre above which grow six to ten wedge-shaped ray-flowers with notched tips. Lance-leaved Tickseed is a perennial of dry woods and stony fields, from Virginia to Florida, west to the Great Lakes region and New Mexico; it is much cultivated and has escaped back into the wild, especially northeastward. It flowers from May to July.

TALL COREOPSIS

PLATE 222

Coreopsis tripteris — *Compositae*

Tall Coreopsis is a much more robust plant than the preceding, growing often to a height of eight or nine feet; the pinnately lobed leaves are divided into three to five segments. The flower-heads are similar in general appearance to those of the lance-leaved tickseed. Tall Coreopsis grows in woods and old fields from New England to Wisconsin and southward to North Carolina, west to Louisiana and Kansas. The flowering period is in August and September.

PINK TICKSEED

Coreopsis rosea — *Compositae*

This is a wiry, slender species one to two feet tall, perennial by means of creeping rootstocks; the small crowded leaves are narrowly linear and opposite. Each flower-head, about an inch in breadth, consists of four to eight rosy-pink or purplish ray-flowers and a disk of yellow tubular flowers. Pink Tickseed grows in damp meadows and hollows from New England south to Georgia. It flowers from July to September.

COMMON TANSY

PLATE 223

Tanacetum vulgare — *Compositae*

A European species which has established itself as a common wayside and field wild flower. Tansy is a strongly spicy-scented plant with deeply lobed fernlike leaves. Stems growing to a height of three feet bear terminal flat-topped clusters of buttonlike heads whose small yellow ray-flowers hardly project beyond the disk. Each head possesses a saucer-shaped involucre and a convex receptacle; the inconspicuous ray-flowers are nearly tubular in structure, forming a compact mass with the disk-flowers. Tansy is found throughout the United States and adjacent Canada. Its flowering period is from July to September.

GOLDEN RAGWORT

PLATE 224

Senecio aureus — *Compositae*

One of the few Composites flowering in spring, Golden Ragwort, also known as Swamp Squaw-weed, is a smooth-stemmed perennial a foot or two in height with ovate or orbicular basal leaves and deeply lobed stem leaves. The flower-heads form a loose cluster, each head being one-half to three-quarters of an inch in diameter. The ray-flowers, eight to twelve in number, have a notched tip; the disk-flowers have a funnel-shaped throat and lobed margin. Golden Ragwort grows in swamps and wet woods from southeastern Canada to the Gulf; it flowers from April to May.

SQUAW-WEED

PLATE 224

Senecio obovatus — *Compositae*

This is a slightly smaller species than golden ragwort, with the obovate basal leaves forming a rosette which is perennial in nature. The flower-heads of the two species are structurally similar. Squaw-weed grows in dry woods and on rocky banks from New England to Michigan and southward toward the Gulf. The flowering period is from April to June.

PLATE 229

Bull Thistle, ***Cirsium vulgare***

PLATE 230

Chicory, *Cichorium intybus*

DANDELION

PLATE 225

Taraxacum officinale

Compositae

It hardly seems necessary to describe this ubiquitous Composite which has become an obnoxious garden and lawn weed throughout the eastern states. Few European species have spread as rapidly in the United States as has this immigrant. Dandelion is a stemless plant with a basal rosette of elongated, pinnately lobed leaves, from which arise smooth, hollow, milky flowering stems bearing solitary showy heads consisting only of ray-flowers. There is a double involucre; after flowering, the inner involucre closes and forms a slender beak while the fruit is maturing. The fruit is the familiar achene with a parachutelike silky pappus. Dandelion "greens" are prized by many as a food.

CYNTHIA

PLATE 225

Krigia biflora

Compositae

Cynthia is an annual, about a foot in height, with chiefly basal leaves which are pinnately lobed or toothed. The flower-heads, borne on slender stems, consist entirely of ray-flowers as in the common dandelion; the involucre, however, is single and the plants branch at the base. Each ray-flower has a five-notched tip. Cynthia grows in sandy places and open woods from New England to Georgia, and west to Arizona. The flowering period is from May to August.

EUROPEAN STAR-THISTLE

PLATE 226

Centaurea maculosa

Compositae

The Star-thistles (which are not true thistles) are characterized by heads containing only tubular flowers, of which the marginal flowers are often larger and thus may be mistaken for ray-flowers. The European Star-thistle is an introduced species which has escaped to fields and roadsides throughout northeastern and north central United States. Wiry stems bear alternate, pinnately lobed leaves and small flower-heads, less than an inch in diameter; the plants reach a height of three feet. The spherical involucre consists of spiny-tipped bracts. European Star-thistle flowers from June to August.

AMERICAN STAR-THISTLE — PLATE 226

Centaurea americana — *Compositae*

This plains species, found from Missouri and Louisiana westward, is a fairly tall plant, up to three feet in height, with the stems thickened beneath the flowering heads. The oblong-lanceolate leaves grow alternately on the stems. Beneath each flower-head is a spiny-tipped and fringed mass forming an involucre bract. American Star-thistles bloom from May to August. This species makes an attractive ornamental, and is often grown in gardens under the name of Basket-flower.

The European species *Centaurea cyanus* is also common as a garden annual; it goes by a variety of names—Bachelor's Button, Cornflower, and Ragged Sailor. Another ornamental of this genus, Dusty Miller (*Centaurea cineraria*) with white-hairy foliage is used as a bedding plant.

SPANISH DAISY — PLATE 228

Helenium tenuifolium — *Compositae*

This is a smooth-stemmed branching annual, one of the numerous sneezeweeds, one to two feet in height, with narrow, alternate leaves, many of which are grasslike in shape. A flattened involucre bears a flower-head an inch or so in diameter, characterized by an elevated and spherical disk of tubular flowers surrounded by a few wedge-shaped ray-flowers with notched tips. The Spanish Daisy grows in fields and along roadsides, either native or naturalized, from southern New England to Michigan, south to Florida and Mexico. It flowers from June to November.

PLATE 231

Cup-plant, *Silphium perfoliatum*

PLATE 232

Joe-Pye-weed, ***Eupatorium maculatum***

SNEEZEWEED

Helenium autumnale — *Compositae*

This is a stout branching plant growing to a height of six feet, with resinous foliage and winged angles along the stems. This Sneezeweed is also known as False Sunflower. Its habitat is wet meadows and shores. The oblong-lanceolate leaves are sessile and toothed. The ray-flowers are yellow, the globose disk of tubular flowers are a yellowish-brown. Sneezeweed is found throughout most of the United States and adjacent Canada.

GUMWEED

PLATE 228

Grindelia lanceolata — *Compositae*

The resinous and sticky nature of the foliage of this species is responsible for such other common names as Tarweed and Sticky-head. Growing to a height of three feet, Gumweed has alternate, lanceolate leaves with spiny-toothed margins. Conspicuous involucres with spreading green tips support flower-heads with both ray- and disk-flowers. Gumweed is found on rocky prairies and other dry grassy habitats from Tennessee and Louisiana westward to Kansas and Texas. It flowers from August to October.

CHICORY

PLATE 230

Cichorium intybus — *Compositae*

Chicory is a European plant which has escaped from cultivation to become a common but attractive wild flower of fields and roadsides throughout the United States and southern Canada. The stem leaves are oblong or lanceolate, with toothed or pinnately lobed margins. A double involucre, the outer circle of which consists of five short spreading bracts, supports a flower-head consisting only of showy ray-flowers. The heads are solitary or few in a cluster, on short thickened branches. Chicory flowers from June to October. The ground and roasted roots are used as an adulterant or substitute for coffee. Another species of Cichorium is endive, believed to be a native of India; this plant is grown for its tender young basal leaves which are usually blanched and used as a salad green.

A Guide to the Flower Families Described in This Book

The publishers, in collaboration with a number of prominent botanists, have prepared this Guide in an effort to help the amateur in flower identification. This is not offered as a complete botanical key to wild flowers, but merely as a guide to the flower families described here. It will not necessarily apply to all other plants in these same families, but has been compiled as a preliminary aid to the identification of the plants *in this book*. An asterisk (*) indicates that the plant part mentioned is illustrated in the Introduction pp. v-xv.

The plant Families in this volume may be classified under the major headings listed below. To use this Guide, first place the plant in one of these main groups. Then following through under that heading on the following pages, the plant may be placed in the proper Family, by checking its distinguishing characteristics. Once the Family is selected, the individual species can easily be identified from the descriptive notes and color plates.

DISTINGUISHING CHARACTERISTICS	FAMILY	PAGE
I PLANTS WITH NUMEROUS MINUTE FLOWERS, CLOSELY PACKED TOGETHER		
Inconspicuous individual flowers tightly packed into a cylindrical or tapering spike *		
Mature spike brown and velvety	Cattail	4
Flower spike fleshy, generally surrounded by a spathe *	Arum	5
Stems with swollen, sheathed joints	Buckwheat	89
Minute or very small flowers in a compact head *		
Flowers shaped like small sweet peas (Clovers)	Bean	189, 192 205, 206
Flowers 2-lipped; stems square	Mint	341
Flowers with pettallike wings formed from 2 sepals; actual petals 3, similarly colored	Milkwort	209
Flowers with 3 petals; leaves linear *	Yellow-eyed Grass	12
Flowers with 5 corolla-lobes, the head generally surrounded by colored rays *	Composite	397
Flowers clustered within a large corollalike cup (an involucre) *		
Each flower containing several stamens * and a pistil *		
Involucre * of generally 5 lobes	Four o'clock	92
Involucre * of 4 separate white bracts *	Dogwood	268
Each flower containing either 1 pistil * or 1 stamen *, never both together; plants with milky juice	Spurge	216
II PLANTS WITH UNUSUAL LEAVES OR NONE		
Plants with modified leaves		
Aquatic plants with large, rounded leaves on or above the surface of the water	Water-lily	104
Bog plants with leaves like pitchers; flowers with an umbrella-shaped structure in center	Pitcher-plant	148
Minute leaves studded with glistening, sticky hairs	Sundew	152
Leaf-blades hinged longitudinally (Venus Flytrap)	Sundew	152
Leafless plants		
Without chlorophyll; stem and blossom white; plants small (Indian Pipe)	Heath	292
With chlorophyll; stems of fleshy, spiny pads	Cactus	241

DISTINGUISHING CHARACTERISTICS	FAMILY	PAGE
III PLANTS OF CLIMBING OR TRAILING HABIT		
Slender twining plants		
Leaves simple *; flowers trumpet-shaped, fragile, twisted when in bud	Morning-glory	313
Leaves compound *; flowers shaped like small sweet peas	Bean	181
Woody vines with compound leaves * and heavy-textured, orange, trumpet-shaped flowers	Bignonia	384
Woody plants, sometimes trailing close to the ground, with tubular flowers in pairs, the pairs sometimes clustered		
Calyx * 5-toothed	Honeysuckle	393
Calyx * 4-toothed (Partridge-berry)	Madder	392
Twining woody plants with bright yellow flowers and 5 (or sometimes 4) broad corolla-lobes and stamens * (Yellow Jessamine)	Logania	304
Clambering vines		
Flowers in heads *; corollas with 5 small lobes (Climbing Hempweed)	Composite	397
Flowers single or loosely clustered		
Flowers of 4 petallike sepals (Clematis)	Buttercup	121, 124
Flowers winged	Fumitory	144
High-climbing vines with 3-lobed brown flowers	Dutchman's-pipe	88
IV FLOWERS WITH WINGS, LIPS, OR SPURS		
Wings		
Flowers shaped like sweet peas—that is, with a wing on each side, one upright petal, and 2 united ones; leaves compound * (except in Crotalaria)	Bean	181
Flowers with also a protruding pouch or lip; leaves with parallel veins	Orchid	64
Flowers with 2 petallike sepals forming wings; the flowers sometimes tightly clustered; leaves simple,* narrow	Milkwort	209
Lips		
Corolla of 5 unequal lobes, sometimes forming two lips		
Ovary * of 4 distinct lobes; stem square	Mint	341
Ovary * 2-celled; stem round (Lobelia)	Bellflower,	381
	also Acanthus	385
	Figwort	360

DISTINGUISHING CHARACTERISTICS	FAMILY	PAGE
Calyx as well as corolla 2-lipped; plants growing in wet places	Bladderwort	376
Leaves with parallel veins	Orchid	64

Spurs

DISTINGUISHING CHARACTERISTICS	FAMILY	PAGE
Flowers with 5 unequal petals, one of them spurred; plants small	Violet	228
Flowers yellow, with a spurred, bulbous sac; fruit curling in fingers when touched; leaves simple *; plants growing in wet places	Touch-me-not	217
Flowers with colored sepals, one of them spurred; leaves palmately cut; plants growing in dry places (Larkspur)	Buttercup	109
Flowers with 2 pairs of petals, the outer pair spurred	Fumitory	141
Flowers with 5 colored spurs (Columbine)	Buttercup	117
Flowers with wings, lips, and also spurs	Orchid	64

V REMAINING PLANTS CLASSIFIED ESSENTIALLY ACCORDING TO NUMBER OF PETALS *

A. Petals 1 or 2 apparently

DISTINGUISHING CHARACTERISTICS	FAMILY	PAGE
One single purple petal in a flower with 5 calyx-lobes; flowers in a compact spike (Leadplant)	Bean	185
Two bright blue petals visible, the third minute (Dayflower)	Spiderwort	16

B. Flower parts in units or multiples of 3

DISTINGUISHING CHARACTERISTICS	FAMILY	PAGE
Petals actually 3 but apparently 5; one fertile stamen	Canna	61
Petals, sepals, or petallike lobes 3 or 6, in an even circle		
Leaves generally linear, with parallel veins	Spiderwort,	16
	also Lily	21
	Amaryllis	52
	Iris	57
Leaves generally broad (Trillium)	Lily	21
(Blue Cohosh)	Barberry	136
	Water-Plantain	13
	Dutchman's-pipe	88
Flowers with generally 6 more or less unequal petals		
Growing in wet places; flowers blue; leaves somewhat erect, generally heart-shaped at base	Pickerelweed	17
Growing in moist or dry ground; flowers purplish; leaves opposite or whorled	Loosestrife	233

DISTINGUISHING CHARACTERISTICS	FAMILY	PAGE
Single flower with 6 to 9 petals; leaves umbrellalike, deeply lobed (May Apple)	Barberry	136
C. Flower parts in units of 4		
Petals * 4 or a multiple of 4		
Petals 8; sepals * 4; leaf of 2 similar leaflets (Twinleaf)	Barberry	135
Petals 4 or 8, fragile; sepals generally 2	Poppy	137
Petals 4; sepals apparently none (Wild Lily of the Valley)	Lily	33
Petals 4; sepals generally 4		
Ovary * inside the corolla		
Stamens 4 (Fringed Gentian)	Gentian	317
Stamens 6		
Leaves simple, or sometimes deeply cleft	Mustard	161
Leaves compound, of 3 leaflets (Spider-flower)	Caper	145
Stamens 8 (Meadow Beauty)	Melastome	244
Ovary beneath the corolla; stamens 8	Evening-primrose	248
Corolla of 4 lobes; stamens 4; leaves opposite or whorled	Madder	388
D. Flower parts in units of 5		
Petals * but not all other flower parts in fives		
Stamens 5		
Small flowers in umbels *		
Fruit, a double seedlike structure	Parsley	261
Fruit, a berry	Ginseng	257
Small clustered flowers with spoon-shaped petals; plants shrubby	Buckthorn	220
Plants mostly with milky juice and (except in Blue Dogbane) feathered seeds		
Petals simple	Dogbane	305
Petals hooded	Milkweed	308
Stamens 10; ovary * within the corolla *		
Petals notched or cleft; leaves opposite and simple;* stems with swollen nodes	Pink	96
Petals rounded or pointed; leaves even, lobed, or notched	Saxifrage	156
Corolla irregular; leaves compound * (Partridge Pea)	Bean	200

DISTINGUISHING CHARACTERISTICS	FAMILY	PAGE
Stamens numerous		
Leaves opposite * and sessile (stalkless)	St. John's-wort	237
Leaves alternate * and stalked		
With stipules (small winged appendages at base)	Rose	168
Without stipules	Buttercup	109
Flowers with all their parts, including cells of ovary,* in fives		
Leaves simple,* succulent, scattered on the stem	Orpine	153
Leaves simple, thickened, basal	Leadwort	301
Leaves deeply palmately cleft *	Geranium	256
Leaves compound,* of 3 small heart-shaped leaflets	Wood Sorrel	208
Five-petaled flowers with stamens united into a central column		
Stamens numerous	Mallow	221
Stamens 5; flowers with a fringed crown around the center	Passion-flower	240
Flowers with 5 petals * and 2 sepals *; leaves fleshy	Purslane	101
Flowers with 5 petallike calyx-lobes; stamens 5	Sandalwood	85
Flowers with 5 petallike sepals; stamens numerous	Buttercup	109
Flowers with 5 regular corolla lobes instead of separate petals		
Lobes expanding at the summit of a definite tube		
Ovary * 2-celled; tube trumpet-shaped	Logania	304
Ovary 3-celled; tube generally slender	Phlox	324
Ovary 4-lobed; flower clusters coiled or arching	Borage	332
Lobes long; tube short		
Ovary 1-celled; leaves deeply cleft	Waterleaf	329
Ovary 2-celled (the flower parts somewhat variable in number); leaves sessile and entire	Gentian	317
Ovary splitting into 5 teeth at summit; leaves basal (European Cowslip)	Primrose	301
Lobes resembling separate petals; leaves opposite * or whorled *	Primrose	296
Flowers saucer-shaped (Ground-cherry)	Nightshade	357
Flowers trumpet-shaped (Jimsonweed)	Nightshade	360
Flowers bell-shaped		
Generally purplish, plants herbaceous	Bellflower	377
Generally waxy-white, occasionally pink	Heath,	269
	also Pyxie	293

DISTINGUISHING CHARACTERISTICS	FAMILY	PAGE
Corolla-lobes reflexed		
Plants small, herbaceous (Shooting Star)	Primrose	296
Plants small, evergreen (Pipsissewa)	Heath	280
Plants sprawling, herbaceous	Nightshade	356
Flowers of apparently 5 but actually 3 petals *; 1 fertile stamen * (southern plants of wet places)	Canna	61
Flowers of 5 corolla lobes, irregular in shape		
Plants shrubby (Rhododendron, Azalea)	Heath	272, 273 276
Plants herbaceous		
Ovary * of 2 or 4 cells (not lobed)	Verbena	337
Ovary of 4 distinct lobes		
Stem rounded; flower clusters coiled or arching (Viper's Bugloss)	Borage	333
Stem square; plants generally aromatic	Mint	341

E. Flower parts variable in number

DISTINGUISHING CHARACTERISTICS	FAMILY	PAGE
Petals * or sepals * (or both) few but variable in number, sometimes falling early; stamens * numerous, often conspicuous	Buttercup	109
Petals 5 to 9, pointed, in flowers occurring above a whorl of pointed leaves (Star Flower)	Primrose	297

Index